D1373281

Moments in Contracts
Text and Cases

Second Edition
Rudy Sandoval, BBA, M.A., J.D., LL.M
University of Texas at San Antonio

Kendall Hunt
publishing company

Kendall Hunt
publishing company

www.kendallhunt.com
Send all inquiries to:
4050 Westmark Drive
Dubuque, IA 52004-1840

Copyright © 2008, 2012 by Rudy Sandoval

ISBN 978-1-4652-0238-3

Kendall Hunt Publishing Company has the exclusive rights to reproduce this work,
to prepare derivative works from this work, to publicly distribute this work,
to publicly perform this work and to publicly display this work.

All rights reserved. No part of this publication may be reproduced, stored in a
retrieval system, or transmitted, in any form or by any means, electronic, mechanical,
photocopying, recording, or otherwise, without the prior written permission of the
copyright owner.

Printed in the United States of America
10 9 8 7 6 5 4 3 2

Chapter Contents

Table of Contents

Chapter 3
The Agreement: Acceptance

Chapter 4
Consideration

Chapter 5
Manifestation of Assent

Chapter 6
The Statutes of Fraud

Chapter 7
Mistake

Chapter 8
Misrepresentation, Duress and Undue Influence

Chapter 9
Performance of Contracts

Chapter 10
Discharge of Contract

Chapter 11
Third Party Beneficiaries, Assignments and Delegation

Chapter 12
Remedies

Acknowledgements

The law has been my life, I loved the law from the moment my law professor said, "You will learn the law on your own; I will teach you to think." It has been my privilege and honor to have traveled life's long journey while doing both.

Moments in Contract, Second Edition is dedicated:

To my father

And to Rudy Jr. and Lisa

Preface

The first edition of *Moments in Contracts* was devoted to the study of contracts law by studying specific cases by breaking them down to the basic framework of *Facts, Issue, Law, Holding* and *Rationale.* This second edition of *Moments in Contracts* continues to emphasis the basic frame work of the cases but focuses more on the fundamentals of critical thinking by comparing and contrasting cases. For this reason many of the cases within each chapter in the first edition have been removed and replaced in the second edition with different set of cases so that they may be compared and contrasted with each other.

We learn the law by reading and studying cases, there is no substitute. We learn how to apply the law to a given set of facts or circumstance by learning how the courts reason to a conclusions in a particular case. It is this critical analysis by the court that teaches us how the law may be applied to other similar facts and circumstances through critical thinking. That is the reason why there is no substitute for reading and studying cases. *Moment in Contracts, Second Edition* is, therefore, designed to teach the law of contracts by utilizing the process of critical thinking.

Chapter 1

Introduction to Contracts

I. Foundations of Contracts

A. Meaning of a Contract

A *contract* is a promise or a set of promises, the performance of which the law in some way recognizes as a duty or provides a remedy for the breach thereof.[1] Sometimes the word contract is used loosely to mean "an agreement or a bargain."[2] But the word "promise" itself makes clear that the promisor's intent is to be bound by the promise. The promise is unequivocal such that the promisee knows that a formal commitment has been stated.

For example, if Sam says, "Joe, I will sell you my 1974 Oldsmobile Cutlass for $500," Sam's statement is an unequivocal promise that manifests itself as an offer to Joe. Joe understands that Sam intended to be bound by his promise. On the other hand, Joe may accept Sam's offer by promising to pay Sam $500. This would be a binding agreement. But if Sam promises through an offer to sell the planet Mars to Joe, the promise is meaningless because there is no available remedy as there is no court with proper jurisdiction to enforce Sam's promise.

A contract can also consist of a "set of promises" which can manifest itself for both parties to the agreement who are making promises to each other. The following case illustrates the basic elements and foundation of a contract.

Robert I. Steinberg v. Chicago Medical School[3] 371 N.E.2d 634 (1977), 1977 Ill. LEXIS 435 Supreme Court of Illinois	**Case 1.1**

OPINION BY: DOOLEY

OPINION: Robert Steinberg received a catalog, applied for admission to defendant, Chicago Medical School, for the academic year 1974–75, and paid a $15 fee. He was rejected. Steinberg filed a class action against the school claiming it had failed to evaluate his application and those of other applicants according to the academic criteria in the school's bulletin. According to the complaint, defendant used nonacademic

---

[1] Restatement (Second) Contracts § 1 (1979).

[2] *Id.* at § 1 cmt. a (1979).

[3] 371 N.E.2d 634 (1977), 1977 Ill. LEXIS 435.

criteria, primarily the ability of the applicant or his family to pledge or make payment of large sums of money to the school.

The 1974–75 bulletin distributed to prospective students contained this statement of standards by which applicants were to be evaluated: "Students are selected on the basis of scholarship, character, and motivation without regard to race, creed, or sex. The student's potential for the study and practice of medicine will be evaluated on the basis of academic achievement, Medical College Admission Test results, personal appraisals by a pre-professional advisory committee or individual instructors, and the personal interview, if requested by the Committee on Admissions."

* * * * *

...Count I alleges Steinberg and members of the class to which he belongs applied to defendant and paid the $15 fee, and that defendant, through its brochure, described the criteria to be employed in evaluating applications, but failed to appraise the applications on the stated criteria. On the contrary, defendant evaluated such applications according to monetary contributions made on behalf of those seeking admission.

A contract, by ancient definition, is "an agreement between competent parties, upon a consideration sufficient in law, to do or not to do a particular thing." *People v. Dummer* (1916), 274 Ill. 637, 640.

An *offer*, an *acceptance*...and *consideration*...are basic ingredients of a contract. Steinberg alleges that he and others similarly situated received a brochure describing the criteria that defendant would employ in evaluating applications. He urges that such constituted an invitation for an offer to apply, that the filing of the applications constituted an offer to have their credentials appraised under the terms described by defendant, and that defendant's voluntary reception of the application and fee constituted an acceptance, the final act necessary for the creation of a binding contract.

This situation is similar to that wherein a merchant advertises goods for sale at a fixed price. While the advertisement itself is not an offer to contract, it constitutes an invitation to deal on the terms described in the advertisement. ...Although in some cases the advertisement itself may be an offer...usually it constitutes only an invitation to deal on the advertised terms. Only when the merchant takes the money is there an acceptance of the offer to purchase.

Here the description in the brochure containing the terms under which an application will be appraised constituted an invitation for an offer. The tender of the application, as well as the payment of the fee pursuant to the terms of the brochure, was an offer to apply. Acceptance of the application and fee constituted acceptance of an offer to apply under the criteria defendant had established.

Consideration is a basic element for the existence of a contract. ...Any act or promise which is of benefit to one party or disadvantage to the other is a sufficient consideration to support a contract. ...The application fee was sufficient consideration to support the agreement between the applicant and the school.

Defendant contends that a further requisite for contract formation is a meeting of the minds. But a subjective understanding is not requisite. It suffices that the conduct of the contracting parties indicates an agreement to the terms of the alleged contract.

..."In the formation of contracts it was long ago settled that secret intent was immaterial, only overt acts being considered in the determination of such mutual assent as that branch of the law requires. During the first half of the nineteenth century there were many expressions which seemed to indicate the contrary. Chief of these was the familiar cliché, still reechoing in judicial dicta, that a contract requires the 'meeting of the minds' of the parties."

* * * * *

Here it would appear from the complaint that the conduct of the parties amounted to an agreement that the application would be evaluated according to the criteria described by defendant in its literature.

* * * * *

A medical school is an institution so important to life in society that its conduct cannot be justified by merely stating that one who does not wish to deal with it on its own terms may simply refrain from dealing with it at all.

As the appellate court noted in a recent case in which this defendant was a party: "A contract between a private institution and a student confers duties upon both parties which cannot be arbitrarily disregarded and may be judicially enforced.

...Here our scope of review is exceedingly narrow. Does the complaint set forth facts which could mean that defendant contracted, under the circumstances, to appraise applicants and their applications according to the criteria it described? This is the sole inquiry on this motion to dismiss. We believe the allegations suffice and affirm the appellate court in holding count I stated a cause of action.

* * * * *

The judgment of the appellate court is affirmed in part and reversed in part, and the judgment of the circuit court of Cook County is affirmed in part and reversed in part. The cause is remanded to the circuit court with directions to proceed in a manner not inconsistent with this opinion.

Appellate court affirmed in part and reversed in part; circuit court affirmed in part and reversed in part; cause remanded.

B. Promises

A *promise* by a promisor is *a manifestation of intention* to act or refrain from acting in a specified way that justifies a promisee's understanding that a commitment has been made.[4] The promise is the promisor's words or acts of assurance that justifies certain expectations on the part of the promisee of performances.[5] Those who claim the existence of a contract must show a valid and enforceable agreement (1) between parties competent to contract, (2) upon a proper subject matter, (3) for a legal consideration, (4) by a mutuality of agreement and (5) with a mutual intent to contract as illustrated in the following case.

---

[4] Restatement (Second) Contracts § 2 (1979).

[5] *Id.* at § 2 cmt. a (1979).

Case 1.2

Deborah L. Baldwin v. University of Pittsburgh Medical Center
636 F.3d 69 (2011); 2011 U.S. App. LEXIS 6305
U. S. Ct. of Appl. for the 3rd Circuit

In 2001, Victoria Trent, biologic mother of three minor children, C.L.D., K.K.D., and C.M.D., began working for appellee University of Pittsburgh Medical Center (UPMC). On June 6, 2003, at Trent's urging, Trent's lifelong family friend, Deborah Baldwin, adopted the children and became their legal guardian. New birth certificates were issued for the children. Notwithstanding the adoption, Trent maintained a parental relationship with the children, who still referred to her as "Mom": she lived with Baldwin and the children for three years after they were adopted by Baldwin and Trent spent all holidays and festivals with Baldwin and the children.

Trent was employed at UPMC from 2001 to 2008. Trent enrolled in four insurance plans offered by UPMC for the year 2008. The premiums for these were deducted from her salary each pay period: (1) a $25,000 basic life insurance policy; (2) a $25,000 basic accidental death and dismemberment (AD&D) insurance policy; (3) a $100,000 supplemental group life insurance policy; and (4) a $200,000 supplemental AD&D insurance policy. Trent designated a beneficiary—Baldwin—for the $25,000 basic life policy, but did not designate a beneficiary for the three remaining policies.

* * * * *

On December 23, 2008, Trent died in an accident at the age of thirty-four. Following Trent's death, Baldwin timely sought payment under each of Trent's insurance policies in accordance with the applicable claims procedure. The insurer, Life Insurance Company of North America (LINA), paid $25,000 due to Baldwin as the designated beneficiary of Trent's basic life policy. However, LINA rejected Baldwin's claims on behalf of the children for the proceeds from the other three policies. LINA explained that as a result of the adoption, the children were no longer considered Trent's "children" for the purposes of the policies' default- beneficiary provisions.

* * * * *

Having exhausted all avenues of administrative review of her claim, Baldwin, as of the children, filed a complaint in the District Court for the District of Western Pennsylvania against UPMC and LINA. In a March 16, 2010, opinion and order, the District Court granted defendants' motion to dismiss with prejudice, holding that Baldwin had neither statutory nor prudential standing to bring her claim under ERISA. Baldwin appeals.

* * * * *

Claims for benefits based on the terms of an ERISA plan are contractual in nature and are governed by federal common law contract principles.

* * * * *

The paramount goal of contract interpretation is to determine the intent of the parties.

* * * * *

The strongest objective manifestation of intent is the language of the contract. [T]he firmly settled principle [is that] the intent of the parties to a written contract is contained in the writing itself'.

* * * * *

Courts are to consider not the inner, subjective intent of the parties, but rather the intent a reasonable person would apprehend in considering the parties' behavior.

* * * * *

The issue here is whether the word "children" presents a latent ambiguity—that is, whether "children," from the objectively manifested linguistic reference point of the parties to the insurance contracts, is susceptible of more than one objectively reasonable meaning. More specifically, is it objectively reasonable to construe "children" to mean "biologic children," or is it only objectively reasonable to construe "children" as "children recognized by state intestacy and adoption law"?

* * * * *

The District Court attempted to resolve the issue before it by seeking to interpret the term "children" in the subject insurance policies. It looked for guidance to *La Bove v. Metropolitan Life Insurance Co.*, in which we examined state law to construe the meaning of "children" in a life insurance policy governed by the Federal Employees' Group Life Insurance Act of 1954. Nonetheless, when a contract term is reasonably argued to be ambiguous, the better approach, and the one that is consistent with the weight of controlling authority, is to allow the parties to proffer evidence in support of alternative interpretations of the term so that the court may properly address the purported ambiguity.[4] That is the approach required by our precedent under ERISA, and it should guide the District Court on remand.

* * * * *

Accordingly, we will vacate the order of March 16, 2010, dismissing the complaint and remand to the District Court for further proceedings consistent with this opinion.

1. Illusory Promises

Where a promise is made by the offeror, which by its terms makes the promise optional by the promisor, there is no promise. Where the promisor reserves the right to change, modify or otherwise revoke the promise, the promise becomes *illusory* and there is no promise because the promisee cannot rely on the expectation of performance.[6] The following case discusses illusory promises.

Frances v. ClearOne Communication Inc.   **Case 1.3**
618 F.3d 1110 (2010), 2010 U.S. App. LEXIS 18113.
U. S. Ct. of Appls. for the 10th Circuit.

Frances Flood formerly served as Chief Executive Officer, President, and Chairman of the Board of Directors of ClearOne. In January 2003, the United States Securities and Exchange Commission and the United States Department of Justice began investigating Ms. Flood's conduct at the company. Roughly a year

---

[6] Restatement (Second) Contracts § 2 cmt. e (1979).

after the government's investigation started, ClearOne and Ms. Flood entered into an "Employment Separation Agreement" (ESA). Under the ESA's terms, Ms. Flood agreed to transfer her shares of common stock, cancel various stock options and her then-existing employment agreement, and release ClearOne from liability for claims she may have had against the company. In exchange, ClearOne promised to pay Ms. Flood $ 350,000, release her from liability for any claims it may have had against her, and *advance and indemnify the legal expenses she had incurred and would continue to incur in defending matters related to her tenure at the company* [*emphasis added*].

* * * * *

The dispute in this case centers on the company's advancement promise. By its express terms that promise came with strings attached:

* * * * *

"The Company's duty to indemnify Flood is further conditioned upon Flood's fulfillment of her duty…to cooperate with the Company and its counsel in connection with the SEC Action and Related Proceedings. Subject to the foregoing ESA limitation:

a. Determination and Authorization. The corporation shall not indemnify a director under this section unless:
1. …the director met the standard of conduct…and
2. payment has been authorized in accordance with the procedures set forth… [and] based on a conclusion that the expenses are reasonable, the corporation has the financial ability to make the payment, …

b. Standards of Conduct. The individual shall demonstrate that:
1. his or her conduct was in good faith; and
2. he or she reasonably believed that his or her conduct was in, or not opposed to, the corporation's best interests; and
3. in the case of any criminal proceeding, he or she had no reasonable cause to believe his or her conduct was unlawful.

Beginning in May 2007, ClearOne's Board found all the various conditions set forth in the ESA and the company's bylaws satisfied and advanced Ms. Flood the costs associated with her criminal defense. Payments continued after Ms. Flood was indicted in July 2007 and through the Spring of 2008. By that time, however, disputes began to arise over certain of her claimed expenses and in April 2008 the company paid only half of the monthly invoice submitted by Ms. Flood's attorneys. Shortly thereafter, the company refused any further advancement.

* * * * *

Ms. Flood sought summary judgment in her favor; ClearOne filed a motion to dismiss or, alternatively, for summary judgment. After hearing argument on the dueling motions, the district court issued…a preliminary injunction requiring ClearOne to advance Ms. Flood's defense costs through at least the conclusion of her criminal trial.

* * * * *

The district court concludes that the conditions render the company's advancement promise illusory, the only possible outcome could be a holding that the company was *never* obligated to provide advancement. An illusory promise, after all, is but a "facade" that imposes no performance obligations on the promisor and affords no consideration to the promisee;

* * * * *

By the phrase 'illusory promise' is meant words in promissory form that promise nothing."

* * * * *

Put differently, if its advancement promise really was illusory, as the district court surmised, ClearOne had no duty to advance Ms. Flood's fees and costs and she was never entitled to receive any. So it is that, if the district court were correct in calling the parties' agreement illusory, the company was the party likely to succeed on the merits of Ms. Flood's contract claim, not the other way around…The proper response to an illusory promise isn't to reform it into an enforceable one…When a party's promise is genuinely illusory, the court must decline to enforce it; the court may not impose on the parties a new deal to which they've never assented.

The district court's preliminary injunction order cannot be saved. [The appellant court ruled in favor of ClearOne Communications [because the promise was illusory and therefore, there was no contract].

2. Opinions and Predictions

There is a distinction between promises that may rise to the level of a legal obligation versus opinions and predictions that will not. The opinion and the prediction differ from a promise in that the offeror's statement is not manifesting an intention to act or refrain from an act that could lead the offeree to understand that a commitment has in fact been made. The offeror's opinions and statement of predictions are not promises.[7] For example, if an offeror states that you will never lose a race by using this particular car, the statement is an opinion and not a promise.

II. Types of Contracts
A. Express and Implied Contracts

A contract may be expressed or implied. An *express contract* may manifest itself either orally or in writing such that the promisor and promisee assent to the contract. The assent itself may be manifested by silence, in course of dealing, or in usage of trade or course of performance.[8]

B. Quasi Contracts

A *quasi contract* is sometimes referred to as an *implied contract*, but in fact it is not. This is a contract implied in law, which means that a court can create a quasi contract to avoid certain injustice. In reality, it is no contract at all, but rather a form of restitution remedy.[9] The following case addresses the issue of implied contracts in law and quasi contracts.

---

[7] Restatement (Second) Contracts § 2 cmt. f (1979).
[8] *Id.* at § 4 cmt. a (1979).
[9] *Id.* at § 4 cmt. b (1979).

Case 1.4

John Marcatante v. City of Chicago, Illinois
657 F.3d 433; 2011 U.S. App. LEXIS 17683
U. S. Ct. of Appls. for the 7th Circuit

JUDGES: Before Posner, Kanne, and Tinder, Circuit Judges.

OPINION BY TINDER, *Circuit Judge.*

The plaintiffs are retired City of Chicago employees who were members of several trade unions. They were offered incentives to retire early under an Early Retirement Incentive Program (ERIP) and did so in early 2004 while their unions were still negotiating new Collective Bargaining Agreements (CBAs) for the 2003–2007 periods. During the negotiation process, the 1999–2003 CBAs governed the parties' relationships. In 2005, after two years of negotiations, the City and unions agreed to make raises retroactive to July 2003, but only for current employees, employees laid off with recall rights, and seasonal employees eligible for rehire, not for the plaintiff retirees. The plaintiffs brought this class action claiming entitlement to retroactive wage increases between July 2003 and their retirement dates. The certified class consists of coalition union members who retired under the ERIP between July 2003 and July 2005.

The parties filed cross-motions for summary judgment. The district court granted the City's motion on the plaintiffs'… state law breach of express contract claim. The court, however, granted summary judgment to the plaintiffs on their state law implied contract claim and awarded the class $1,773,502 in retroactive pay, plus attorney's fees. The City appeals the district court's grant…on the plaintiffs' implied contract claim and the plaintiffs cross-appeal on…breach of express contract claims; …

The plaintiffs' primary argument on appeal is that they continued to work for the City after the 1999-2003 CBAs expired with the mutual understanding and expectation that the City would later reach a final agreement regarding their wage rate. They claim an *implied contract* formed because "the City had entered into an agreement with Plaintiffs under which the City accepted Plaintiffs' work but left the final rate of pay unstated pending agreement at a later date." Because no final agreement was ever reached for their wages, they assert that the court must imply a contract term for a reasonable rate of pay. The plaintiffs claim that the following facts gave rise to an *implied contract* for raise increases: employees who continued working for the City in the same job classifications received retroactive wage increases for the time period at issue; the plaintiffs' wages were generally tied to "prevailing wage rates"; the City offered wage increases shortly before and after the 1999–2003 CBAs were set to expire; the City agreed to make any wage increases retroactive in the June 26, 2003 letter agreement; and the plaintiffs, and past retirees who had retired during contract negotiations, had historically received retroactive pay increases. The district court found the plaintiffs' argument persuasive, concluding that the City breached an *implied contract* under Illinois law and reasoning that the City's acceptance of plaintiffs' services entitled them to reasonable pay from July 2003 through the date of their retirement. Reasonable pay, the court found, was the rate the City was willing to pay retroactively to other employees.

* * * * *

A contract implied in fact is one in which a contractual duty is imposed by a promissory expression which may be inferred from the facts and circumstances and the expressions [on] the part of the promisor which show an intention to be bound.

* * * * *

Such a contract "consists of obligations arising from an agreement where an agreement has not been expressed in words."

* * * * *

It is "a true contract, containing all necessary elements of a binding agreement; it differs from other contracts only in that it has not been committed to writing or stated orally in express terms, but rather is inferred from the conduct of the parties in the milieu in which they dealt. *But [A]n implied contract cannot coexist with an express contract on the same subject.*

* * * * *

We pause here to consider the plaintiffs' express contract claim because it dovetails into their argument that there was a mutual understanding for retroactive wages. The plaintiffs contend that the 2003 letter agreement required the City, if it agreed to give raises, to apply them retroactively to *all* employees as of July 2003 and that by only giving active or laid-off employees retroactive wage increases, the City violated the agreement. The district court properly rejected this argument.

* * * * *

The letter is unambiguous; it merely contemplated that the City and the unions would continue to negotiate wage increases and made *agreed-upon* wage increases, if any, retroactive to July 2003 (unless they agreed otherwise). After extensive negotiations, the parties didn't agree to give plaintiff retirees retroactive wage increases; this deal was entirely consistent with the terms of the 2003 letter agreement, which in essence, was an agreement to negotiate.

* * * * *

The plaintiffs' argument similarly falters under an implied-in-law theory, sometimes referred to as a claim in quantum meruit, *quasi-contract,* or one for unjust enrichment. Unlike contracts implied in fact, contracts *implied in law* arise notwithstanding the parties' intentions, and are no contracts at all. They are instead governed by equitable principles. Under this theory, a plaintiff asks the court to remedy the fact that the defendant was 'unjustly enriched' by imposing a contract. To succeed, the plaintiffs must show (1) that they performed a service to benefit the defendant; (2) they performed the service non-gratuitously; (3) the defendant accepted their services; and (4) *no contract existed to prescribe payment for this service.* Similar to the implied-in-fact theory of recovery, there can be no contract implied in law where an express contract or a contract implied in fact exists between the parties and concerns the same subject matter.

* * * * *

Because there is an express contract that governed the plaintiffs' wages, there can be no implied-in-law contract, nor would equity require finding an implied contract here…The City has not been unjustly enriched by accepting the plaintiffs' services in exchange for existing wage rates. The plaintiffs were paid for their services, received enhanced pension benefits for taking early retirement, and were not subject to the new cost-saving concessions that apply to active employees who received retroactive raises.

We AFFIRM…to enter summary judgment for the City on the plaintiffs' implied contract claim.

C. Formal Contracts

A *formal contract* is one in which certain criteria must necessarily be met in order to crystallize the agreement into a contract. For example, a contract that falls within the statute of frauds requires that the contract be in writing. The sale of land, for example, falls within the statute of frauds and a formal contract in writing is required to consummate an enforceable contract. An *informal contract* is therefore one that does not require the formalities of a formal contract such as the sale of a computer or a bicycle.[10]

---

[10] Restatement (Second) Contracts § 6 (1979).

Chapter 1
Vocabulary

1. Contract
2. Promises in Contracts
3. Manifestation of Intention
4. Unilateral Contract
5. Bilateral Contract
6. Illusory Promises
7. Express Contract
8. Implied Contract
9. Quasi Contract
10. Formal Contract

Review Questions

1. What is the issue in the *Steinberg v. Chicago Medical School* case?
2. What is the applicable law in the *Steinberg* case?
3. What is the issue in the *Deborah L. Baldwin v. University of Pittsburgh Medical Center* case?
4. What is the applicable law in the *Deborah L. Baldwin v. University of Pittsburgh Medical Center* case?
5. What is the issue in the *Frances v. ClearOne Communication Inc.* case?
6. What is the applicable law in the *Frances v. ClearOne Communication Inc.* case?
7. What is the issue in the *Marcatante v. City of Chicago, Ill.* case?
8. What is the applicable law in the *Marcatante v. City of Chicago, Ill.* case?

Chapter 2

The Agreement: The Offer

I. The Offer

The agreement is composed of an offer by the promisor and an acceptance by the promisee. An *offer* is the manifestation of willingness to enter into a bargain that leads the promisee to understand that his assent to that bargain is invited and, by accepting the offer, will conclude it.[1]

For example, Sally needs $1000 to pay for her college tuition. She offers to sell her Oldsmobile to Butler for $1000. Sally has manifested her willingness to enter into a bargain to obtain $1000 for her college tuition. The offer is clear, definite and explicit. If Butler accepts the offer, the parties have concluded an agreement.

A manifestation of an offer occurs when the offeror has the requisite *intent* to make the offer, and where the offer is *clear, definite, and explicit,* and leaves nothing open for negotiation, it constitutes an offer. The following case illustrates the issue as to whether or not an advertisement manifested into an offer.

Morris Lefkowitz v. Great Minneapolis Surplus Store, Inc. 86 N.W.2d 689 (1957), 1957 Minn. LEXIS 684 Supreme Court of Minnesota	**Case 2.1**

Murphy J.

This case grows out of the alleged refusal of the defendant to sell to the plaintiff a certain fur piece which it had offered for sale in a newspaper advertisement. It appears from the record that on April 6, 1956, the defendant published the following advertisement in a Minneapolis newspaper:

> "Saturday 9 a.m. sharp
> 3 Brand New
> Fur Coats
> Worth to $100.00
> First Come, First Served
> $1 Each"

---

[1] Restatement (Second) Contracts § 24 (1979).

On April 13, the defendant again published an advertisement in the same newspaper as follows:

"Saturday 9 a.m.
2 Brand New Pastel
Mink 3 Skin Scarf's
Selling for $89.50
Out they go
Saturday. Each $1.00
1 Black Lapin Stole
Worth $139.50 for $1.00
First Come, First Served"

…The record supports the findings of the court that on each of the Saturdays following the publication of the above-described ads the plaintiff was the first to present himself at the appropriate counter…in the defendant's store and on each occasion demanded the coat and the stole so advertised and indicated his readiness to pay the sale price of $1. On both occasions, the defendant refused to sell the merchandise to the plaintiff, stating on the first occasion that by a "house rule" the offer was intended for women only and sales would not be made to men, and on the second visit that plaintiff knew defendant's house rules.

* * * * *

…The defendant contends that a newspaper advertisement offering items of merchandise for sale at a named price…is a "unilateral offer" which may be withdrawn without notice. He relies upon authorities which hold that, where an advertiser publishes in a newspaper that he has a certain quantity or quality of goods which he wants to dispose of at certain prices and on certain terms, such advertisements are not offers which become contracts as soon as any person to whose notice they may come signifies his acceptance by notifying the other that he will take a certain quantity of them. Such advertisements have been construed as an invitation for an offer of sale on the terms stated, which offer, when received, may be accepted or rejected and which therefore does not become a contract of sale until accepted by the seller; and until a contract has been so made, the seller…may modify or revoke such prices or terms. …

The defendant relies principally on *Craft v. Elder & Johnston Co. supra.* In that case, the court discussed the legal effect of an advertisement offering for sale, as a one-day special, an electric sewing machine at a named price. The view was expressed that the advertisement was…"not an offer made to any specific person but was made to the public generally. Thereby it would be properly designated as a unilateral offer and not being supported by any consideration could be withdrawn at will and without notice." It is true that such an offer may be withdrawn before acceptance. Since all offers are by their nature unilateral because they are necessarily made by one party or on one side in the negotiation of a contract, the distinction made in that decision between a unilateral offer and a unilateral contract is not clear. On the facts before us we are concerned with whether the advertisement constituted an offer, and, if so, whether the plaintiff's conduct constituted an acceptance.

There are numerous authorities which hold that a particular advertisement in a newspaper or circular letter relating to…a sale of articles may be construed by the court as constituting an offer, acceptance of which would complete a contract. …The test of whether a binding obligation may originate in advertisements addressed to the general public is "whether the facts show that some performance was promised in positive terms in return for something requested."

…The authorities above cited emphasize that, *where the offer is clear, definite, and explicit, and leaves nothing open for negotiation, it constitutes an offer,* (emphasis added) acceptance of which will complete the contract. The most recent case on the subject is *Johnson v. Capital City Ford Co.* (La. App.) 85 So. (2d) 75, in which the court pointed out that a newspaper advertisement relating to the purchase and sale…of automobiles may constitute an offer, acceptance of which will consummate a contract and create an obligation in the offeror to perform according to the terms of the published offer.

Whether in any individual instance a newspaper advertisement is an offer rather than an invitation to make an offer depends on the legal intention of the parties and the surrounding circumstances. …We are of the view on the facts before us that the offer by the defendant of the sale of the Lapin fur was clear, definite, and explicit, and left nothing open for negotiation. The plaintiff having successfully managed to be the first one to appear at the seller's place of business to be served, as requested by the advertisement, and having offered the stated purchase price of the article, he was entitled to performance on the part of the defendant. We think the trial court was correct in holding that there was in the conduct of the parties a sufficient mutuality of obligation to constitute a contract of sale.

The defendant contends that the offer was modified by a "house rule" to the effect that only women were qualified to receive the bargains advertised. The advertisement contained no such restriction. This objection may be disposed of briefly by stating that, while an advertiser has the right at any time before acceptance to modify his offer, he does not have the right, after acceptance, to impose new or arbitrary conditions not contained in the published offer. Affirmed.

A. Bilateral and Unilateral Agreements

The offeror, being the master of his offer, may request a bilateral agreement from the offeree. A *bilateral agreement* is one in which the offeror makes a promise in return for a promise. For example, when Sam says to Joe, "I promise to sell you my Cutlass Oldsmobile if you promise to pay me $500," if Joe then promises to pay the requested amount, a bilateral agreement is created by the parties.

Alternatively, the offeror may request a *unilateral agreement* wherein the offeror makes a promise to sell the car in return, not for a promise, but for *an action* such as requesting that Joe place $500 into Sam's checking account.

B. Meeting of the Minds

Where one or more terms to the bargain are left open or uncertain, the manifestation of intent is lacking, there is no meeting of the minds and therefore the offer will fail. For example, if the parties leave open the price term, then it is intended that there is no offer until such time as the price is determined.

Where there is a series of terms in the bargain, the more definite the terms, the more likely that the offer is good.[2] In the following case, the court addresses the issue of *meeting of the minds*.

Case 2.2

Isaac Esmay v. Truman B. Gorton
18 Ill. 483 (1857); 1857 Ill. LEXIS 64

Bill in Chancery

By the answer of the defendant, and by the testimony of M. B. Osborn, it appears that Esmay was the owner of the several quarter sections of land in Henry county, as alleged in the bill, and that, at that time, and long previous, Osborn was his agent in respect to said lands, for the purpose of paying taxes and effecting sales, though not authorized by power of attorney to make deeds. From his testimony it appears that the complainants, some six months anterior to the 1st of May, 1854, applied to the witness and agent, Osborn, to purchase three quarter sections, all of which defendant owned or had power to sell, as was then supposed. This application was, by Osborn, communicated by letter to defendant, and, while awaiting a reply, Osborn went to New York, and, at defendant's request, called on him, in the city of Albany, some time in the month of January, 1854. The defendant, at this interview with Osborn, instructed him to sell all his lands in Henry county at $ 3 per acre. These terms of sale Osborn, on his return to Rock Island, about the middle of February following, communicated to complainants, and requested them to examine said lands (the ten quarter sections in question), with a view to the purchase of the whole. At his request, the complainants did so, and, after such examination, *offered to purchase* the lands at $ 3 per acre, one quarter down, and the balance in one, two and three years. Osborn communicated this offer, by letter, to the defendant, some time previous to May, 1854. The defendant, in his reply, by letter, to his agent, did not accept complainants' proposition in terms, but made a *counter proposition*, modified only by exacting from them to pay the taxes on the land, due 1st of December, 1853, and amounting, as afterward ascertained, to $ 62.79. This letter of defendant, addressed to the agent, Osborn, containing such modified proposition to complainants, was received by Osborn some time between the 1st and 9th days of May, 1854, and was by him immediately communicated to complainants, and the letter shown to them, that they might accept or reject the proposition therein contained. The complainants thereupon at once *accepted the proposal* of defendant, as contained in said letter, namely: Complainants to pay the last year's taxes on said land (being the taxes due 1st of December, 1853), $ 1,250 down; balance, $ 3,600, in one, two and three years, with six per cent. interest; complainants to give note, with mortgage on the land, to secure said sum of $ 3,600, and interest; and the papers all to bear date [**4] the 1st day of May, 1854. Defendant also, in said letter, enclosed a form of deed, which he was willing to give, the like of which he agreed to forward to his said agent, properly made out, acknowledged and ready for record.

* * * * *

[2] Restatement (Second) Contracts § 33 cmt. c (1979).

> A contract need not be on one piece of paper, nor entered into at the same time by both parties. It will be sufficient to connect the several pieces of paper containing the whole of the contract, and which, when connected, show the parties, property, terms and consideration.
>
> * * * * *
>
> The minds of the contracting parties must meet upon the terms. Where a proposition is made on one side, it must be simply and fully accepted by the other. Where it is submitted in and sent by letter, it must be accepted as sent, within the time named, if any, and answered as required. If the terms, time or other part be changed or modified, the case becomes a new proposition, and, until simply accepted, there is no agreement or mutual **meeting of minds.**
>
> * * * * *
>
> In the strictest sense, we think defendants have established their alleged contract. They first submitted a proposition, through plaintiff's agent, Osborn, which plaintiff modified, by requiring them to refund to Osborn the taxes advanced for plaintiff for the year past. This was simply accepted, and these taxes refunded within a reasonable time. *Decree affirmed* for defendant.

C. Certainty of the Offer

Another *element of the offer* requires that it be definite.[3] The offer must contain certainty about the nature of what is being offered. The offer must begin with clarity if it is to rise to the level of manifestation of mutual assent. An offer does not necessarily fail if it is indefinite if it can be given a dimension of precision via a course of dealing or usage of trade.[4] However, if the essential terms are missing or are so uncertain that it becomes problematic to ascertain whether or not an agreement exists, then it is probable that the offer is deficient and there is not a contract.[5] Finally, the offer must be communicated to the offeree.

D. Preliminary Negotiations

If the offeree has reason to know that the offeror does not intend to conclude the bargain, then the offer is a *preliminary negotiation* and not a good offer.[6] For example, the offeror may not have the requisite intent to make an offer or the offer is not properly addressed to the offeree or the transaction contemplates a gift instead of a bargain.[7] Great care should be taken not to construe the

---

[3] Restatement (Second) Contracts § 33 cmt. a (1979).

[4] *Id.* at § 33 cmt. a

[5] *Id.* at § 33 cmt. a

[6] *Id.* at § 26 (1979).

[7] *Id.* at § 26 cmt. a (1979).

conduct, declarations or letters of a party as proposals when they are intended only as **preliminary negotiations.** The question is does the offeror mean to submit a proposition, or is he only settling the terms of an agreement on which he proposed to enter after all its particulars are adjusted? If it is intended merely to start negotiations which may subsequently result in a contract, or is intended to call forth an offer from the one to whom it is addressed, its acceptance does not consummate a contract. Whether a writing will constitute a definite offer which the other party may turn into an obligation by acceptance, depends upon the intent and purpose of the writer[8]

E. Advertisements

Advertisements manifest through newspapers, pamphlets, radio, television, billboards, signs and other media. They are intended to invite consumers to purchase goods and services. However, advertisements are generally *not* considered offers.[9] They are, instead, an invitation by the advertiser to the consumer to make an offer. Where the advertisement provides a "quotation" or a seller states, "I quote you $50,"[10] or "Make me an offer,"[11] the statements are considered invitations for an offer rather than an offer.[12] However, advertisements may rise to become offers if they are clear, specific and intended to be offers. In the following case, the court rules on whether or not an advertisement rises to an offer.

Case 2.3

> Leonard v. PepsiCo Inc.
> 88 F. Supp 2d 116 (1999); 1999 U.S. Dist. LEXIS 11987
> U. S. Dist. Ct. (S. D. N.Y.)
>
> WOOD, U.S.D.J.
>
> Plaintiff brought this action seeking, among other things, specific performance of an alleged offer of a Harrier Jet, featured in a television advertisement for defendant's "Pepsi Stuff" promotion. Defendant has moved for summary judgment pursuant to Federal Rule of Civil Procedure 56. For the reasons stated below, defendant's motion is granted.

---

[8] *See* Andrew Bakke v. Columbia Valley Lumber Co. 298 P. 2d 849 (1956).

[9] Restatement (Second) Contracts § 26 cmt. b (1979).

[10] *Id.* at § 26 cmt. c (1979).

[11] *Id.* at § 26 cmt. d (1979).

[12] *Id* at § 26 cmt. c (1979).

I. Background

This case arises out of a promotional campaign conducted by defendant, the producer and distributor of the soft drinks Pepsi and Diet Pepsi. …The promotion, entitled "Pepsi Stuff," encouraged consumers to collect "Pepsi Points" from specially marked packages of Pepsi or Diet Pepsi and redeem these points for merchandise featuring the Pepsi logo. …Before introducing the promotion nationally, defendant conducted a test of the promotion in the Pacific Northwest from October 1995 to March 1996. …A Pepsi Stuff catalog was distributed to consumers in the test market, including Washington State. …Plaintiff is a resident of Seattle, Washington. …While living in Seattle, plaintiff saw the Pepsi Stuff commercial…that he contends constituted an offer of a Harrier Jet.

*****

A. The Alleged Offer

Because whether the television commercial constituted an offer is the central question in this case, the Court will describe the commercial in detail. The commercial opens upon an idyllic, suburban morning, where the chirping of birds in sun-dappled trees welcomes a paperboy on his morning route. As the newspaper hits the stoop of a conventional two-story house, the tattoo of a military drum introduces the subtitle, "MONDAY 7:58 AM." The stirring strains of a martial air mark the appearance of a well-coiffed teenager preparing to leave for school, dressed in a shirt emblazoned with the Pepsi logo, a red-white-and-blue ball. While the teenager confidently preens, the military drumroll again sounds as the subtitle "T-SHIRT 75 PEPSI POINTS" scrolls across the screen. Bursting from his room, the teenager strides down the hallway wearing a leather jacket. The drumroll sounds again, as the subtitle "LEATHER JACKET 1450 PEPSI POINTS" appears. The teenager opens the door of his house and, unfazed by the glare of the early morning sunshine, puts on a pair of sunglasses. The drumroll then accompanies the subtitle "SHADES 175 PEPSI POINTS." A voiceover then intones, "Introducing the new Pepsi Stuff catalog," as the camera focuses on the cover of the catalog. …

The scene then shifts to three young boys sitting in front of a high school building. The boy in the middle is intent on his Pepsi Stuff Catalog, while the boys on either side are each drinking Pepsi. The three boys gaze in awe at an object rushing overhead, as the military march builds to a crescendo. The Harrier Jet is not yet visible, but the observer senses the presence of a mighty plane as the extreme winds generated by its flight create a paper maelstrom in a classroom devoted to an otherwise dull physics lesson. Finally, the Harrier Jet swings into view and lands by the side of the school building, next to a bicycle rack. Several students run for cover, and the velocity of the wind strips one hapless faculty member down to his underwear. While the faculty member is being deprived of his dignity, the voiceover announces: "Now the more Pepsi you drink, the more great stuff you're gonna get."

The teenager opens the cockpit of the fighter and can be seen, helmetless, holding a Pepsi. "Looking very pleased with himself,"…the teenager exclaims, "Sure beats the bus," and chortles. The military drum roll sounds a final time, as the following words appear: "HARRIER FIGHTER 7,000,000 PEPSI POINTS." A few seconds later, the following appears in more stylized script: "Drink Pepsi—Get Stuff." With that message, the music and the commercial end with a triumphant flourish.

Inspired by this commercial, plaintiff set out to obtain a Harrier Jet. Plaintiff explains that he is "typical of the 'Pepsi Generation'…he is young, has an adventurous spirit, and the notion of obtaining a Harrier Jet appealed to him enormously." …Plaintiff consulted the Pepsi Stuff Catalog. The Catalog features youths dressed in Pepsi Stuff regalia or enjoying Pepsi Stuff accessories, such as "Blue Shades" ("As if you need another reason to look forward to sunny days. "), "Pepsi Tees" ("Live in 'em. Laugh in 'em. Get in 'em."), "Bag of Balls" ("Three balls. One bag. No rules."), and "Pepsi Phone Card" ("Call your mom!"). The Catalog specifies the number of Pepsi Points required to obtain promotional merchandise. …The Catalog includes an Order Form which lists, on one side, fifty-three items of Pepsi Stuff merchandise redeemable for Pepsi Points. …Conspicuously absent from the Order Form is any entry or description of a Harrier Jet. …The amount of Pepsi Points required to obtain the listed merchandise ranges from 15 (for a "Jacket Tattoo" ("Sew 'em on your jacket, not your arm.") to 3300 (for a "Fila Mountain Bike" ("Rugged. All-terrain. Exclusively for Pepsi."). It should be noted that plaintiff objects to the implication that because an item was not shown in the Catalog, it was unavailable. …

…The Catalog notes that in the event that a consumer lacks enough Pepsi Points to obtain a desired item, additional Pepsi Points may be purchased for ten cents each; however, at least fifteen original Pepsi Points must accompany each order.

Although plaintiff initially set out to collect 7,000,000 Pepsi Points by consuming Pepsi products, it soon became clear to him that he "would not be able to buy (let alone drink) enough Pepsi to collect the necessary Pepsi Points fast enough."…Reevaluating his strategy, plaintiff "focused for the first time on the packaging materials in the Pepsi Stuff promotion,"…and realized that buying Pepsi Points would be a more promising option. …Through acquaintances, plaintiff ultimately raised about $700,000. …

B. Plaintiff's Efforts to Redeem the Alleged Offer

On or about March 27, 1996, plaintiff submitted an Order Form, fifteen original Pepsi Points, and a check for $700,008.50. …Plaintiff appears to have been represented by counsel at the time he mailed his check; the check is drawn on an account of plaintiff 's first set of attorneys. …At the bottom of the Order Form, plaintiff wrote in "1 Harrier Jet" in the "Item" column and "7,000,000" in the "Total Points" column. …In a letter accompanying his submission, …plaintiff stated that the check was to purchase additional Pepsi Points "expressly for obtaining a new Harrier jet as advertised in your Pepsi Stuff commercial."…

On or about May 7, 1996, defendant's fulfillment house rejected plaintiff's submission and returned the check, explaining that: The item that you have requested is not part of the Pepsi Stuff collection. It is not included in the catalogue or on the order form, and only catalogue merchandise can be redeemed under this program. The Harrier jet in the Pepsi commercial is fanciful and is simply included to create a humorous and entertaining ad. We apologize for any misunderstanding or confusion that you may have experienced and are enclosing some free product coupons for your use. …Plaintiff's previous counsel responded on or about May 14, 1996, as follows: Your letter of May 7, 1996 is totally unacceptable. We have reviewed the video tape of the Pepsi Stuff commercial…and it clearly offers the new Harrier jet for 7,000,000 Pepsi Points. Our client followed your rules explicitly. …This is a formal demand that you honor your commitment and make immediate arrangements to transfer the new Harrier jet to our client. If we do not receive transfer instructions within ten (10) business days of the date of this letter you will leave us no choice but to file an appropriate action against Pepsi. ...

* * * * *

1. Advertisements as Offers

The general rule is that an advertisement does not constitute an offer. The Restatement (Second) of Contracts explains that: Advertisements of goods by display, sign, handbill, newspaper, radio or television are not ordinarily intended or understood as offers to sell. The same is true of catalogues, price lists and circulars, even though the terms of suggested bargains may be stated in some detail. ...It is of course possible to make an offer by an advertisement directed to the general public, ...but there must ordinarily be some language of commitment or some invitation to take action without further communication.

...Similarly, a leading treatise notes that: It is quite possible to make a definite and operative offer to buy or sell goods by advertisement, in a newspaper, by a handbill, a catalog or circular or on a placard in a store window. It is not customary to do this, however; and the presumption is the other way. ...Such advertisements are understood to be mere requests to consider and examine and negotiate; and no one can reasonably regard them as otherwise unless the circumstances are exceptional and the words used are very plain and clear.

...*See Lovett v. Frederick Loeser & Co.*, 124 Misc. 81, 207 N.Y.S. 753, 755 (Mun. Ct. N.Y. City 1924) (noting that an "advertisement is nothing but an invitation to enter into negotiations, and is not an offer which may be turned into a contract by a person who signifies his intention to purchase some of the articles mentioned in the advertisement"); ...*People v. Gimbel Bros. Inc.*, 202 Misc. 229, 115 N.Y.S.2d 857, 858 (Ct. Spec. Sess. 1952) (because an "advertisement does not constitute an offer of sale but is solely an invitation to customers to make an offer to purchase,"...

An advertisement is not transformed into an enforceable offer merely by a potential offeree's expression of willingness to accept the offer through, among other means, completion of an order form. ...In *Mesaros v. United States*, 845 F.2d 1576 (Fed. Cir. 1988), for example, ...The court began by noting the "well-established" rule that advertisements and order forms are "mere notices and solicitations for offers which create no power of acceptance in the recipient." ...("A manifestation of willingness to enter a bargain is not an offer if the person to whom it is addressed knows or has reason to know that the person making it does not intend to conclude a bargain until he has made a further manifestation of assent.")...

* * * * *

The exception to the rule that advertisements do not create any power of acceptance in potential offerees is where the advertisement is "clear, definite, and explicit, and leaves nothing open for negotiation," in that circumstance, "it constitutes an offer, acceptance of which will complete the contract."

* * * * *

The Court finds, in sum, that the Harrier Jet commercial was merely an advertisement...

* * * * *

III. Conclusion

In sum, there are three reasons why plaintiff's demand cannot prevail as a matter of law. First, the commercial was merely an advertisement, not a unilateral offer. Second, the tongue-in-cheek attitude of the commercial would not cause a reasonable person to conclude that a soft drink company would be giving away fighter planes as part of a promotion. Third,...

For the reasons stated above, the Court grants defendant's motion for summary judgment...

F. Auctions Manifesting Offers

As a general rule, an auctioneer invites offers from bidders, which he, the auctioneer, may accept or reject.[13] There are two types of auctions—with reserve and without reserve. An *auction with reserve* is one in which the auctioneer may withdraw the goods from the block unless the bid is at or above the price requested at the opening of the bid. This protects the owner of the goods from selling the goods at a price lower than the one requested.[14] An *auction without reserve* is one in which once the goods are placed on the block, the auctioneer may not withdraw the goods. Offers made by the bidder may be withdrawn at the bidder's option until the auctioneer closes the bidding process. A bidder's offer is said to be withdrawn at the moment that a higher bid is made.[15] The following case illustrates the distinction between auctions with reserve and those without reserve.

Case 2.4

L. M. Coleman v. John Duncan and Jerry Bartle
540 S.W.2d 935 (1976), 1976 Mo. App. LEXIS 2188

The basic statute governing sales by auction is § 400.2-328, V.A.M.S. As pertinent here, it states: "(2) A sale by auction is complete when the auctioneer so announces by the fall of the hammer or in other customary manner. (3) Such a sale is **with reserve** unless the goods are in explicit terms put up **without reserve**. In an auction with reserve the auctioneer may withdraw the goods at any time until he announces completion of the sale. In an auction **without reserve**, after the auctioneer calls for bids on an article or lot, that article or lot cannot be withdrawn unless no bid is made within a reasonable time. ..."

＊ ＊ ＊ ＊ ＊

---

[13] Restatement (Second) Contracts § 28 cmt. a (1979).

[14] *Id.* at § 28 cmt. b (1979).

[15] *Id.* at § 28 cmt. d (1979).

> ...In addition to "the fall of the hammer," expressions such as "'going, going, gone'", "sold", etc. constitute "other customary manner[s]" for demonstrating the completion of a sale by auction. ...
>
> * * * * *
>
> "It is the right of the owner of property sold at auction to prescribe, within reasonable limits, the manner, conditions, and terms of sale. ...Usually the auctioneer, at the time and place appointed for the auction, announces these terms and conditions which, when so announced, are generally deemed to supersede all others and to bind the purchaser even though he did not hear or understand the announcement, or was not present at the time of the announcement and such terms [or conditions] were not brought to his actual attention." ..."Where the seller reserves the right to refuse to accept any bid made, a binding sale is not consummated between the seller and the bidder until the seller accepts the bid. Furthermore, where a right is reserved in the seller to reject any and all bids received, the right may be exercised by the owner even after the auctioneer has accepted a bid, and this applies to the auction of public as well as private property." ...

G. The Power of the Offeror

The offeror is the master of his offer and may place conditions on it.[16] The offeror is entitled to determine the specific mode of manifestation of assent by the offeree. For example, the offeror may determine and designate the person to accept the offer. The offeror may also empower the promisee or promisees with broad or narrow authority to accept the offer,[17] and the offer may invite an acceptance which may manifest itself by performance or a return promise.[18] The offeror may require that an affirmative answer or some act or performance[19] be communicated back to the offeror by some specific mode,[20] but it is generally understood that that the acceptance may be communicated back to the offeror in any manner or by any reasonable means so long as the offeror does not restrict the means in his offer.[21] In the following case, the offeror, having the power to revoke the offer, did not, resulting in an enforceable contract.

---

[16] *See* Kroueze v. Chloride Group Ltd., 572 F.2d 1099 (5th Cir. 1978).
[17] Restatement (Second) Contracts § 29 cmt. a (1979).
[18] *Id.* at § 32 cmt. a (1979).
[19] *See* Hamer v. Sidway 124 N.Y. 538, 27 N.E. 256 (1891).
[20] *Id.* at § 30 (1) (1979).
[21] Restatement (Second) Contracts § 30 (2) (1979).

Case 2.5

Rolla Carr v. Mahaska County Bankers Association
222 Iowa 411 (1936); 269 N.W. 494 (1936)

JUSTICE RICHARDS, J.—

On January 10, 1935, defendant Farmers Savings Bank of Leighton, Iowa, in Mahaska County, was robbed. Plaintiffs discovered and furnished information that led to the arrest and conviction of the offenders. In so doing plaintiffs relied upon an offer of reward which they claim had been made for such information by the Mahaska County Bankers Association. This action at law was brought against the association and several banks located in Mahaska county, alleged members of such association, to recover the amount of the reward. A jury being waived the case was tried to the court and a judgment was entered for $1,000 with interest and costs against three of the defendant banks, including the Taintor Savings Bank, the sole appellant herein.

* * *

Revocation of an offer of reward is ordinarily within the power of the offeror at any time before it is accepted by performance. Appellant says the facts disclosed by the testimony of its cashier conclusively established that the offer made by the posting by appellant was revoked. Appellees challenge such conclusion and claim that the record is such that the trial court could properly find as a fact that as to plaintiffs there had been no *revocation*, nor any communication to plaintiffs of any alleged revocation.

* * *

And if from the nature of the offer the public could in reason assume that continuity was an intended element of the offer, then it would seem necessary to abandon appellant's contention that the element of continuity must have been additionally given to the offer by uninterrupted posting. Such lack of an uninterrupted or continuous posting is the ultimate fact on which appellant must rely to establish *revocation*, because to the public could be imputed no knowledge that the cashier turned down the sight-draft nor that the poster was thrown into the wastebasket, and these incidents of self-serving testimony must be rejected so far as chargeable to the knowledge of the public on the question of a revocation. There seems no avoidance of the conclusion that appellant did not effectively *revoke* the offer in the manner in which it was made, as perhaps by posting in its bank a notice of *revocation*, nor can it be said there was a revocation in any other manner that gave the alleged revocation like publicity as the offer. For aught that appears in the record there was warrant for a finding by the trial court that the public could rightfully assume that the offer remained in force at the time of the robbery.

The motion for directed verdict and to dismiss was properly overruled and the judgment below is *affirmed* for the Plaintiff.

H. Time for Performance

When no time for performance is articulated in the offer, then the *time for performance* is understood to be a "reasonable time."[22] The time for payment

---

[22] Restatement (Second) Contracts 33 cmt. d (1979).

is whenever the service is completed or when the goods are delivered.[23] For example, Sam offers to sell his computer to Joe for $500 and Joe accepts. Joe must make payment on the computer within a reasonable period of time that will give Sam the opportunity to sell the computer to another person if Joe does not perform. Likewise, Sam cannot wait for the delivery of the computer indefinitely.

I.   Indefinite Price

Where the parties agree not to be bound by the bargain until such time as the price is determined, then there is no contract until the price is ascertained.[24] But where the parties agreed to be bound on the bargain and the price has not yet been determined, the price will be a reasonable price upon delivery.[25]

J.   Other Indefinite Terms

There are other terms besides time and price that may be left open and indefinite. But the more terms that are left indefinite, the more likely it is that the bargain will collapse because of the lack of definiteness to the bargain.[26] The following case illustrates that the intent of the parties is the controlling factor when the contract itself is indefinite.

<table>
<tr><td>

Southern Fire & Casualty Company v. Teal
287 F. Supp. 617 (1968), 1968 U.S. Dist. Lexis 10149

DONALD RUSSELL, District Judge.

   On Friday night, March 11, 1966, James Lawrence Teal, Sr., and his wife attended an automobile show at the Spartanburg (South Carolina) Auditorium. While there, they visited the booth of the local franchised Oldsmobile dealer, Glover Oldsmobile, Inc., and discussed with the latter's sales manager, one Baker, a possible trade for a used Oldsmobile car...Mr. Baker took the Teals to the car and provided both of them an opportunity to drive the car. ...The Teals stated to Mr. Baker that they wanted to consider the proposed trade.
   The Teals walked about the auditorium for "a few minutes", talked over the proposed trade, decided that "it looked like a good deal", and determined, by their own statement, "that we (they) would go ahead and take it." Returning to Glover's booth, they told Baker that they had decided to take the deal. ...

</td><td>

Case 2.6

</td></tr>
</table>

---

[23] *Id.* at 33 cmt. d (1979) *See also* San Francisco Brewing Corp. v. Bowman, 343 P. 2d 1 (1959).

[24] *Id.* at § 33 cmt. e (1979).

[25] *Id.* at 33 cmt. e (1979).

[26] *Id.* at § 33 cmt. f (1979).

...It is clear, therefore, that the parties on the evening of Friday, March 11, 1966, had reached agreement upon the terms of the chattel mortgage...In the mean-time, however, and as an interim arrangement, Baker prepared a sales agreement and chattel mortgage covering the transaction, in which the monthly payments and face amount were left blank, and Mrs. Teal signed this. The purpose of this interim arrangement, as explained by the Teals, was to assure that "in case somebody ran into us on the way home we (the Teals) would be covered with insurance." ...The Teals returned home, told their married son, who, with his family, had come from their home to visit his parents, that they had purchased the car and that, since his own car was being repaired, authorized "him to drive it over the weekend."

* * * * *

The real question in issue, as I have observed, is whether responsibility in the damage suits arising out of the accident occurring on Saturday falls on the insurance carrier of Glover Oldsmobile, Inc., or that of the Teals. This, in turn, will be determined, it is conceded by the parties, by the resolution of the issue of ownership of the car at the time of the accident.

Under the law of South Carolina, which is controlling in this situation...a sale of personal property is complete and "Change of title takes place when the bargain is struck." ...Whether a bargain has been "struck" and passage of title had is a matter of the intention of the parties.

* * * * *

"The cardinal factor, according to both the Uniform Sales Act and the common law, upon which the passing of title between a seller and buyer depends is the intention of the parties. The Uniform Sales Act provides that where there is a contract to sell specific or ascertained goods, the property in them is transferred to the buyer at such time as the parties to the contract intend it to be transferred, and that for the purpose of ascertaining the intention of the parties, regard shall be had to the terms of the contract, the conduct of the parties, usages of trade, and the circumstances of the case."

Delivery of possession is strong, if not conclusive evidence of such an intention. ... "A delivery to the buyer with authority to use the goods immediately should be *conclusive evidence* of transfer of the property in the absence of clear evidence showing an intention to reserve the title."

...The actual delivery of the goods is of the greatest importance as evincing an intention to pass title. If unaccompanied by an explanation or the specification of any condition, the buyer generally has a right to regard it as passing title. ...

* * * * *

In this case, there can be no dispute that the parties intended a completed sale or that they struck a bargain on Friday night. Baker affirmed that there was a sale then. Teal testified they had "agreed" at such time. In affirmance of such sale and by way of completion thereof, they exchanged delivery, without any reservations. Baker told the Teals the car was theirs. They executed interim papers to attest such ownership so that the Teals' liability insurance would attach to the car's operation—an act, incidentally, intended to avoid this very controversy. The Teals delivered to Baker not merely their truck but also the only evidence of title, i.e., the registration card, they had. After receiving the car, the Teals proceeded to turn it over to their married son for his use, assuring him the car was theirs. Every act of the parties was thus consistent solely with the conclusion that ownership of the car passed on Friday night to the Teals.

* * * * *

> The Teals intended to purchase and Glover intended to sell them the car in question on Friday night. That intention was abundantly evidenced by the conduct of the parties. Such intent will not be frustrated by any technical attempt by the insurance carrier to read a disagreement or indefiniteness into an arrangement thoroughly understood and agreed upon by the parties themselves.
>
> *****
>
> I am of the opinion that the liability properly was assumed by the plaintiff and it is not entitled to any recovery of the defendant Glens Falls Insurance Company. Let order of judgment be entered that the defendant Glens Falls Insurance Company is free of any liability on account of the accident involved in this proceeding.
>
> *And it is so ordered.*

K. Duration of the Power to Accept

The power of the offeree to accept the offer is created when the offeror's manifestation of assent is complete.[27] Once the offeree's power to accept is created, it continues until it is terminated.[28] Once the offeree exercises his power of acceptance, the bargain or the agreement is then crystallized.[29]

L. Termination of the Power to Acceptance
1. Counteroffer and Meeting of the Minds

A *counteroffer* is one where the offeree agrees with the same subject matter in the bargain but proposes a substitute in the terms of the offer from the one offered by the offeror.[30] The counteroffer stating a substituted proposal will not be effective until it is received by the offeror.[31] A counteroffer is generally considered a rejection of the original offer by the offeror and it destroys the power of the offeree to accept.[32] For example, Sam says to Joe, "I will sell you my car for $2000." Joe then states, "Sam, I will give you $1500 for the car." Sam's original offer of $2000 no longer exists after Joe has made his counter offer of $1500. Joe becomes the new offeror by proposing a counteroffer of $1500, which Sam may or may not accept.[33] However, an inquiry about the terms of the offer, or a request for a better offer, will *not* rise to the level of a counteroffer.[34] The following case addresses the issue of a counteroffer

---

[27] Restatement (Second) Contracts § 35 cmt. b (1979).

[28] *Id* at § 35 cmt. b (1979).

[29] *Id.* at § 35 cmt. c (1979)

[30] *Id.* at § 39 cmt. a (1979)

[31] *Id.* at § 40 cmt. a (1979)

[32] *Id.* at § 39 cmt. a (1979)

[33] *Id.*

[34] *Id.* at § 39 cmt. b (1979)

Case 2.7

> Shaw, as Shaw & Co. v. Ingram-Day Lumber Co;
> 153 S.W. 431 (1913), 152 Ky. 329 (1913)

MR. JUSTICE, O. HOLMES

On the merits the only question is whether the alleged contract was made. The first material step was the following offer, dated December 4, 1911:

"Mr. W. Borck, Real Estate Agent, Manila, P.I. Sir: In compliance with your request I herewith give you an option for three months to buy the property of Mr. Benito Legarda, known as the Nagtahan hacienda, situated in the district of Sampaloc, Manila, and consisting of about 1,993,000 square meters of land, for the price of its assessed government valuation. B. Valdes."

On January 17, 1912, Borck wrote to Valdes:

"In reference to our negotiations regarding" the property in question, "I offer to purchase said property for the sum of three hundred and seven thousand (307,000.00) pesos, Ph. C., cash, net to you, payable the first day of May, 1912, or before and with delivery of a Torrens title free of all encumbrances as taxes and other debts."

No answer was received, and on January 19 Borck wrote again, saying that he was ready to purchase the property at the price and that full payment would be made on or before March 3, provided all documents in connection with the hacienda were immediately placed at his disposal and found in good order. On January 23, Borck wrote again that he could improve the condition of payment and would pay ten days after the documents had been put at his disposal for inspection, &c., and finally, on February 28, wrote that the price was ready to be paid over and requesting notice when it was convenient to allow inspection of all papers. Before this last letter was written Valdes had indicated that he regarded compliance as an open question by saying in conversation that he wished to communicate with Mr. Legarda. Subsequently conveyance was refused.

The letter of January 17 plainly departed from the terms of the offer as to the time of payment and was, as it was expressed to be, a **counter offer**. In the language of a similar English case, "plaintiff made an offer of his own ... and he thereby rejected the offer previously made by the defendant. ... It was not afterwards competent for him to revive the proposal of the defendant, by tendering an acceptance of it." *Hyde* v. *Wrench*, 3 Beavan, 334. Langdell, Cont., § 18.

*   *   *   *   *

The right to hold the defendant to the proposed terms by a word of assent was gone, and after that all that the plaintiff could do was to make an offer in his turn. It would need a very much stronger case than this to induce us to reverse the decision of the court below.

Judgment affirmed.

2. Rejection of an Offer

When the offeror makes an offer, his normal preparations to perform are premised on the acceptance of the offer by the offeree. Hence, when the offeree rejects the offer, the offeror changes his position with respect to performance, and therefore the offer is terminated.[35] The following case illustrates the *rejection of an offer.*

Smaligos v. Fireman's Fund Insurance Company
247 A.2d 577 (1968), 1968 Pa. LEXIS 497
Supreme Court of Pennsylvania

Case 2.8

JUDGES: Opinion by Mr. Justice Jones.

Elizabeth Smaligos, the decedent—a high school graduate who had also attended night classes at Duquesne University—had been gainfully employed as a secretary by Westinghouse Electric Corporation from 1949 until October, 1962, when she was admitted to Western Psychiatric Hospital and there diagnosed as schizophrenic. Later she was committed to Mayview State Hospital and, at the time of her death, was still so committed though permitted to visit her home on weekends and holidays. During such a home week-end stay she was struck by a hit-and-run driver on March 27, 1967. Smaligos then made claim against their insurance company under the terms of the Uninsured Motorist Provisions of an automobile liability policy that had been issued to them by that company wherein the company had agreed to pay "all sums which the insured or his legal representative shall be legally entitled to recover as damages." The company refused to pay the $9750 asked by Smaligos in settlement and on July 27, 1967 the company notified Smaligos' counsel by letter as follows: "We concede that there is a settlement value to the case but that it is not worth $9750 as demanded by you. In an effort to avoid further expenses and time to both, I will now make an offer to conclude this claim on an amicable basis and for the sum of $7500 which you may convey to your clients. If the offer of $7500 is not acceptable, I would then suggest that your arbitration papers be prepared as we have no intention of increasing this offer, feeling that it is fair and just to all parties concerned."

On August 30, 1967, Smaligos' counsel made a demand for arbitration to the American Arbitration Association and on October 11, 1967 Thomas J. Reinstadtler, Jr., Esquire, was appointed as arbitrator. A hearing was held on December 18, 1967 which, as before stated, resulted in the arbitrator awarding only $243, being one-third of the cost of a family memorial monument. The arbitrator determined that the funeral bill of $1016.30 was payable under the Medical Payment Clause of the policy and thus not recoverable under the Uninsured Motorist Clause.

* * * * *

Smaligos further argue that there was an offer and acceptance of a settlement in the amount of $7500. However, we are constrained to agree with the reasoning of the lower court that, when Smaligos filed for arbitration of the dispute, they rejected the offer of settlement. The letter hereinbefore quoted offering the said $7500 clearly stated that the company was "now" offering the same and that if it is not acceptable then Smaligos should proceed to arbitration. By proceeding to arbitration, Smaligos showed the offer was not acceptable and such conduct clearly showed that Smaligos did not intend to accept the offer nor take it under further advisement. As stated in

---

[35] Restatement (Second) Contracts § 38 cmt. a (1979).

> section 36 of the Restatement of the Law of Contracts: "An **offer is rejected** when the offeror is justified in inferring from the words or conduct of the offeree that the offeree intends not to accept the offer or to take it under further advisement." We cannot agree with Smaligos' interpretation of the phrase "as we have no intention of increasing this offer" as meaning that the offer was to stand firm at $7500 even though arbitration was sought. The company, as stated in the letter, made the offer "in an effort to avoid further expenses and time to both;" certainly that offer cannot be viewed as still standing after the company was required to proceed to arbitration.
>
> *Order affirmed.*

3. Lapse of Time

Where the offer contains a specified time for acceptance, upon the lapse of that specified time, the offer will terminate[36] (*Kurio v. United States*),[37] or, where no time period is specified, the offer will terminate within a reasonable time. It is fundamental that an offer, if not accepted promptly, may be terminated by lapse of time.[38] Where no time is fixed in the offer within which acceptance must be made, it is a rule of law that acceptance must be made within a reasonable time. What is considered a reasonable time may vary with the circumstances and is an issue of fact to be resolved upon trial. There are instances, no doubt, where a court would be warranted in holding that the failure of an offeree to respond within a reasonable time terminated the offer as a matter of law. Such was the holding in *Staples v. Pan-American Wall Paper & Paint Co.* (63 F. 2d 701) where a period of 101 days lapsed between the receipt of an offer and its purported acceptance.[39]

4. Revocation

A *revocation* occurs when the offeror revokes his offer and denies the power of acceptance to the offeree.[40] As a general rule, most offers are revocable.[41] For example, Sam says to Joe, " I will sell you my bicycle for $100." Joe says, "I am going home to retrieve my checkbook and will be right back." As Joe is leaving, Sam says, "Joe, I revoke my offer." The result is that Sam has revoked his offer

---

[36] *See* Kurio v. United States, 429 F. Supp. 42, 63–66 (S.D. Tex. 1970) (stating termination of the power of acceptance by lapse of a specified time).

[37] Restatement (Second) Contracts § 41 (1979).

[38] Restatement (Second) Contracts § 35 (1979).

[39] *See* Modern Pool Products, Inc. v. Rudel Machinery Company, Inc.294 N.Y.S.2d 426 (1968), 1968 N.Y. Misc. LEXIS 1630.

[40] Restatement (Second) Contracts § 42 cmt. a (1979).

[41] *Id.* at § 42 (1979).

to sell his bicycle and Joe then has no offer to accept. But suppose that Sam had promised Joe that he would not revoke the offer. The offer does not become irrevocable unless and until Joe gives consideration by paying Sam $100. The offer is therefore revocable notwithstanding Sam's promise to not revoke the offer.[42]

5. Irrevocable Offers

The act of revocation does not necessitate the word "revoke." Revocation can occur either directly by a pronouncement by the offeror or indirectly by implication. Any act by the offeror which is inconsistent with his manifestation of intent to make an offer will constitute a revocation of an offer.[43] But once the offeree has exercised his power to accept the offer, the offer has been captured, and the offeror is deprived of his power to revoke the offer.[44]

6. Option Contracts Create Irrevocable Offers

As a general rule, the offeror's promise is revocable until the offer is accepted.[45] What may keep an offer open is an option contract. An *option contract* is a promise which meets the requirements for the formation of a contract and limits the promisor's power to revoke an offer.[46] The notion of the option generally has the characteristic that it may keep the offer open even though the offer is revocable. For example, Sam has a large plot of real estate. He needs cash and decides to divide his property into two parcels, A and B. He offers to sell parcel B to Joe and keep parcel A for himself. Joe promises to purchase parcel B, but also gives Sam $1000 for an option to purchase parcel A if ever Sam decides to sell it. Joe wants the option of first refusal. This option contract limits Sam's power to revoke the offer until he has first offered Joe the opportunity to purchase parcel A.

An option contract prevents the offeror from retracting his offer and thus the offer remains open until the offeree decides to exercise it.[47] It binds the offeror's commitment to the offer and his obligation to performance will be binding upon the acceptance of the offer by the offeree.[48] The following case illustrates the legal enforcement of option contracts that create irrevocable offers.

---

[42] *Id.* at § 42 cmt. a (1979).
[43] *Id.* at § 42 cmt. d (1979). *See also* Tatsch v. Hamilton-Ericson Mfg. Co., 76 N.M. 729, 418 P. 2d 187 (1966) (1979).
[44] *Id.* at § 42 cmt. c (1979).
[45] *Id.* at § 24 cmt. a (1979).
[46] *Id.* at § 25 (1979).
[47] *Id.* at § 37 cmt. a (1979).
[48] *Id.* at § 37 cmt. b (1979).

Case 2.9

> ## Fred Y. Boyer v. George M. Karakehian
> ### 915 P.2d 1295 (1996); 1996 Colo. LEXIS 159
>
> Chief Justice. Vollack
>
> On May 1, 1991, Boyer and Karakehian executed a written agreement entitled "Lease and Option" (the "Agreement"). The agreement provided that Boyer was to rent Karakehian's house for the four month period from May 8, 1991 through September 8, 1991 for $ 1,750 per month. The Agreement also stated that Boyer was to provide Karakehian a security deposit of $ 1,750. The Agreement further provided that Boyer had the option to purchase the property at any time during the term of the lease for the sum of $ 275,000.[1] Boyer then gave Karakehian a check for $ 3,500, representing the first month's rent and security deposit, and moved into the house.
>
> * * * * *
>
> Boyer and Karakehian met for lunch on September 9, 1991. The parties are in dispute over what occurred at that meeting. Karakehian claims the parties set a closing date at the meeting, while Boyer maintains that he told Karakehian that he was unsure at that time whether he wanted to purchase the property. When Karakehian was subsequently unable to contact Boyer in order to set a closing date, Karakehian served Boyer with a notice to quit on September 27, 1991, terminating Boyer's tenancy effective October 8, 1991. Karakehian also notified Boyer that he was retaining Boyer's security deposit of $ 1,750.
>
> * * * * *
>
> Boyer then filed suit in county court demanding return of the security deposit, and Karakehian counterclaimed for breach of contract and promissory estoppel. The cases were consolidated and transferred to district court, where, after a trial, a jury rendered a verdict in favor of Karakehian on the breach of contract claim and against Boyer on the security deposit claim. ***Boyer appealed.
>
> * * * * *
>
> A purchase option in a lease is an **irrevocable offer** to sell the leased property to the lessee for a specified consideration. *Polemi v. Wells*, 759 P.2d 796, 798 (Colo. App. 1988), cert. denied, No. 88SC249 (Colo. Aug. 22, 1988). As a purchase option is a contract for the sale of an interest in land, it is required by statute to be in writing.
>
> * * * * *
>
> The Agreement is unambiguous. It bound Boyer to a four- month lease of the subject property with an option to purchase the property within that time period. It does not, on its face, bind Boyer to purchase the property.
>
> * * * * *
>
> We thus affirm in part and reverse in part, and remand this case for a new trial.

7. Death or Incapacity

Death or incapacity of the offeror destroys the power of the offeree to accept the offer because there is no longer a manifestation of mutual assent.[49] Similarly, death and incapacity of the offeree prevents the offeree from manifesting acceptance.[50]

---

[49] *Id.* at § 48 (1979).

[50] *Id.* at § 48 cmt. c (1979).

Chapter 2

Vocabulary

1. Offer
2. Bilateral Agreements
3. Unilateral Agreements
4. Meeting of the Minds
5. Elements of an Offer
6. Preliminary Negotiations
7. Offer v. Advertisements
8. Offers v. Auctions
9. Time for Performance
10. Counteroffer
11. Rejection of an Offer
12. Revocation
13. Irrevocable Offer
14. Option Contracts

Review Questions

1. What is the issue in the *Lefkowitz v. Great Minneapolis Surplus Store* case?
2. What is the applicable law in the *Lefkowitz* case?
3. What is the issue in the *Isaac Esmay v. Truman B. Gorton* case?
4. What is the applicable law in *Isaac Esmay* case?
5. What is the issue in the *Leonard v. PepsiCo* case?
6. What is the applicable law in the *Leonard* case?
7. What is the issue in the *Coleman v. John Duncan* case?
8. What is the applicable law in the *Coleman* case?
9. What is the issue in the *Rolla Carr v. Mahaska County Bankers Association* case?
10. What is the applicable law in the *Rolla Carr* case?
11. What is the issue in the *Southern Fire & Casualty v. Teal* case?
12. What is the applicable law in the *Teal* case?
13. What is the issue in the *Shaw & Co. v. Ingram-Day Lumber Co.* case?
14. What is the applicable law in the *Shaw* case?
15. What is the issue in the *Smaligos v. Fireman's Fund* case?
16. What is the applicable law in the *Fireman's Fund* case?
17. What is the issue in the *Fred Y. Boyer v. George M. Karakehian* case?
18. What is the applicable law in the *Karakehian* case?

Chapter 3

The Agreement: Acceptance

I. Acceptance
A. Acceptance of the Offer

Acceptance by the offeree of an offer by the offeror is the manifestation of assent by the offeree to the terms communicated by the offeror to the offeree.[1]

The offeror is the master of his offer and, by virtue of his manifested intention, has the right to designate the offeree. Therefore, only the designated offeree has the power to accept the offer from the offeror.[2] An offer can be accepted by the offeree only if the offeror invites such an offer.[3]

B. Acceptance by Performance or Promise

Acceptance may manifest itself either by a *promise* or by *performance*. An acceptance by a promise is the manifestation of assent by the offeree of the same bargain that is advanced by the offeror.[4] The promise may be made in words or other symbols of assent, or it may be implied by conduct, other than a performance.[5] A promise for a performance is called a *unilateral contract*.[6]

The acceptance must assent to the terms and conditions articulated in the offer, and must be accepted in the mode and manner requested by the offeror.[7] Because a bargain is one in which there are mutual promises, the offeror may require the acceptance by the offeree to be manifested by a return promise, which can be an oral acceptance[8] such as saying "I accept," or some conduct other than a performance, which indicates acceptance by the offeree, such as nodding of the head or a movement of the hand.

When the offeror make an offer that requires performance on the part of the offeree, the offer can only be accepted by the offeree upon performing the act requested.[9] The acceptance is complete when the offeree either initiates or

---

[1] Restatement (Second) Contracts § 50 (1) (1979).
[2] *Id.* at § 52 (1979).
[3] *Id.* at § 53 (1979).
[4] *Id.* at § 50 (1979).
[5] *Id.* at § 50 cmt. c (1979).
[6] *Id.* at § 50 (1979).
[7] *Id.* at § 50 cmt. a (1979).
[8] *Id.* at § 50 cmt. c (1979).
[9] *Id.* at § 45 cmt. a (1979), *See also* § 50 cmt. b (1979).

completes the performance.[10] The offeree may accept by performing the act requested by the offeror, giving rise to a unilateral contract. But only the performance requested by the offeror will give rise to a good acceptance. For example, suppose the offeror, Sam, makes an offer such as, "Joe, if you run across the London Bridge, I will pay you 50 pounds." Joe then starts to run and gets to the middle of the bridge when the offeror yells, "Joe, I reject my offer" but Joe ignores Sam and continues to run all the way across the bridge. Joe's performance satisfies the conditions of the offer, which manifests into an acceptance of the offer by running across the London Bridge. The offer is not revoked and the acceptance is good.

The case below illustrates the principle that acceptance is good only when the terms of the offer are met.

Case 3.1

> Bowlerama of Texas v. John Miyakawa
> 449 S.W.2d 357 (1969), 1969 Tex. App. LEXIS 2141
> Civil Ct. Appls. of Texas, 4th Dist., San Antonio
>
> OPINION BY: CADENA J.
>
> OPINION: Plaintiffs, John Miyakawa and Jo Ann Goldman, filed this suit to recover $500 which they alleged they won as a Jackpot prize in a bowling tournament sponsored by defendant, Bowlerama of Texas, Inc. Defendant appeals from a judgment rendered in favor of plaintiffs by County Court at Law No. 3 of Bexar County, following a non-jury trial.
>
> The tournament in question involved, in fact, two separate competitions. First, there was a doubles tournament, with defendant awarding ten prizes weekly, guaranteed to total at least $300, with first prize in the weekly doubles competition being $100. In addition, there was a "Jackpot" competition in which any team of a man and woman bowler who scored in excess of 1,440 in three games would be awarded $500. Only one Jackpot prize of $500 could be won in any one week, and, of course, there was no guarantee that any team would win the Jackpot during any given week.
>
> The announcement of the competition advised prospective entrants that "house rules" would be applicable to both the doubles tournament and the Jackpot competition. Some of the "house rules" were applicable to all contests, but five of the rules were, by their language, applicable only to the Jackpot competition. Insofar as this controversy is concerned, we need only note that while teams which kept their own scores were eligible to win one of the ten weekly prizes, only those contestants whose scores were kept by a scorer selected by the clerk in charge of the control desk and approved by defendant's manager were eligible for the Jackpot award. The more stringent scoring rules applicable to the Jackpot competition were due to the fact that the guaranteed ten weekly prizes in the doubles tournament were paid from a prize fund made up of a portion of the entry fee paid by the contestants, while the $500 Jackpot prize was to be paid entirely from defendant's funds.

---

[10] *Id.* at § 45 cmt. d (1979), *See also* § 50 cmt. b (1979).

It is undisputed that plaintiffs' score was not kept by a scorekeeper selected by the clerk in charge of the control desk and approved by defendant's manager. When plaintiffs paid their entry fee they did not request the appointment of an official approved scorekeeper, and, although the Jackpot competition rules specifically stated that the official scorekeeper must keep the score beginning with the first ball rolled in the first frame of the first game of the three-game series, plaintiffs kept their own score for the first two frames, after which a third party, at plaintiffs' request, kept score for the remaining twenty-eight frames of the three games. The rules applicable to the Jackpot competition expressly stated that no bowlers would be allowed to keep their own scores.

The "house rules" had been reduced to writing and had been posted on the bulletin board at defendant's bowling establishment for almost five months prior to the time that plaintiffs alleged they won the Jackpot. One of the plaintiffs confessed familiarity with all of the house rules except that which required that Jackpot scores be kept by an official scorer.

Under these circumstances plaintiffs cannot recover. The rights of a contestant who has performed the act required in the promoter's offer are limited by the terms of the offer, that is, by the conditions and rules of the contest as made public. …In order to recover, it was incumbent on plaintiffs to show either that they had complied with the terms of the offer or that the promoter accepted their performance as sufficient compliance…this plaintiff failed to do.

Plaintiffs contend that defendant paid prizes to contestants whose scores had not been kept by an official scorer. This is true as far as the doubles competition, as distinguished from the Jackpot contest, is concerned, but as already pointed out; the rules relating to the presence of an official scorekeeper were applicable only to the Jackpot contest. There is no evidence that defendant, since adoption of the rule governing score keeping in the Jackpot contest, had ever awarded a prize to contestants whose score was not kept by an official scorekeeper.

The judgment of the trial court is *reversed* and judgment is here rendered that plaintiffs take nothing.

C. Acceptance Before Knowledge of the Offer

Where the offeree provides information and is unaware that an offer has been made for such information, then there is no acceptance. Such is the case when an offeree provides information to an officer of the law to apprehend a criminal but is unaware that there is a reward for his apprehension. Providing the information without knowledge of the offer does not create acceptance when the offeree later discovers the existence of the reward.[11] But where the offeree tenders part performance without knowledge of the offer and later receives knowledge of the offer before completing the performance, an acceptance may manifest itself by completion of the remaining performance.[12]

The following case illustrates the principle that the offeree must have knowledge of the reward before acceptance is good.

[11] Restatement (Second) Contracts § 51 cmt. a (1979).
[12] *Id.* at § 51 cmt. b (1979).

Case 3.2

James Williams v. The W. Chicago St. R.R. Company
61 N.E. 456 (1901), 1901 Ill. LEXIS 2394

Mr. JUSTICE HAND delivered the opinion of the court:

This is an action of assumpsit brought by the appellant, against the appellee, in the circuit court of Cook County, to recover a reward offered by the appellee for the arrest and conviction of the murderer or murderers of C. B. Birch, who was killed while in the service of the appellee, which, as published, was in the following terms:

"$5,000 Reward"
"OFFICE WEST CHICAGO STREET RAILROAD Co., "*June 24, 1895.*
"The above reward will be paid by the West Chicago Street Railroad Company for the arrest and conviction of the murderer or murderers of C. B. Birch, who was fatally shot while in discharge of his duty as receiver, on the morning of June 23, at the Armitage avenue barn.
CHARLES T. YERKES, Pres't."

* * * * *

At about two o'clock on Sunday morning, June 23, 1895, Birch, whose duty it was to receive the money brought in by the conductors, was fatally shot at the barn of appellee located at Armitage avenue, in the city of Chicago. The appellant, who was also an employee of the appellee, and whose duty consisted of going from barn to barn each night to inspect the cash registers, was in the barn from midnight until two 'clock in the morning, and left just before the killing of Birch. As he drove away in his buggy he noticed two men coming across the street toward the barn. They looked sharply at him and he looked at them. On Monday morning, June 24, the appellant went to the appellee's office, where he met its general superintendent, who inquired of him if he saw any men near the barn as he drove away. Appellant told him that he had seen two men and that he thought he could identify them, whereupon the superintendent gave him a note and told him to go and see Capt. Larson of the police force. He called upon Capt. Larson that afternoon, told him what he had seen and gave him a description of the two men, whereupon the officer said that he had a man in custody at that time who he thought answered the description of one of the men described by him. The man, whose name was Julius Mannow, was brought up and was identified by the appellant as one of the men he had seen near the barn as he drove away. Capt. Larson told him to come to the station the next day, and in the meantime he would hunt up and have arrested the other man he had described. The murder or Birch led the police authorities to at once issue what was termed a "drag-net order,"—that is, an order to the various patrolmen to arrest all suspicious characters in their respective districts and bring them in for examination as to their whereabouts at the time of the commission of the crime. Mannow was thus arrested and brought to the station. A police officer named Jurs testified upon the trial of this cause that about two months before the time of the murder Mannow had narrated to him a plan for the robbing of a coal office in the manner in which the Armitage avenue robbery was accomplished, and had described Joseph Windrath as concerned in the plan, and that after the Armitage avenue robbery and the murder of Birch the witness at once recalled this fact and suspected Mannow and Windrath and took steps to cause their arrest. This was before the information was given by the appellant.

On Tuesday morning, the 25th day of June, the appellant for the first time learned of the offered reward by reading the same as published in the *Chicago Tribune*. Afterwards, on that day, he went again to the police station and identified Windrath, who had been arrested in the meantime, as the man he had seen in company with Mannow near the barn just before the killing. The services rendered by the appellant in connection with the arrest and conviction of Mannow and Windrath after he knew of the offered reward, consisted in his identification of Windrath, and his testifying before the coroner's jury, the grand jury, and upon the trial in the criminal court, that he had seen Mannow and Windrath together near the Armitage avenue barn on the night and near the time of the commission of the crime. Other information was obtained by the police authorities shortly after the identification of Mannow and Windrath which fastened the crime upon the two men. Mannow pleaded guilty and Windrath was tried and convicted. The offered reward was paid by the appellee to another claimant.

The offer of a reward remains conditional until it is accepted by the performance of the service, and one who offers a reward has the right to prescribe whatever terms he may see fit, and such terms must be substantially complied with before any contract arises between him and the claimant. Thus, if the reward is offered for the arrest and conviction of a criminal, or for his arrest and the recovery of the money stolen, both the arrest and conviction or arrest and recovery of the money are conditions precedent to the recovery of the reward; and when the offer is for the delivery of a fugitive at a certain place the reward cannot be earned by the delivery of him at another place, and an offer for a capture of two is not acted upon by the capture of one. The reward cannot be apportioned. The offer is an entirety, and as such must be enforced, or not at all. ...

* * * * *

We are of the opinion that the appellant is not entitled to recover in this case for the further reason that the services performed by him were substantially all rendered before the reward was offered or at a time when he was ignorant of the fact that a reward had been offered. [There was no offer to accept]. After the appellant had informed the superintendent of appellee and the captain of police that he had seen Mannow and his companion near the scene of the murder at about the time the same was committed, he did nothing towards securing the conviction of the prisoners other than what he could have been required to do as a witness. The reward was not offered for information which was already in the possession of the officers nor for witnesses who would come forward and testify to facts which were then known to be within their knowledge, but for the arrest and conviction of the murderer or murderers. The right to recover a reward arises out of the contractual relation which exists between the person offering the reward and the claimant, which is implied by law by reason of the offer on the one hand and the performance of the service on the other, the reason of the rule being that the services of the claimant are rendered in consequence of the offered reward, from which an implied promise is raised on the part of the person offering the reward to pay him the amount thereof by reason of the performance by him of such service, and no such promise can be implied *unless he knew at the time of the performance of the service that the reward had been offered*, and in consideration thereof, and with a view to earning the same, rendered the service specified in such offer. ...

* * * * *

And in *Howlands v. Lounds, supra,* the court says, "In order to entitle a party to recover a reward offered, he must establish between himself and the person offering the

> reward, not only the offer and his acceptance of it, but his performance of the services for which the reward was offered; and upon principle, as well as upon authority, the performance of this service by one who did not know of the offer and could not have acted in reference to it cannot recover."
>
> We are of the opinion the appellant failed to make out a cause of action, and that the trial court, for the reasons above suggested, properly directed a verdict for the appellee. The judgment of the Appellate Court will therefore be *affirmed*.

D. Rejection and Revocation of the Offer

The offeree does not have to accept the offer and can manifest his intentions by revoking or rejecting it and communicating his intentions to the offeror. However, the rejection does not terminate the offeree's power of acceptance until the rejection or revocation is communicated and received by the offeror.[13] Receipt is manifested when the rejection or revocation comes into the possession of the offeror or is delivered to his agent.[14] Hence the offer may be accepted if the acceptance reaches the offeror before the rejection. For example, suppose Sam offers to sell Joe a painting for $5000. Joe sends a note to Sam rejecting the offer to purchase the painting, but before Sam receives the rejection note, Joe calls Sam and accepts the offer to purchase the painting for $5000. Joe's acceptance is good since the acceptance was received by Sam before the rejection note was received.

E. Notice of Acceptance

In the usual course of striking a bargain, the offeror expects to receive prompt notification of the acceptance.[15] Notice of the acceptance to the offeror is essential unless the offer indicates otherwise or if it is the custom or tradition in the industry *not* to give notice.[16] It is essential to an acceptance that the offeree exercise reasonable diligence to notify the offeror of the acceptance[17] because the offeror is entitled to know, in clear terms, whether the offeree accepts his offer.[18] In cases of communication by mail or telegram, the acceptance is effective when placed in the mailbox even if the acceptance fails to reach the offeror.[19] Where the offer requires performance instead of a promise, there is no requirement to give notice since performance will serve the same purpose as notice to the offeror.[20]

---

[13] Restatement (Second) Contracts § 53 cmt. b (1979).
[14] *Id.* at § 68 (1979).
[15] *Id.* at § 54 cmt. a (1979).
[16] *Id.* at § 54 (1979).
[17] *Id.* at § 56 (1979).
[18] *Id.* at § 57 cmt. b (1979).
[19] *Id.* at § 56 cmt. b (1979).
[20] *Id.* at § 54 cmt. c (1979).

The question raised in the following case is whether or not in a unilateral contract performance will manifest in an acceptance.

F. C. Scott v. J. F. Duthie & Company
216 P. 853 (1923); 125 Wash. 470 (1923)

OPINION BY: J. MACKINTOSH

This appeal arises from the sustaining of a demurrer to a complaint which alleges that, on December 23, 1918, the appellant was a department foreman in the shipyard owned and operated by the respondents; that the employment was for an indefinite term; that, on that date, the respondents made a promise as follows:

For the purpose of inducing the general department foremen of this company to continue their work with this company and to refrain from accepting employment elsewhere until this company shall complete the ships which it has contracted to build for the United States Shipping Board, Emergency Fleet Corporation, J. F. Duthie & Company promises the general department foremen now in its employment that upon the completion of its contract with the shipping board, the company will divide as a bonus one-half million dollars among those of its general department foremen who continue in its employment until the completion of that contract."

The complaint alleged further that, in reliance on this promise, the appellant remained continuously in the respondent's employment until October 15, 1920, when the contract referred to had been completed; that the appellant would not have continued in such employment except in reliance upon the promise, and that he has not been paid the bonus.

As stated by the appellant, the question here is, "where an employer promises a bonus or a share of the profits to an employee employed for an indefinite term, to be paid if he works continuously for a given period, is the employer bound by his promise when the employee accepts the offer by performance?"

A binding and enforceable contract to pay a reward rests, on one side, upon a valid offer, and, on the other side, upon an acceptance of such offer, including its terms and conditions, by a performance of the services requested in the offer before the offer lapses or is revoked. Until **acceptance by performance** of the services, it is merely a proposition; but when accepted by performance it becomes a binding contract, subject to the laws governing contracts generally.

* * * * *

"Performance constitutes acceptance of the offer, and after performance it cannot be revoked, so as to deprive a person who has acted on the faith thereof of compensation. It is not necessary that the person performing the service for which a reward is offered generally should give notice to the offeror that he accepts the offer; for in such case the party making the offer impliedly dispenses with actual notice, and the doing of the act completes the contract.

The judgment is reversed [in favor of the employees] with instructions to overrule the demurrer

F. Characteristics of Acceptance

1. Compliance With the Terms of the Offer

Since the offeror is the master of his offer, the offer may be conditioned in any manner requested by the offeror. For example, the offeror may specifically state the date, time, place or manner of acceptance.[21] Therefore, a good acceptance requires that the offeree comply with all the terms of the offer unless otherwise agreed by the parties.[22] Where the offeree places qualification on the acceptance, in other words, changes or modifies the terms of the original offer, then there is no acceptance[23] because the acceptance must be unequivocal.[24] If the acceptance is not unequivocal, the modified acceptance becomes a counteroffer. However, the offeree may request a change or modification to the terms of the offer from the offeror without changing the terms of the offer. Requesting information does not give rise to a counteroffer. In this situation, the offeree is requesting additional information about the terms of the offer *without* rejecting the initial offer.

The following case illustrates a fact pattern wherein the court attempts to determine whether there was a proper acceptance or not.

Case 3.4

Town of Lindsay, Texas v. Cooke Co. Electric Coop. Asso.
502 S.W.2d 117 (1973), 1973 Tex. LEXIS 222

JUDGE: Ruel C. Walker,

Petitioner was incorporated as a town in 1959. Respondent, which had been serving inhabitants of the area since 1938, prepared and submitted to the Town Council a proposed ordinance granting respondent a franchise for a period of 50 years from acceptance of the ordinance. The ordinance was enacted by the council on March 24, 1960, but was not immediately effective. The final section provided:

Section 8: The Electric Cooperative Association shall file its written acceptance of this franchise within thirty (30) days after the passage of this ordinance, and this ordinance shall take effect and be enforced from and after its passage, approval and acceptance.

The ordinance further provided that the franchise was conditioned upon payment by respondent on April 1, 1960, and annually thereafter, of two per cent of the gross

---

[21] Restatement (Second) Contracts § 60 (1979).

[22] *Id.* at § 58 cmt. a (1979).

[23] *Id.* at § 59 (1979).

[24] *Id.* at § 61 cmt. a (1979).

receipts from the sale of electric energy within the corporate limits during the preceding calendar year. Within a few days after March 25, 1960, respondent mailed its check for $12.45 to petitioner. The check was accompanied by a statement of the 1959 receipts from inhabitants of the town and by a voucher showing that the check was in payment of "2 percent Gross Receipts Tax for the Year 1960." The check was endorsed by petitioner's Secretary-Treasurer and deposited in petitioner's bank account. It was paid by the drawee bank on April 4, 1960. On April 20, 1960, the ordinance was considered at a meeting of respondent's Board of Directors, which unanimously approved the franchise agreement. Respondent's attorney was instructed to file a formal written acceptance of the ordinance with petitioner, but there is no evidence that this was ever done.

On June 9, 1960, after expiration of the 30-day acceptance period, respondent's manager appeared before the Council and requested that the ordinance be allowed to stay in effect. No action on the matter was taken on that meeting. On June 30, 1960, the franchise ordinance was repealed and the Council at the same time ordered that the franchise tax be refunded to respondent. Petitioner thereupon issued its check for $12.45 to respondent, and the check was accepted by respondent and deposited in its bank account. In July or August, 1960, and again in 1963 and in 1970, respondent's manager appeared before the Council and requested a franchise, but the request was denied.

Under the provisions of Art.1436a, V.A.T.S., respondent was entitled to continue operating within the corporate limits and without a franchise for ten years after the date of the petitioner's incorporation. In 1970, after the expiration of the 10-year period, petitioner requested respondent to remove its poles and lines from the streets and alleys of the Town. Respondent declined to do so, and this suit followed.

In response to the two special issues that were submitted, the jury found: (1) that the cooperative filed its written acceptance of the franchise within 30 days after March 24, 1960, and (2) respondent's payment of the gross receipts tax by writing its check with the accompanying voucher and statement was intended by both parties as an acceptance of the franchise.

Where, as here, an offer prescribes the time and manner of acceptance, its terms in this respect must be complied with to create a contract. The use of a different method of acceptance by the offeree will not be effectual unless the original offeror thereafter manifests his assent to the other party. ...Petitioner's Mayor and Secretary-Treasurer testified that there had never been a written acceptance of the franchise. While their testimony may not be conclusive, there is no evidence to the contrary. If the manner of acceptance had not been specified in the ordinance, respondent's act in paying the gross receipts tax might constitute an implied acceptance of the franchise. Its conduct in this respect was not, however, a written acceptance within the meaning of the ordinance, and the record does not suggest that petitioner assented to an implied acceptance. In our opinion there is no evidence to support the jury's findings, and the trial court erred in overruling petitioner's motion for judgment non obstante veredicto.

The judgments of the courts below are reversed, and the cause is remanded to the district court with instructions to render judgment for petitioner.

2. The Moment That Acceptance Becomes Effective

A good acceptance to the offer completes the manifestation of mutual assent at the moment that the offeree dispatches the acceptance to the offeror, regardless of whether or not the acceptance reaches the offeror.[25] The "mailbox" rule is applicable here, i.e. the acceptance is complete when the offeree drops the acceptance letter in the mailbox.[26] But the acceptance by mail is ineffective unless the correspondence is properly addressed to the offeree.[27] However, an ineffective acceptance resulting from an improper address becomes effective at the time that it is received by the offeror because once the acceptance is in the hands of the offeror, the means of transmission of acceptance becomes immaterial.[28] Otherwise, acceptance can be made by any reasonable medium. A "reasonable medium" is one ordinarily used by the offeror or one customarily used in the trade.[29]

Moreover, the moment that an acceptance by telephone, teletype or e-mail is manifested is considered the same moment when the parties are in the presence of one another.[30] The advantage to being in the presence of each other is that any ambiguities or misunderstanding with respect to the terms of the offer can be cleared immediately.[31]

There are several circumstances in which silence operates as an acceptance. First, where the offeree has an obligation to speak but does not will result in an acceptance by silence. This occurs when the offeree receives a benefit that requires compensation and the offeree, by his silence, nevertheless accepts the benefit. The second circumstance of acceptance by silence occurs when the offeror is led to understand that the offeree will accept the offer by silence. A third type of acceptance by silence is manifested when the parties, because of previous dealings, understand that silence on the part of the offeree means acceptance. Finally, an offeree who exercises dominion of the offeror's property may manifest and assent in silence to an acceptance.[32]

The following case illustrates an attempt to bind the parties to a contract by silence.

---

[25] Restatement (Second) Contracts § 63 (1979).

[26] *Id.* at § 63 cmt. a (1979).

[27] *Id.* at § 66 cmt. b (1979).

[28] *Id.* at § 66 cmt. a (1979).

[29] *Id.* at § 65 cmt. a (1979).

[30] *Id.* at § 64 (1979).

[31] *Id.* at § 64 cmt. b (1979).

[32] *Id.* at § 69 cmt. e (1979).

Phaedra R. Shively v. Santa Fe Preparatory School, Inc.
21 Fed. Appx. 875 (2001); 2001 U.S. App. LEXIS 24578

OPINION BY: MICHAEL R. MURPHY

Plaintiff Phaedra R. Shively was employed by defendant Santa Fe Preparatory School as a French teacher for many years. The school signed and offered her a full-time contract for the 1994–95 school year which included the following as the last sentence: "The School may refuse to reemploy the teacher without cause, and this contract shall not give rise to any entitlement to or expectation of reemployment." Plaintiff signed and returned the contract with the following notation: "I agree with all of the last paragraph except the last sentence. I deserve and expect just cause for non-renewal of continuation of my teaching." Defendant did not respond to plaintiff's notation, but did employ plaintiff as a teacher during the 1994–95 school year. Defendant did not offer plaintiff a contract for the 1995–96 school year. Plaintiff then filed this suit asserting claims under the Age Discrimination in Employment Act (ADEA) and for breach of contract under New Mexico law

* * * * *

Defendant argues, in the alternative, that it did not accept plaintiff's counteroffer as a matter of law. This argument is without merit, as New Mexico law recognizes acceptance by silence or by performance. *See Garcia v. Middle Rio Grande Conservancy Dist.*, 99 N.M. 802, 664 P.2d 1000, 1005 (N.M. Ct. App. 1983) (discussing acceptance by silence). Defendant argues that an offeree's silence does not evidence acceptance unless the offeree has a duty to speak. While this is true as far as it goes, defendant ignores the proposition that silence operates as an acceptance "where because of previous dealings or otherwise, it is reasonable that the offeree should notify the offeror if he does not intend to accept," We have found no cases explaining how a duty to speak arises under New Mexico law, but also no case indicating that New Mexico would not follow the Restatement on this point.

* * * * *

We reverse the award of damages, however, and remand for further fact-finding on that issue. The magistrate judge awarded plaintiff $ 60,000 in damages, representing "one year's full salary, as well as a declining, lesser amount for each subsequent year …tempered…with the amount Plaintiff had earned in mitigation of her damages," id. Plaintiff claims damages of $ 325,270.00. Appellant's Br. at 11. The magistrate judge did not explain what evidence supported his conclusion that $ 60,000 was the correct amount to be awarded. Without an explanation tying the magistrate judge's award to the evidence, however, we cannot provide meaningful review. On remand, the magistrate judge should determine the length of the amended contract and the damages to be awarded as a consequence of that determination, specifically tying his conclusions to the evidence.

The judgment of the United States District Court for the District of New Mexico is AFFIRMED in part and REVERSED in part, and the case is REMANDED for additional proceedings consistent with this decision.

* * * * *

Chapter 3

Vocabulary

1. Acceptance
2. Rejection
3. Revocation
4. Acceptance by Performance
5. Acceptance by Promise
6. Acceptance by Silence
7. Notice of Acceptance

Review Questions

1. What is the issue in the *Bowlerama of Texas v. John Miyakawa* case?
2. What is the law in the *Bowlerama* case?
3. What is the issue in the *James Williams v. The West Chicago Street* case?
4. What is the law in the *Williams* case?
5. What is the issue in the *F. C. Scott v. J. F. Duthie & Company* case?
6. What is the law in the *Scott* case?
7. What is the issue in the *Town of Lindsay, Texas v. Cooke Co.* case?
8. What is the law in the *Cooke* case?
9. What is the issue in the Phaedra R. Shively case?
10. What is the law in the Phaedra case?

Chapter 4

Consideration

I. Contracts Requiring Consideration
A. Exchange of Promise for Performance

Consideration is something bargained for and given in exchange for a promise.[1] As a general rule, any performance which is bargained for is consideration.[2] That something can be a performance that can manifest itself as an act, forbearance,[3] or the creation, modification or destruction of a legal relation.[4]

The following case illustrates a performance that manifests itself into consideration.

<table>
<tr><td align="center">Hamer v. Sidway
27 N.E. 256 (1891); 1891 N.Y. LEXIS 1396
Court of Appeals of New York</td><td align="right">Case 4.1</td></tr>
</table>

JUDGES: Parker, J. All concur.

The question which provoked the most discussion by counsel on this appeal, and which lies at the foundation of plaintiff's asserted right of recovery, is whether by virtue of a contract defendant's testator William E. Story became indebted to his nephew William E. Story, 2d, on his twenty-first birthday in the sum of five thousand dollars. The trial court found as a fact that "on the 20th day of March, 1869, ...William E. Story agreed to and with William E. Story, 2d, that if he would refrain from drinking liquor, using tobacco, swearing, and playing cards or billiards for money until he should become 21 years of age then he, the said William E. Story, would at that time pay him, the said William E. Story, 2d, the sum of $5000 for such refraining, to which the said William E. Story, 2d, agreed," and that he "in all things fully performed his part of said agreement."

The defendant contends that the contract was without consideration to support it, and, therefore, invalid. He asserts that the promisee by refraining from the use of liquor and tobacco was not harmed but benefited; that that which he did was best for him to do independently of his uncle's promise, and insists that it follows that unless the promisor was benefited, the contract was without consideration. A contention, which

---

[1] Restatement (Second) Contracts § 71 (1979).
[2] *Id.* at § 72 (1979).
[3] *Id.* at § 71 cmt. d (1979).
[4] *Id.* at § 71 (3) (1979).

if well founded, would seem to leave open for controversy in many cases whether that which the promisee did or omitted to do was, in fact, of such benefit to him as to leave no consideration to support the enforcement of the promisor's agreement. Such a rule could not be tolerated, and is without foundation in the law. The Exchequer Chamber, in 1875, defined consideration as follows: "A valuable consideration in the sense of the law may consist either in some right, interest, profit or benefit accruing to the one party, or some forbearance, detriment, loss or responsibility given, suffered or undertaken by the other." Courts "…will not ask whether the thing which forms the consideration does in fact benefit the promisee or a third party, or is of any substantial value to anyone. It is enough that something is promised, done, forborne or suffered by the party to whom the promise is made as consideration for the promise made to him…"

"In general a waiver of any legal right at the request of another party is a sufficient consideration for a promise." …"Any damage, or suspension, or forbearance of a right will be sufficient to sustain a promise. …"

* * * * *

Now, applying this rule to the facts before us, the promisee used tobacco, occasionally drank liquor, and he had a legal right to do so. That right he abandoned for a period of years upon the strength of the promise of the testator that for such forbearance he would give him $5000. We need not speculate on the effort which may have been required to give up the use of those stimulants. It is sufficient that he restricted his lawful freedom of action within certain prescribed limits upon the faith of his uncle's agreement, and now having fully performed the conditions imposed, it is of no moment whether such performance actually proved a benefit to the promisor, and the court will not inquire into it, but were it a proper subject of inquiry, we see nothing in this record that would permit a determination that the uncle was not benefited in a legal sense. Few cases have been found which may be said to be precisely in point, but such as have been support the position we have taken.

* * * * *

"Dear Uncle—I am now 21 years old to-day, and I am now my own boss, and I believe, according to agreement, that there is due me $5000. I have lived up to the contract to the letter in every sense of the word." A few days later, and on February sixth, the uncle replied, and, so far as it is material to this controversy, the reply is as follows:

"Dear Nephew—Your letter of the 31st came to hand all right saying that you had lived up to the promise made to me several years ago. I have no doubt but you have, for which you shall have $5000 as I promised you. I had the money in the bank the day you was 21 years old that I intended for you, and you shall have the money certain. Now, Willie, I don't intend to interfere with this money in any way until I think you are capable of taking care of it, and the sooner that time comes the better it will please me. I would hate very much to have you start out in some adventure that you thought all right and lose this money in one year. …This money you have earned much easier than I did, besides acquiring good habits at the same time, and you are quite welcome to the money. Hope you will make good use of it.
W. E. STORY.
"P. S. —You can consider this money on interest."

The trial court found as a fact that "said letter was received by said William E. Story, 2d, who thereafter consented that said money should remain with the said

William E. Story in accordance with the terms and conditions of said letter." And further, "That afterwards, on the first day of March, 1877, with the knowledge and consent of his said uncle, he duly sold, transferred and assigned all his right, title and interest in and to said sum of $5000 to his wife Libbie H. Story, who thereafter duly sold, transferred and assigned the same to the plaintiff [Hamer] in this action."

* * * * *

The order appealed from should be reversed and the judgment of the Special Term affirmed, with costs payable out of the estate. [The court ruled in favor of Hamer.]

B. Adequacy of Consideration

As a general rule, courts do not inquire into the adequacy of consideration. The argument that the consideration is of insufficient value for the promise is of no consequence. For example, in determining whether a promissory note is supported by a valuable consideration, the courts do not concern themselves with the relative value of the property for which the note was given. If the consideration for which a note was given is deemed valuable, then such note is valid.[5] It is not required that consideration have an economic value equivalent to that of the promise.[6] The court will only look to determine whether consideration exists, not whether it is adequate.

The following case illustrates this issue.

Chastain v. Texas Christian Missionary Soc.
78 S.W.2d 728 (1935)

Case 4.2

J. HIGGINS

The decedent, Silas R. Dale, deceased, executed a promissory note to the payee, Texas Christian missionary society, in which he agreed to submit to the payee the sum of $ 5,000 to be deposited into the payee's permanent memorial fund. The payee presented its claim to the administrator, Chastain, who rejected the claim. Within 89 days of the rejection, the payee commenced a lawsuit to recover the sum of the note. In his appeal, the administrator argued that the lawsuit was barred by limitation. The court rejected the argument, finding that the payee filed the action within 90 days of the claim's rejection. Moreover, the payee's amended petition did not set up a new cause of action. The administrator also contended that the note was invalid for **want of consideration** and certainty in date of payment. The court held that the promises set forth in the bond issued by the payee imposed obligations upon the payee that constituted **valuable consideration**. For example, the payee promised that the net income from the memorial fund would be devoted to its evangelical work.

* * * * *

---

[5] Chastain v. Texas Christian Missionary Soc. 78 S.W.2d 728 (1935), 1935 Tex. App. LEXIS 50.
[6] Restatement (Second) Contracts § 72 cmt. d (1979).

> In determining whether a promissory note is supported by a **valuable consideration**, the courts do not concern themselves with the relative value of the property for which the note was given. If, in law, the consideration for which a note was given is deemed valuable, then such note is valid.
>
> * * * * *
>
> Mutual promises concurrent in time constitute a **valuable consideration**, and the promises in the bond imposed obligations upon the society which, in our opinion, constitute a **valuable consideration** for the note sued upon.
>
> The case was *affirmed* in favor of the payee Texas Christian Missionary Society.

C. Gifts

However, a gift is generally not treated as a bargain; it is a gratuitous transfer. Therefore, the party that accepts the gift does so without giving consideration.[7] For example, a father says to his son, "Here are the keys to the car; it is now yours." The son says, "Thanks, dad, I accept." There is no bargain, the car is a gift, and the son has given no consideration.

To constitute a valid gift, there must be an *intention* by the donor, an *acceptance* by the donee, and a *delivery* of the gift by the donor to the donee. "If the donation is of a substantial benefit, the law will presume the acceptance, unless the contrary is shown."[8] Actual delivery is not essential to the validity of a gift. Any act which shall indicate a renunciation of dominion by the donor, and the transfer of dominion to the donee, is constructive delivery. "All are agreed that to constitute a gift there must be a present intention to give, and that this intention must be accompanied with delivery. Actual delivery is not essential in all cases. Constructive and symbolical delivery has been held to be sufficient under certain circumstances. If the property is bulky and the present intention to give is clear, and the donee, as soon thereafter as practicable, reduces the property to his possession and exercises dominion over it, the gift will be upheld."[9]

Indeed, it has been held that even the delivery of a key to a chest or trunk is sufficient, if all the other elements are present.[10] It has also been upheld that "the gift was complete when the donor pointed out to the donee several places where money was buried, the donee afterwards going to the places thus indicated, digging up the treasure, and reducing it to possession. There must be, in every case, a delivery of some sort, such a delivery as would put it beyond the power of the

---

[7] Restatement (Second) Contracts § 71 cmt. c (1979).
[8] Croxton v. Barrow 194 S.E. 24 (1937), 1937 Ga. App. LEXIS 539.
[9] Harrell v. Nicholson, 119 Ga. 458 (1904), 46 S.E. 623 (1904).
[10] Thomas's v. Lewis, 15 S.E. 389 (1892), 89 Va. 1 (1892).

donor to revoke the gift. He must relinquish all dominion and control over it as owner, and part absolutely with the title."[11]

D. Performance of a Preexisting Duty

Where the promisor is acting under a preexisting duty, then the act by the promisor is not consideration. For example, a police officer works for the city. He is informed that an award for $1000 is available for persons capturing Sam, the bad guy. While patrolling the city, the police officer spots Sam, gives chase and apprehends him. The officer's action in capturing Sam is not consideration because he already had a duty, as a police officer, to capture the bad guys of the world.[12]

In the following case, the court discusses the duties of a husband and wife in determining whether or not there is a preexisting duty that squelches consideration.

Case 4.3

Frank F. Campbell v. L. R. Prater
191 P.2d 160 (1948), 1948 Wyo. LEXIS 6
Supreme Court of Wyoming

KIMBALL, Justice.

Plaintiff is the executor of the will of Nellie Campbell Prater, who died in 1945; defendant is the surviving husband of the testatrix. The will deprives the husband of more than one-half of the wife's property. The testatrix is not survived by any child. The statute, cited above, by an amendment of 1915, provides that in such a case "it shall be optional with the surviving spouse after the death of the…testatrix to accept the condition of the will or one-half of the estate, real and personal, of the deceased spouse." Defendant seeks to exercise this option by electing to take one-half of the estate, and has filed in the probate proceedings the writing required by the statute to signify that election.

Thereafter, plaintiff brought this action for a declaration of rights under the Uniform Declaratory Judgments Act, claiming that defendant is barred from making such election by his promise not to do so. The promise was made in a transaction evidenced by a writing, called "Memorandum of Agreement," signed by the husband and wife March 11, 1931.

Defendant in his answer admits that he signed the writing, but alleges that it is void or unenforceable for want of consideration; because he was induced to sign it by coercion, and because the bargain shown by the writing is inequitable. …

* * * * *

---

[11] Williams v. McElroy, 133 S.E. 297 (1929), 35 Ga. App. 420 (1929).
[12] Restatement (Second) Contracts § 73 cmt. b (1979).

[The writing in part says,] "That upon the execution of this agreement and as a part of the consideration moving from the second party to the first party hereunder second party will return to the home of first party and resume the marital relation in all respects."

* * * * *

"That the parties hereto will henceforth endeavor seriously and in good faith to live together as man and wife, and will continue their ranching and livestock operations with the determination and the hope that no further difficulties of a serious nature will arise between them."

* * * * *

The husband and wife had become separated when the wife voluntarily left the home. The cause of her leaving was a disagreement in regard to the property rights, particularly with reference to the desire of the wife to make a will that would effectively deprive her surviving husband of more than one-half of her property, notwithstanding the optional right of the husband under the statute. There is no hint of any other cause of separation.

It was the desire and purpose of the husband to induce the wife to return to him, and the promise of the wife to return to the home and "resume the marital relation in all respects" was all that the husband obtained by the agreement except possibly the recited money consideration of $100. ...

The wife, as a consideration for her promise to return, exacted among other things, the promise of the husband to waive and relinquish his right as surviving spouse under section 6-301, supra. She retained her correlative right under the same statute, and was careful not to surrender any interest she might have in her own or her husband's property during marriage, upon future separation or divorce, or after the husband's death. We think, however, that the fact that the wife did return to the home following the signing of the writing was not in dispute. Defendant in his answer alleged that the wife left the home because he had refused to release all his rights in her property, and that she "refused to return until this defendant yielded to her demands" by signing the writing. This evidently means that the wife did not refuse to return after the writing was signed. ...

* * * * *

The wife's promise to return to the husband and resume marital relations was not a sufficient consideration for the husband's promises, unless she had just cause for leaving him. ... These cases and many others are cited in note on "Resumption of Marital Relations as Consideration" ... in support of the principle that an agreement to resume marital relations made by one spouse who has deserted the other without just cause is not a consideration for an exchange promise [because there is a preexisting duty to continue the marital relations when the parties are married]. ...

* * * * *

It is the [preexisting] legal duty of the wife [or husband] to live with her husband in the absence of any reasonable cause justifying her separation from him.

"There seems to be no reason why a bargain to resume marital relations where one of the parties has just cause for divorce should not be sustained, and it is generally held that a promise made in consideration of such resumption and of the dismissal or forbearance to bring justified proceedings for divorce, or in compromise of legal proceedings for nonsupport, is binding."

"On the other hand, if there is no justification for divorce or separation, a bargain to continue or resume marital relations is certainly insufficient consideration and is probably also unenforceable on grounds of policy."

* * * * *

The courts, referring to bargains like that in the case at bar, frequently state not only that the promise to continue or resume marital relations is insufficient consideration, but also that the bargain is invalid or unenforceable or grounds of public policy [since she had a preexisting duty]. ...

* * * * *

In this case, as explained above, the wife in leaving the husband had deprived him of the most important personal right to which he was entitled as an incident of the marriage contract. It is necessarily implied that she threatened to continue the separation unless the husband signed the writing of March, 1931. ...He was forced to choose between alternatives, either to endure the separation, or sign the agreement. The wife obtained the agreement by creating a motive from which the husband ought to have been free, and which was intended to be, and in fact was, sufficient to produce the result. ...

* * * * *

That appeal [by the wife] will be dismissed.

E. Illusory Promises

Where the offeror utters words of promise that make performance optional on the part of the offeror, the promise is illusory and does not constitute a promise that rises to good consideration.[13] As a general rule, if a contract in which one party has an absolute and unrestricted right to cancel or terminate the contract at will at any time, or where both parties have such right, the contract is invalid because the promise is illusory and unenforceable for lack of mutuality.[14] On the one hand, an illusory promise of performance invalidates a bilateral contract. A bilateral contract is one in which there are mutual promises between two parties to the contract, each being both a promisor and a promisee. A bilateral contract must be premised upon a valid consideration—in other words, mutuality of obligation. A promise is illusory when it fails to bind the promisor who retains the option of discontinuing performance. In fact, an illusory promise is no promise at all. Because an illusory promise fails to bind the promisor, it provides no consideration for a contract.[15]

A unilateral contract, on the other hand, may be formed when one of the parties makes an illusory promise and the other party makes a non-illusory promise. The non-illusory promise can serve as the offer for a unilateral contract, which the promisor who made the illusory promise can then accept by performance.[16]

---

[13] Restatement (Second) Contracts, § 77 cmt. a (1979).

[14] 52 Wis. 2d 1 (1971), 188 N.W.2d 454 (1971), 1971 Wisc. LEXIS 957.

[15] Ed Vanegas v. American Energy Services 224 S.W.3d 544 (2007), 2007 Tex. App. Lexis 3562.

[16] *Id.*

For example, promises that depend on continued employment of at-will employees are illusory: At-will employees may contract with their employers on any matter except those which would limit the ability of either employer or employee to terminate the employment at will. Consideration for a promise, by either the employee or the employer in an at-will employment, cannot be dependent on a period of continued employment. Such a promise would be illusory because it fails to bind the promisor, who always retains the option of discontinuing employment in lieu of performance. Any promise made by either employer or employee that depends on an additional period of employment is illusory because it is conditioned upon something that is exclusively within the control of the promisor. Thus, an employer's promise of a raise to an at-will employee is illusory because it depends upon a period of continued employment. After promising the raise, the employer could fire the at-will employee and, therefore, avoid the obligation to perform the promise.[17]

F. Past Consideration

As a general rule, past consideration is no consideration because past consideration is not sufficient to support an express promise and, therefore, is insufficient to support a contractual obligation. The practical application of the doctrine gives rise to certain exceptions, but validity must at least be denied to a promise made in consideration of benefits rendered in the past. Past consideration—unless requested by the promisor express or implied,—is not sufficient to support any promise. But a promise to perform an act in consideration of some act to be done by the promisee, in the present or the future, implies a request, and compliance on the part of the latter closes the contract and makes it binding.[18]

The following case addresses the issue of past consideration.

Case 4.4

> Purselley V. Lockheed Martin Corp.
> United States Court Of Appeals For The Fifth Circuit
> 322 Fed. Appx. 399 (2009); 2009 U.S. App. LEXIS 8483
>
> JUDGES: Before DAVIS, GARZA, and PRADO, Circuit Judges.
>
> Lockheed's Weight Incentive Program ("WIP") offered monetary awards to spur employees' weight-reduction suggestions for the F-35 aircraft under development for the government. Purselley states in late 2003 or early 2004 he submitted his idea to eliminate a piece of equipment to reduce weight and cost and the company began

---

[17] *Id.*

[18] The Union Bank of Louisiana v. Executors of John G. Coster. 3 N.Y. 203 (1850), 1850 N.Y. LEXIS 8.

studying how to implement the idea. Lockheed states that the idea immediately became its property because when he was hired, Purselley signed an agreement assigning any employee inventions to the company.

In April 2004, Lockheed planned Weight Stand Down Day ("WSDD"), a half-day project to focus on F-35 weight-savings ideas, and contemplated monetary awards for WSDD ideas implemented into the project. The company also considered awards with different scales of payment for two cost-savings components based on indirect weight savings—system development and design ("SDD") and unit recurring flyaway ("URF") components. Ultimately, Lockheed opted not to offer cost-savings awards. It notified participants, including Purselley, before WSDD began that cost-savings awards were "off the table." However, Purselley relies on preliminary documents posted before this decision, contemplating awards for SDD and URF cost-savings.[1]

During WSDD, Purselley resubmitted the earlier-submitted suggestion. Lockheed initially rated his WSDD suggestion as "not recommended." But Purselley still argued for a weight-savings award, and a year later he received $ 7500. In this suit, he initially sought hundreds of millions of dollars in a Texas state court on breach of contract and quantum meruit claims, arguing he also was due an SDD cost-savings award. He now claims Lockheed owes him an URF cost-savings award. Lockheed removed the action to federal district court. The district court granted Lockheed's motion for summary judgment. This appeal followed.

Purselley first argues there is a fact issue as to whether he gave consideration to support a unilateral contract. Specifically, Purselley asserts there was no requirement that WSDD suggestions be original and unique and that by his performance— expending time and effort to resubmit an idea—he accepted Lockheed's offer to compensate employees for ideas suggested during WSDD. Lockheed argues that providing already-disclosed information is **past consideration** and, thus, no consideration. Granting Lockheed's motion for summary judgment, the district court found "[t]o whatever extent [Purselley] [**5] claims a breach of contract," he gave no new consideration to Lockheed. Lockheed received nothing new from Purselley upon which it could act.

In Texas, "[c]onsideration is a present exchange bargained for in return for a promise."

* * * * *

The formation of a unilateral contract in the employment context requires that "(1) the performance must be bargained-for so that it is not rendered **past consideration**… and (2) acceptance must be by performance"

* * * * *

We agree with the district court. No fact issue as to consideration remains. The evidence showed the company indeed was looking for new ideas, not ideas previously submitted. While the company still sought ideas despite notifying WSDD participants it was forgoing cost-savings awards, Purselley's resubmission of the earlier suggestion was **past consideration**; the parties do not dispute that the company already owned the idea and had acted upon it when Purselley resubmitted it for WSDD. Therefore, the WSDD submission was not new consideration and was unable to support any new promise Lockheed made, as Purselley claims, to pay cost-savings awards under a unilateral contract. For the foregoing reasons, we AFFIRM the district court's order granting summary judgment.

G. Moral Obligation

A previous moral obligation is insufficient as a consideration to support an action needed to enforce an executory contract. A *moral obligation* is one, for example, when a father promises to give his daughter a family heirloom in consideration for all the love and affection that he has received from the daughter. Promises made in consideration of love and affection do not give rise to consideration because there is no legal duty to provide love and affection from one person to another. A distinction is drawn between moral obligations and equitable obligations. An *equitable obligation* rests on some actual duty that is unenforceable legally, such as an infant's obligations or debts being barred by the statute of limitations or bankruptcy. But a mere moral or conscientious obligation, unconnected with a prior legal or equitable claim, implies no duty and is therefore not a sufficient consideration to support a promise.[19] *Goulding v. Davidson*, 26 N.Y. 604; *McGuire v. Hughes*, 207 N.Y. 516.

II. Contracts Without Consideration
A. Promise to Pay an Antecedent Debt

Sometimes the law recognizes that certain contracts are legally binding even when consideration is lacking. For example, when the promisor makes a promise while admitting the present existence of an antecedent contract debt, the promise is binding without consideration if the debt is still enforceable.[20] Also, where the promisor makes part payment on an antecedent debt, the new promise is binding without consideration.[21] However, under these circumstances, some states have passed legislation stating that such a debt, without consideration, must be in writing and must be signed by the promisor.[22] If the promisor makes an unqualified admission that a debt is due, and makes a promise to pay for an antecedent debt after the statutes of limitations have run, it is sufficient to revive the debt.

The following case shows the revival of an antecedent debt after the statutes of limitations have run.

---

[19] Charlotte E. Pershall v. Hiram Elliott, 249 N.Y. 183 (1928), 163 N.E. 554 (1928), 1928 N.Y. LEXIS 785.
[20] Restatement (Second) Contracts § 82 (1) (1979).
[21] *Id.* at § 82 cmt. e (1979).
[22] *Id.* at § 82 cmt. a (1979).

George Sneed v. Charles V. Parker
262 Ill. App. 333 (1931), 1931 Ill. App. LEXIS 184
Court of Appeals of Illinois

Case 4.5

OPINION BY: BARRY

JUSTICE BARRY delivered the opinion of the court.

In 1921, appellee was a tenant in possession of 20 or 25 acres of land upon which he had raised a crop of corn. In September of that year, appellant purchased the land and procured a deed from the landlord. There can be no question but that appellee was entitled to his share of the crop of corn. When he started to gather the corn appellant procured an injunction, gathered the corn and converted it to his own use. Sometime later, and long before the statute of limitations had run, appellant told his employee, Robert Gross, to go to the courthouse and see appellee and see if he could not settle with appellee for the corn, pay him for it, get it out of the way, or words to that effect. It is quite evident that Mr. Gross would have paid appellee for the corn at that time if he had then had the weights. It was then agreed that Mr. Gross would get the weights and take them to the office of the attorney for appellee so that the matter could be settled the next morning. In the meantime appellant talked to Mr. Gross and suggested that there was a line dispute between him and appellee and that Mr. Gross should also try to settle that matter at the same time. No settlement was reached but we think the evidence shows that there was no controversy then existing between the parties as to appellant's liability for the corn.

Appellee testified that on several occasions he spoke to appellant about the matter and that appellant promised to pay him for the corn. After the statute had run appellee asked appellant when he was going to settle and pay him for that corn and appellant said that he would be ready to settle any day after Monday. An unqualified admission that the debt was due and unpaid, accompanied by nothing said or done to rebut the presumption of a promise to pay it, is sufficient to revive the debt against the statute of limitations [without consideration].[23]

* * * * *

In our opinion the evidence was sufficient to show an unqualified admission that the debt was due and unpaid, and there was nothing said or done to repute the presumption of a promise to pay it. There was no error in the giving or refusing of instructions and the judgment is affirmed [in favor of the appellee].

Affirmed.

---

[23] West Publishing Co. v. Lasley, 165 Ill. App. 256 (1911), *see also* Herdien v. Jones, 202 Ill. App. 172 (1911).

B. Enforceable Contracts Without Consideration

The law recognizes that there are circumstances in which contracts can be binding notwithstanding lack of consideration. In other words, a court will enforce a contract without consideration where a new promise is made for a debt that has been discharged by bankruptcy.[24] For example, Joe owes Sam $10,000 on a debt that has since been discharged when Joe was adjudged bankrupt. After the adjudication, Joe promises Sam that he will pay back the $10,000 debt. Joe's promise is binding without consideration, and he must pay Sam the debt.

Similarly, a promise made by the promisor for a benefit previously received by the promisor is enforceable without consideration, unless the promise is disproportionate to the value of the benefit.[25] Where a contract has not been fully performed on either side, a promise modifying a duty under the contract is binding without consideration if (1) the modification is fair and equitable, (2) allowed by statute and (3) the modification manifests material changes of position in reliance of the promise.[26]

No consideration is required to enforce a contract where the promisor, by his promise, reasonably expects to induce some action or forbearance on the part of the promisee, induces such action or forbearance, and only if enforcement of the promise could avoid injustice.[27] In the case of *Hamer v. Sidway*, the uncle promised his nephew that if he did not drink, smoke or play cards, that he, the uncle, would pay the nephew $5000. The nephew promised and did not drink, smoke or play cards. The court held that while the nephew did not provide the uncle any benefit, the promise by the uncle was enforceable because the forbearance constituted consideration.[28]

The following case examines the issue of whether or not there existed forbearance that gave rise to consideration in order to create a legally binding contract.

---

[24] Restatement (Second) Contracts § 82 (1979).
[25] *Id.* at § 86 (1979).
[26] *Id.* at § 89 (1979).
[27] *Id.* at § 90 (1979).
[28] Hamer v. Sidway, 27 N.E. 256 (1891), 124 N.Y. 538 (1891), 1891 N.Y. LEXIS 1396.

Case 4.6

Benjamin B. Strong v. Louisa A. Sheffield
39 N.E. 330 (1895), 1895 N.Y. LEXIS 541
Court of Appeals of New York

JUDGES: Andrews, Ch. J.

The contract between a maker or endorser of a promissory note and the payee forms no exception to the general rule that a promise, not supported by a consideration, is *nudum pactum.*

*****

The debt of the husband was past due at the time, and the only consideration for the wife's indorsement, which is or can be claimed, is that as part of the transaction there was an agreement by the plaintiff when the note was given to forbear the collection of the debt, or a request for forbearance, which was followed by forbearance for a period of about two years subsequent to the giving of the note.

There is no doubt that an agreement by the creditor to forbear the collection of a debt presently due is a good consideration for an absolute or conditional promise of a third person to pay the debt, or for any obligation he may assume in respect thereto. Nor is it essential that the creditor should bind himself at the time to forbear collection or to give time. If he is requested by his debtor to extend the time, and a third person undertakes in consideration of forbearance being given to become liable as surety or otherwise, and the creditor does in fact forbear in reliance upon the undertaking, although he enters into no enforceable agreement to do so, his acquiescence in the request, and an actual forbearance in consequence thereof for a reasonable time, furnishes a good consideration for the collateral undertaking. In other words, a request followed by performance is sufficient, and mutual promises at the time are not essential, unless it was the understanding that the promisor was not to be bound, except on condition that the other party entered into an immediate and reciprocal obligation to do the thing requested. …

The general rule is clearly, and in the main accurately, stated in the note to *Forth v. Stanton* (1 Saund. 210, note b). The learned reporter says: "And in all cases of forbearance to sue, such forbearance must be either absolute or for a definite time, or for a reasonable time; forbearance for a little, or for some time, is not sufficient." The only qualification to be made is that in the absence of a specified time a reasonable time is held to be intended. (*Oldershaw v. King*, 2 H. & N. 517; *Calkins v. Chandler*, 36 Mich. 320.) The note in question did not in law extend the payment of the debt. It was payable on demand, and although being payable with interest it was in form consistent with an intention that payment should not be immediately demanded, yet there was nothing on its face to prevent an immediate suit on the note against the maker or to recover the original debt.

In the present case the agreement made is not left to inference, nor was it a case of request to forbear, followed by forbearance, in pursuance of the request, without any promise on the part of the creditor at the time. The plaintiff testified that there was an express agreement on his part to the effect that he would not pay the note away, nor put it in any bank for collection, but (using the words of the plaintiff) *"I will hold it until such time as I want my money, I will make a demand on you for it."* And again: *"No, I will keep it until such time as I want it."* Upon this alleged agreement the defendant indorsed the note. It would have been no violation of the plaintiff's promise if, immediately on receiving the note, he had commenced suit upon it. Such a suit would have been an assertion that he wanted the money and would have fulfilled the condition of forbearance. The debtor and the defendant, when they became parties to the note, may have had the hope or expectation that forbearance would follow, and there was forbearance in fact. But there was no agreement to forbear for a fixed time or for a reasonable time, but an agreement to forbear for such time as the plaintiff should elect. The consideration is to be tested by the agreement, and not by what was done under it. It was a case of mutual promises, and so intended. We think the evidence failed to disclose any consideration for the defendant's indorsement, and that the trial court erred in refusing so to rule.

The order of the General Term reversing the judgment should be affirmed, and judgment absolute directed for the defendant on the stipulation, with costs in all courts.

C. Option Contracts

Suppose that Sam has a parcel of real estate and Joe offers to buy it. Sam does not want to sell the property outright but offers to sell it to Joe in the future. Joe accepts the offer, saying, "I want the option to purchase whenever you decide to sell it." Several years later, Sam sells the property to a third party and Joe brings a law suit to assert his option of first refusal.

There are three methods to bind an offer on an option contract. First, the option is enforceable if it is made irrevocable by statute.[29] Second, it is enforceable if the option is in writing, signed by the offeror, and recites the consideration given in exchange for the offer.[30] And finally, the option is binding where the offeror reasonably expects to induce action or forbearance of a substantial nature on the part of the offeree and the offeror does induce action or forbearance. In this case, Joe would be unable to recover on the option to purchase the property because there is no available statute to enforce the option. There is no evidence of a writing and the offer for the option did not induce an action or forbearance on Joe's part.

---

[29] Restatement (Second) Contracts § 87 (1)(b) (1979).
[30] *Id.* at § 87 (1)(a) (1979).

Chapter 4

Vocabulary

1. Consideration
2. Adequacy of Consideration
3. Gifts
4. Preexisting Duty
5. Illusory Promises
6. Past Consideration
7. Moral Obligations
8. Antecedent Debt
9. Forbearance
10. Option Contracts

Review Questions

1. What is the issue in the *Hamer v. Sidway* case?
2. What is the principle of law in the *Hamer v. Sidway* case?
3. What is the issue in the *Chastain v. Texas Christian Missionary Soc.* case?
4. What is the principle of law in the *Chastain v. Texas Christian* case?
5. What is the issue in the *Frank Campbell v. Prater* case?
6. What is the principle of law in the *Campbell* case?
7. What is the issue in *Purselley V. Lockheed Martin*?
8. What is the law in *Purselley V. Lockheed Martin*
9. What is the issue in the *George Sneed v. Charles Parker* case?
10. What is the principle of law in the *Sneed* case?
11. What is the issue in the *Benjamin Strong v. Louisa Sheffield* case?
12. What is the principle of law in the *Strong* case?

Chapter 5
Manifestation of Assent

I. Manifestation of Mutual Assent
A. Serious Intent

The notion of manifestation of mutual assent in negotiating a serious bargain necessitates that each of the parties to the bargain makes or begins a promise, or renders some type of performance.[1]

It is a prerequisite to the creation of a contract that the offeror as well as the offeree assent to the bargain. The assent begins as a promise by the offeror, who may request the offeree to either make a promise or render a performance in return. When promises have been exchanged or when a promise is made with a return performance, a manifestation of mutual assent exists.[2] A qualification of the rule is that an apparent *manifestation* of assent will not operate to make a contract if the other party knows—or as a reasonable person should know—that the apparent acceptor does not intend what his words or other acts ostensibly indicate.[3]

B. Promises Made in Jest

When either or both parties make a promise that is not to be taken seriously or the promises are made in jest, then there is no manifestation of mutual assent. If only one of the parties is joking but the other takes the promise seriously, the offer is a sham because the non-joking party has been deceived. Therefore, there is no manifestation of mutual assent.[4]

To determine whether one or both of the parties are joking, "We must look to the outward expression of a person as manifesting his intention rather than to his secret and unexpressed intention. The courts will look to the objective not the subjective actions of the parties to determine the real intent of the parties. 'The law imputes to a person an intention corresponding to the reasonable meaning of his words and acts.'" *First Nat. Bank* v. *Roanoke Oil Co.*, 169 Va. 99, 114, 192 S.E. 764, 770. The law, therefore, judges an agreement between two persons exclusively from those expressions of their intentions which are

---

[1] Restatement (Second) Contracts § 18 (1979).
[2] *Id.* at § 18 cmt. b (1979).
[3] Frederich v. Union Electric Light & Power Co. (Mo.), 82 S.W.2d 79, 86 (1935).
[4] Restatement (Second) Contracts § 18 cmt. c (1979).

communicated between them. So a person cannot set up that he was merely "jesting" when his conduct and words would warrant a reasonable person believing that he intended a real agreement. Even where one of the parties entered into the contract *in jest,* he is bound by it if the other party believed, and from the acts and statements of the jesting party was warranted in believing, that the contract represented a serious and good faith sale and purchase. Mental assent is not essential for the formation of a contract; if the words and acts of a party, reasonably interpreted, manifest an intention to agree, his contrary but unexpressed state of mind is immaterial.[5]

C. Assent by Conduct

Manifestation of mutual assent is not limited to oral or written promises. Assent may or may not arise as a result of a party's conduct, such as an action or inaction.[6] Where the actions of one party lead the other party to perform based on the belief that a contract is in existence, the court may or may not deem it as a *contract implied in fact.* The following case illustrates this principle.

Case 5.1

> Russel Blad v. Richard K. Parris, Jr.
> 2010 Minn. App. Unpub., 2010 LEXIS 417
>
> JUDGE Peterson
>
> In a January 2006 letter, respondents requested that appellant notify them of any rent increase for the upcoming year by October 1st of the contract year because land is fertilized in the fall after crop harvesting. Viewing the evidence in the light most favorable to the verdict, the jury apparently did not find credible appellant's testimony that respondents stated that they would not be renting from appellant and instead believed that appellant did not notify respondents about a rent increase, rented the land to a third party in a lease agreement that was fully executed by February 15, 2007, and then did not respond to respondents' February 27, 2007 letter and did not promptly return the $ 1,000 check that he received on April 6, 2007. This view of appellant's conduct, considered in light of the nature of the farming business and respondents' request to be notified by October 1st of the contract year of any rent increases, is sufficient to support the finding of a contract. *See Holt v. Swenson,* 252 Minn. 510, 516, 90 N.W.2d 724, 728 (1958) (stating that "[i]t is well settled that acceptance of an offer may be by **conduct,** and where the relation between the parties is such that the offeror is justified in expecting a reply, or where the offeree is under a duty to reply, the latter's silence will be regarded as an acceptance" and finding acceptance by **conduct** when party allowed other party to perform contract without objection). Respondents Russel

---

[5] Lucy v. Zehmer, 196 Va. 493 (1954), 84 S.W. 2d 516 (1954).
[6] Restatement (Second) Contracts § 19 cmt. a (1979).

and Nancy Blad farm about 3,500 acres of land, most of which is leased property. Since about 1997, respondents have leased 180 acres of property that appellant Richard K. Parris became the owner of in 2001. Each year, from 2002 through 2006, there was a written lease agreement between the parties.

All of the lease agreements between appellant and respondents were executed through the mail. Near the beginning of each year, appellant would send respondents a proposed lease agreement for the upcoming year. Respondents would sign the lease agreement and return it to appellant with a deposit. Respondents' signatures on the lease agreements are all dated in January or February of the year to which the agreement applies. Every lease agreement was for a one-year term, described as the "crop year," and no lease contained any automatic renewal or extension option.

The proposed lease agreement for crop year 2006 contained a rent increase from $ 87 per acre to $ 90 per acre. Respondents signed and returned the lease agreement to appellant along with a $ 1,000 deposit and a letter that stated: "I noticed that the rent was increased by $ 3.00 per acre. In the future we would like to be notified by October 1st as to any increase in land rent due to the fact that we apply fall fertilizer after the crop is harvested for the next crop year." Appellant testified that he had two telephone conversations with respondents in 2006 and that respondent Russel Blad stated that respondents would not be renting from appellant anymore. After October 1, 2006, respondents applied manure and other fertilizer to the land. On February 27, 2007, having not received a proposed lease agreement from appellant for crop-year 2007, respondents sent appellant a letter that stated: "I tried calling the telephone directory service to find a phone number for you, but you must have an unlisted phone number. We have not received a renewal on the land rent contract for 2007. We applied fall fertilizer on the land after the crop was harvested last fall." The letter provided Russel Blad's cell-phone number to appellant and requested that appellant call Russel Blad. Respondents were not contacted by appellant after sending the letter. In April 2007, respondents sent a $ 1,000 deposit to appellant by certified mail. The receipt showed that the check was delivered to appellant on April 6, 2007. On May 1, 2007, respondents planted 100.3 acres of corn and sent appellant a check for rent for the first half of the year, as had been the custom under the written lease agreements.

On May 2, 2007, respondents received a phone message from appellant stating that he had rented the land to someone else. The lease agreement between appellant and the third party was signed by appellant on January 25, 2007, and by the third party on February 15, 2007. Respondents brought breach-of-an-implied-contract and equitable-estoppel claims against appellant. The case was tried to a jury, which found that (1) a contract existed between the parties; (2) appellant breached the contract; and (3) as a result of the breach, respondents incurred damages in the amount of $ 35,081.69. The district court denied appellant's motion for a new trial, and remittitur. This appeal followed.

Appellant argues that the evidence is insufficient to prove the existence of a contract for crop-year 2007 because all previous agreements were in writing and were executed near the beginning of the crop year, there was no written agreement for 2007, there was no evidence of an express oral agreement between the parties, and the essential price term had not been agreed on.

The form of the assent, whether it be written, oral, or by conduct, is not relevant as long as objective standards are applied and the essential finding of mutual assent is made. The Restatement (Second) of Contracts § 19 (1979) provides: "(1) The manifestation of assent may be made wholly or partly by written or spoken words or by other acts or by failure to act. (2) The **conduct** of a party is not effective as a manifestation of his assent unless he intends to engage in the **conduct** and knows or has reason to know that the other party may infer from his **conduct** that he assents."

Comment c to section 19 provides: "[E]ven though the intentional **conduct** of a party creates an appearance of assent on his part, he is not responsible for that appearance unless he knows or has reason to know that his **conduct** may cause the other party to understand that he assents."

In a January 2006 letter, respondents requested that appellant notify them of any rent increase for the upcoming year by October 1st of the contract year because land is fertilized in the fall after crop harvesting. Viewing the evidence in the light most favorable to the verdict, the jury apparently did not find credible appellant's testimony that respondents stated that they would not be renting from appellant and instead believed that appellant did not notify respondents about a rent increase, rented the land to a third party in a lease agreement that was fully executed by February 15, 2007, and then did not respond to respondents' February 27, 2007 letter and did not promptly return the $ 1,000 check that he received on April 6, 2007. This view of appellant's conduct, considered in light of the nature of the farming business and respondents' request to be notified by October 1st of the contract year of any rent increases, is sufficient to support the finding of a contract. *See Holt v. Swenson*, 252 Minn. 510, 516, 90 N.W.2d 724, 728 (1958) (stating that "[i]t is well settled that acceptance of an offer may be by **conduct**, and where the relation between the parties is such that the offeror is justified in expecting a reply, or where the offeree is under a duty to reply, the latter's silence will be regarded as an acceptance" and finding acceptance by **conduct** when party allowed other party to perform contract without objection).

Judgement is Affirmed.

D. Mutual Misunderstanding

Where parties misunderstand the true meaning of their promises, the misunderstanding may prevent the formation of a contract because there is no manifestation of mutual assent. Such was the case in the *Kyle* decision below.

Case 5.2

Winslow S. Kyle v. Edward Kavanagh
103 Mass. 356 (1869), 1869 Mass. LEXIS 88

JUDGES: Morton, J.

The defendant contended and introduced evidence tending to show that, either by the fraud or misrepresentation of the plaintiff, or by mistake, the land conveyed by the deed was not the land which he bargained for, and that what he had agreed to purchase was a lot of land on another Prospect Street in Waltham, in no way connected with that mentioned in the deed, and a long way off; and he also contended that he was entitled to a warranty deed.

* * * * *

The judge, at the commencement of his charge, instructed the jury that, "if the defendant was negotiating for one thing and the plaintiff was selling another thing, and if their minds did not agree as to the subject matter of the sale, they could not be said to have agreed and to have made a contract;" and furthermore, after the conclusion of his charge and at the request of the defendant, also instructed the jury that, "if the plaintiff or the defendant were in fact mistaken as to the location of the land, it was a good defenses, although there was no fraud or misrepresentation on the part of the plaintiff," and that "mistake alone, if proved, was a good defense." The jury returned a verdict for the defendant, and the plaintiff alleged exceptions.

DISPOSITION: Exceptions sustained.

* * * * *

In an action for the price of land, in which the defendant set up as a defence [defense] that the land conveyed to him was not that which he agreed to purchase, the judge instructed the jury that "if the defendant was negotiating for one thing and the plaintiff was selling another, and their minds did not agree as to the subject matter, they could not be said to have agreed and made a contract, although there was no fraud on the part of the plaintiff," and that "mistake alone, if proved, was a good defence [defense]."

Held, that the plaintiff had no ground of exception.

E. Intentions to be Legally Bound

It is of no consequence that the parties are unaware whether their promises are legally binding or not. However, if the one party's intention is that their promises are not to be legally bound, then there will be no manifestation of mutual assent.[7] Sometimes a contract is drawn such that one of the parties is of the opinion that the contract has no legal authority, but a closer analysis of the contract will reveal that notwithstanding the intentions of one of the parties, the contract will legally bind him.[8]

The issue of whether a written statement where an employer makes certain disclaimers is legally binding is found in the following case.

Case 5.3

The Mabley & Carew Co. v. Borden
195 N.E. 697 (1935), 1935 Ohio LEXIS 335

OPINION BY: STEPHENSON

Ida C. Borden brought an action in the Court of Common Pleas of Hamilton county against the Mabley & Carew Company, alleging in her petition that Anna

---

[7] Restatement (Second) Contracts § 21 (1979).
[8] The Mabley & Carew Co. v. Borden, 129 Ohio St. 375 (1935), 195 N.E. 697 (1935), 1935 Ohio LEXIS 335.

Work, her sister, now deceased, was and had been for some years an employee of such company and that it promised and agreed in writing to pay to such person as was designated by Anna Work on the back of a certificate issued to her a sum equal to the wages received by her from the company for the year next preceding the date of her death. The plaintiff in error further alleges that she is the person designated on the back of the certificate; that Anna Work continued in the employ of the company until the date of her death; that her wages for the year preceding were $780, and she prays judgment for this amount with interest from the date of the death of Anna Work.

The Mabley & Carew Company in effect denies these allegations and states affirmatively that if the certificate was issued as claimed, it was issued voluntarily and gratuitously and without consideration, and was issued to Anna Work and accepted by her with the express understanding that it carried no legal obligation.

* * * * *

The following is a copy of the certificate upon which the action was predicated:

"No. 378.
"THE MABLEY & CAREW CO.

(emphasis added) *"To Mrs. Anna Work."*

"In appreciation of the duration and faithful character of your services heretofore rendered as an employee of this Company, there will be paid in the event of your death, if still an employee of this Company, (except under those circumstances which would give rise to an obligation on the State of Ohio under any Workmen's Compensation Act to reimburse your Estate for your death,) to the party or parties designated by you on the back of this certificate a sum equal to the wages you have received from this Company for the year next preceding the day of your death, but in no event to exceed the sum of Two Thousand Dollars.
"The issue and delivery of this certificate is understood to be purely voluntary and gratuitous on the part of this Company and is accepted with the express understanding that it carries no legal obligation whatsoever or assurance or promise of future employment, and may be withdrawn or discontinued at any time by this Company.

The Mabley & Carew Co.

"Adolph C. Weiss, Secy.
"Cincinnati, Ohio, Dec. 24, 1919."

"ENDORSEMENT. [written on the back of the agreement].
"The Mabley & Carew Co.   *Date, …*

"Gentlemen: — It is my desire that you make all benefits payable under this Certificate to the following and in the proportions here indicated:

Name	Relation to Beneficiary	Address
Mrs. Ida Borden	*Sister*	

"Signature…

* * * * *

It is contended by the Mabley & Carew Company that there is no proof of the designation of Ida C. Borden as beneficiary under the certificate in question. The name appears on the back of the certificate and, while it is typewritten, it is certainly a sufficient designation, taken in connection with the fact that Anna Work had it in her possession until her death.

There is just one question in this case, and that is the consideration for the issuance of this certificate. It is true that Anna Work could not maintain an action on this certificate in her lifetime, as no right of action existed in her favor; but that fact did not prevent it from being enforceable, after her death, in the hands of Ida C. Borden.

This certificate was not a pure gratuity on the part of the Mabley & Carew Company, as there was a provision in the certificate to the effect that the payment would not be made in the event of death unless Anna Work was still an employee of the company. This was an inducement to Anna Work to continue in the employ of the company. That is not the only consideration, as it is expressed at the outset that the company appreciates the duration and faithful character of the services of the employee theretofore rendered. The employee, by virtue of the issuance of the certificate, had a right to expect that the person nominated by her would in the event of her death receive the amount designated by the certificate. This was certainly an incentive to remain in the service of the company.

It is not a tenable proposition that, because Anna Work had no enforceable right during her life, her beneficiary could take no more than she had. We think the learned Court of Appeals was right in holding that Anna Work, by continuing in the service of the company until her death, created a binding obligation upon the company to pay to her designated beneficiary the sum mentioned in the certificate.

It is stated in the certificate: "The issue and delivery of this certificate is understood to be purely voluntary and gratuitous on the part of this Company." That was a part of the contract so far as Anna Work was concerned. She had no right that she could possibly assert, as she had to die before the right would ripen in anyone.

* * * * *

"While the practice initiated by the defendant is beneficial to its employees, it is not difficult to see wherein it is also beneficial to the employer. It tends to induce employees to remain continuously in the employ of the same master and to render efficient services so as to minimize the possibility of discharge. It also tends to relieve the employer of the annoyance of hiring and breaking in new men to take the place of those who might otherwise voluntarily quit, and to insure a full working force at times when jobs are plentiful and labor is scarce."

True, Anna Work by reason of this certificate was under no obligation to continue in the service of the Mabley & Carew Company if she did not see fit so to do; neither was the company, by reason of the certificate, obligated to give her continuous or definite employment. But neither of these facts in any wise affected the right of the beneficiary, so far as Anna Work was concerned after this contract was executed.

* * * * *

The acceptance of the certificate by the employee, the designation of a beneficiary on the back thereof, together with the fact that the employee remained in the employment of the company until death, constituted an executed contract and vested in the beneficiary a right to the amount provided for therein. We find no trouble in upholding this contract.

The judgment of the Court of Appeals is hereby affirmed [*in favor of the beneficiary*].

F. The Mode of Manifestation of Mutual Assent

As a general rule, manifestation of mutual assent in an exchange of promises to a bargain arises in the form of an offer by the offeror and an acceptance by the offeree.[9] When both parties expressly manifest their intent to be bound to their promises, there is a manifestation of mutual assent.[10] However, there are instances where the courts will enforce such contracts when an implied promise is made by a party that does not understand the substance of the contract written in English as illustrated in the case below.

Case 5.4

> Juan Morales v. Sun Constructors, Inc.
> 541 F.3d 218 (2008); 2008 U.S. App. LEXIS 18513
> U.S. Court of Appeals for the 3rd Circuit
>
> CHAGARES, Circuit Judge
>
> Juan Morales (Morales) was employed by Sun Constructors, Inc. (Sun). The employment relationship between Morales and Sun was governed by a signed employment agreement (the Agreement) that contained an arbitration clause. Morales was terminated by Sun, and he filed a wrongful termination suit against his former employer in the District Court of the Virgin Islands. Sun moved to stay the proceedings pending arbitration, but the District Court denied the motion, finding that Morales signed the Agreement without realizing it contained an arbitration clause. The Agreement was written in English, a language Morales cannot understand, and the District Court concluded that the arbitration clause was unenforceable because Morales did not assent to the clause. On appeal, Sun argues that Morales is bound by the entire Agreement, even if he is ignorant of its terms. We agree and will reverse the decision of the District Court and remand the case with instructions to enter a stay pending arbitration.
>
> This case requires us to determine whether an arbitration clause in an employment agreement is enforceable where one party is ignorant of the language in which the agreement is written.
>
> * * * * *
>
> On April 6, 2005, Sun fired Morales for allegedly dumping a bottle of urine from a great height on another contractor's employees in violation of safety standards. Morales filed a wrongful termination suit against Sun in the District Court on December 20, 2006, seeking relief under eight causes of action all covered by the Agreement's arbitration clause. The District Court determined that mutual assent to the arbitration clause did not exist and denied Sun's motion to stay the proceedings pending arbitration. This appeal followed.
>
> * * * * *

---

[9] Restatement (Second) Contracts § 22 (1979).
[10] *Id.*

It is well-settled under the Restatement (Second) of Contracts (the Restatement) that mutual assent between parties is necessary for the formation of a contract. ("[T]he formation of a contract requires 'a bargain in which there is a **manifestation of mutual assent** to the exchange and a consideration.'") (quoting RESTATEMENT § 17). While mutual assent "is sometimes referred to as a 'meeting of the minds,'" RESTATEMENT § 17 cmt. c, this phrase must not be construed too literally. Acceptance is measured not by the parties' subjective intent, but rather by their outward expressions of assent. As the Restatement explains:

* * * * *

The parties to most contracts give actual as well as apparent assent, but it is clear that a mental reservation of a party to a bargain does not impair the obligation he purports to undertake. The phrase used here, therefore, is **"manifestation of mutual assent."**

* * * * *

See *New York Life Ins. Co. v. Kwetkauskas*, 63 F.2d 890, 891 (3d Cir. 1933) (recognizing that "[i]t is true that an illiterate man may bind himself by contract by negligently failing to learn the contents of an instrument which he has executed"); *Hoshaw v. Cosgriff*, 247 F. 22, 26 (8th Cir. 1917) (holding that every contracting party has the duty "to learn and know the contents of a contract before he signs and delivers it"). Arbitration agreements in the employment context are not exempt from this principle. *See e.g., Booker v. Robert Half Int'l, Inc.*, 315 F. Supp. 2d 94, 101 (D.D.C. 2004) (stating that "[f]ailure to read or understand an arbitration agreement, or an employer's failure to explain it, simply will not constitute 'special circumstances' warranting relieving an employee from compliance with the terms of an arbitration agreement that she signed").

* * * * *

For the foregoing reasons, the judgment of the District Court will be reversed and the case remanded for the District Court to enter a stay pending arbitration.

Chapter 5

Vocabulary

1. Manifestation of Mutual Assent
2. Promises Made in Jest
3. Assent by Conduct
4. Mutual Misunderstanding

Review Questions

1. What is the issue in the *Russel Blad vs. Richard K. Parris, Jr.,* case?
2. What is the principle of law in the *Russel Blad* case?
3. What is the issue in the *Winslow S. Kyle v. Edward Kavanagh* case?
4. What is the principle of law in the *Kavanagh* case?
5. What is the issue in the *Mabley v. Borden* case?
6. What is the principle of law in the *Mabley* case?
7. What is the issue in the *Juan Morales v. Sun Constructors, Inc.* case?
8. What is the principle of law in the *Juan Morales* case?

Chapter 6

The Statute of Frauds

I. Introduction

There are certain contracts that are required to be in writing in order to be enforceable. These contracts are said to fall within the statute of frauds. If a contract does not fall within the statute of frauds, then the contract is enforceable even if it is not in writing.

A contract that falls within the *statute of frauds* is enforceable if it is evidenced with writing and signed by the party to be charged.[1]

The writing must reasonably identify the subject matter of the contract.[2] There must be some written indication of a contract between the parties[3] and have a statement with respect to the essential terms of the promises made in the contract.[4] The writing may be composed of several memorandums and the memorandums must have some reference to one another.[5] The signature placed on a memorandum can consist of any symbol made by the signor with the intention to authenticate the writing,[6] and the contract will only be enforceable against the signors.[7]

There are several classes of contracts that fall within the statute of frauds. And unless there is evidence of writing, the contract will be unenforceable.

A. Interest in Land

The first class that falls within the Statutes of Fraud is a contract for the sale of an interest in land.[8] The sale of an interest in land—which may include a lease, a sale, or a transfer of land—falls within the statute of frauds and must be in writing to be enforceable.

The following case illustrates the requirements of the statute of frauds with respect to an interest in land.

---

[1] Restatement (Second) Contracts § 131 (1979).
[2] *Id.* at § 131 (a) (1979).
[3] *Id.* at § 131 (b) (1979).
[4] *Id.* at § 131 (c) (1979).
[5] *Id.* at § 132 (1979).
[6] *Id.* at § 134 (1979).
[7] *Id.* at § 135 (1979).
[8] *Id.* at § 110 (1)(e) (1979).

Case 6.1

> Reedy v. Ebsen
> 242 N.W. 592 (1932), 60 S.D. 1 1932
> S.C. of South Dakota

JUSTICE Roberts

The complaint alleges that plaintiff paid defendant $ 1,000 on an oral agreement for the purchase of a tract of 160 acres in Lincoln county, S.D. Defendant in his answer admits the receipt of the money, but affirmatively alleges that, when the verbal agreement was made and entered into, and at all times up to the commencement of the action, defendant was able, ready, and willing to comply with the terms of the verbal agreement and to convey the premises upon compliance with the terms of the contract. Judgment was entered upon findings in favor of the plaintiff for the purchase money paid with interest. From this judgment defendant has appealed.

* * * * *

The question presented for decision is the right of a vendee to recover back money paid upon an oral contract for the sale of land when the vendor is ready, willing, and able on payment of the balance of the purchase money to convey title. It is the settled law that the purchaser of land under a contract which does not satisfy the **statute of frauds** may recover, as upon an implied promise, the amount he has paid upon the purchase price, when, without fault on the part of the vendee, the vendor refuses or is unable to perform the contract by conveying such title or interest as he has agreed to convey. The rule does not give effect to the oral agreement contrary to the statute. In such instance, the law implies a promise on the part of the vendor to refund the amount that he has received in consideration of the agreement which cannot be enforced against him and which he is unwilling to perform.

* * * * *

Contracts within the **statute of frauds** in this state are not merely voidable, but are void. The statute does not prescribe a mere rule of evidence, but is a matter of substantive law.

* * * * *

The original English **statute of frauds** provides that no action shall be brought upon contracts which are specified therein, unless the parties comply with the requirements of the statute. This form in substance has been adopted in a great many states, and under this form of statute a contract specified therein is valid, but not enforceable, and relates only to the remedy. Under this type of statute, it is manifest that the vendee may not recover money paid in part performance if the vendor is ready, able, and willing to perform the oral agreement on his part.

* * * * *

The parol contract, being void, furnishes no consideration for the payment. A consideration, to be sufficient, must be either a benefit to one party or damage to the other. The purchaser can derive no benefit from the supposed contract. Nothing passes to him by virtue of it; he obtains no **interest in the land**, and no promise or agreement on the part of the seller to convey him any; and he can never derive any advantage from what has transpired, except it be as a matter of favor on the seller's part.

* * * * *

The reason given for not allowing the purchaser under the English statute, and those like it, to repudiate the agreement and recover back what he has paid, so long as the seller is in no default, is very obvious. But it cannot be given here. It is that the agreement is not void but voidable, or, to speak more correctly, not actionable.

* * * * *

Under our statute there is no contract; nothing which can be the foundation of any legal or equitable obligation; and how can the court create one?

* * * * *

It finds one party in the unexplained possession of the money of another, which he knowingly received without any legal equivalent, and not as a gift, and which he has no legal or equitable right to retain; and why should he not refund?"

* * * * *

The settled construction of the **statute of frauds** in this state seems to us to compel the conclusion that the parol agreement, being in all respects a nullity, did not constitute a consideration for the partial payment and that the plaintiff was entitled to judgment.

* * * * *

The judgment appealed from is affirmed [and the purchaser can recover his money].

B. Answering for the Debt of Another

The second class of contracts that requires writing is a contract to answer for the debt of another.[9] For example, Junior goes to the bank and asks for a loan to go to college. The bank refuses to make the loan because Junior does not have any collateral. Junior calls his father and the father orally tells the bank officer on the phone to lend the money to Junior and that if Junior defaults on his loan, the father will pay. The bank makes the loan to Junior. Later, when Junior defaults on the loan, the bank calls upon the father to make his promise good and to pay for Junior's debt. The father refuses to pay. In this case the transaction falls within the statute of frauds because there was a promise to answer for the debt of another. Therefore, the promise by the father must be in writing to satisfy the statute of frauds. Since the promise by the father was oral, and not in writing, the contract is not enforceable.

However, suppose that the father orally tells the bank that he wants to borrow $10,000 from the bank for his own personal use and, in addition, he agrees to be a surety for $3000 for Junior's college tuition. In this case the primary reason for the loan is for the benefit of the father and not Junior. Therefore, the transaction falls under the "Main Purpose Rule"[10] and the contract falls outside the statute of frauds. Hence a writing is not required to enforce the promise to pay for Junior's debt. The following case illustrates this issue.

---

[9] Restatement (Second) Contracts § 110 (1)(b) (1979).
[10] Id. at § 116 (1979).

Case 6.2

> Garland Company, Inc. v. Roofco Company and George Rasor,
> 809 F.2d 546 (1987); 1987 U.S. App. LEXIS 1140
> U S. Ct. of Appl. for the 8th Circuit
>
> OPINION BY: BOWMAN
>
> George Rasor, the president and principal stockholder of the Roofco Company, appeals from a judgment holding him personally liable to the Garland Company, a supplier of materials used in Roofco's business.
>
> Garland sold $48,517 worth of roofing materials to Roofco. Roofco failed to pay. In conversations between Rasor and Garland, Rasor personally guaranteed that he would pay the debt. When after some nine months the debt remained unpaid, Garland brought suit to enforce the oral promise. As an affirmative defense, Rasor invoked the Missouri **Statute of Frauds**, asserting that since his promise was not in writing it was not enforceable. Garland countered, arguing that Rasor's promise was an original promise and thus was not within the **Statute of Frauds.** The District Court found for Garland and entered judgment against Rasor for the amount of the debt.
>
> * * * * *
>
> The tests to be applied to determine whether an agreement is an original undertaking, and not within the **statute of frauds**, are laid down as follows: (1) Credit must be given by the promisee to the promisor alone; and (2) the leading or **main purpose** of the promisor in making the promise must be to gain some advantage for himself, rather than to become the mere guarantor or surety of another's debt, and [3] the promise must be supported by a consideration beneficial to the promisor.
>
> The District Court properly applied the three-part Missouri test to the present case and found: 1) following Rasor's promise to pay Roofco's debt, Garland had extended further credit to Rasor alone; 2) Rasor, as principal shareholder and president of Roofco, had a unique and personal interest in Garland's credit extensions (in the form of delay in filing suit) which allowed Roofco to continue its operations and to realize money from several jobs; and 3) Rasor received beneficial consideration in the form of Garland's grant of credit extensions to Roofco and of Garland's forbearance from levying on a performance bond when absent such forbearance, Roofco's name would have been removed from a list of approved contractors.
>
> * * * * *
>
> Having reviewed the record, we are satisfied that none of the findings of the District Court is clearly erroneous. Under Missouri law, these findings amply support the District Court's ultimate conclusion that Rasor's promise was original and thus not within the **Statute of Frauds.** Accordingly, the judgment of the District Court is affirmed.

C. Upon Consideration of Marriage

The third class of contracts that falls within the statute of frauds is a contract made upon consideration of marriage.[11] For example, to induce Mary to marry him, Sam offers Mary certain personal property. Mary agrees. Such an

---

[11] Restatement (Second) Contracts § 110 (1)(c) (1979).

agreement falls within the statute of frauds and writing is required to enforce the agreement. On the other hand, if Mary simply promises to marry John, the agreement falls outside the statute of frauds and the promise is enforceable without writing. Promises made in consideration of marriage, which consist only of mutual promises of two persons to marry each other, do not require writing.[12]

The following case elucidates a relationship wherein the husband alleges that the wife agreed to have her mother-in-law live with the couple in contemplation of marriage.

Case 6.3

Ruth Koch v. George Koch
232 A.2d 157 (1967), 1967 N.J. Super. LEXIS 577
Superior Court of New Jersey

JUDGE: Lewis, J.A.D.

Plaintiff sued her husband for maintenance and support for herself and the infant child of their marriage. The Chancery Division entered judgment for defendant. Plaintiff appeals.

The parties were married on March 1, 1959. Plaintiff had a 15-year-old daughter by a previous marriage. It was planned that she would live with them and that defendant's mother, then residing in Hungary, would be brought to this country and that she would likewise live in their home. In September 1961 a daughter was born of the marriage.

The mother-in-law arrived on September 11, 1964; she was cordially received and took up residence with her son and daughter-in-law, they having obtained larger quarters for this purpose. It is undisputed that during the previous 5½ years the marriage "was a very loving relationship;" in the words of the wife, "We had as perfect a marriage as any marriage could be." Discord, however, soon developed. It is unnecessary to recount the details that generated an atmosphere of irritation. Suffice it to say, within a very short time after the arrival of the mother-in-law the incompatibility between her and plaintiff caused a disintegration of the marriage.

The only witnesses at the trial were the litigants themselves. The wife testified that her husband's attitude toward her changed, she lost 20 pounds in weight, and the situation became "as good as unbearable." A marriage counsellor and a psychiatrist were consulted, both of whom suggested that the mother-in-law move out of the apartment. When the wife told her husband that the prevailing conditions could not continue and that he would have to choose between living with her or living with his mother, "He chose to live with his mother." She stated that upon her suggestion that the mother-in-law "could live in a furnished room and eat with us and visit with us and stay with us during the day," defendant said "he didn't bring his mother over from Hungary so she could live in a furnished room."

Plaintiff, with her two daughters, left defendant on July 9, 1965. To a question whether her mother-in-law was present at the time she moved out, plaintiff replied,

---

[12] *Id.* at § 124 (1979).

"when the movers came, my husband was ready to leave for work. He kissed me goodbye with tears in his eyes, and his mother just sat there and laughed out loud."

Defendant testified that his mother did not interfere with the functions of the household; he stated that he would accept his wife back if she would live up to her agreement. He was interrogated from the bench as follows:

THE COURT: …As I understand it, prior to the time you got married, your wife agreed that your mother could come to live with you.

THE WITNESS: Yes.

THE COURT: Now, supposing she hadn't agreed to let your mother come to live with you, would you have gotten married to her?

THE WITNESS: I don't think so.

THE COURT: Well, now, if your wife would live up to her first agreement that your mother can live with you and her, would you want to go back to her again?

THE WITNESS: Yes."

It appears that this testimony weighed heavily in the deliberations of the trial judge who declared in his oral opinion: "…Under ordinary circumstances, …[following] the holding of the Court in *Fraser vs. Fraser* [*infra*], a wife would be the mistress of her own home, and where the presence of a mother-in-law would—or father-in-law would prohibit that, then, of course, she will have the prerogative of saying that one roof is not big enough for two females to reside under, and she would then be in a position to give her husband the choice of either herself or his mother, as in this case. However, here we have a factor which does not, in my opinion, bring it within the perfect view of the ruling in *Fraser vs. Fraser*. …[T]he marital contract was entered into conditioned upon the mother being a part of the household. …"

We find the evidence insufficient to establish a contract. There was no more than planning and an expression of intent. In addition, under the statute of frauds, **oral agreements in contemplation of marriage are unenforceable**, …and marriage is not such a part performance "as will avert the operation of the statute and render it enforceable in equity." …Moreover, plaintiff carried out the pre-marriage arrangement to accept her mother-in-law into her house, and there is nothing in the record to suggest that she did not act in good faith. Rarely, however, will affirmative promises, indefinite as to duration, be interpreted as calling for perpetual performance. …That salutary legal concept is certainly applicable in matters of domestic relations where the policy of our law is to preserve the marriage and eliminate contentious elements that do violence to it. "The home which a husband is obligated to provide for his wife must be one where she is free from abuse, violence, and interference by other persons, including his relatives…" For that reason the understanding between the parties, to the extent that it may be considered as one to keep the parent in the household indefinitely, may not be enforced.

* * * * *

Here, the trial judge seemed to think that plaintiff had to prove positive, affirmative interference by the mother-in-law to justify her leaving. That is not so. While the evidence fails to establish direct interference on the part of defendant's mother in the wife's management of the physical and functional operations of the apartment, it abundantly demonstrates that the mother's presence, and the effect thereof upon plaintiff, constituted such a serious psychological interference with the wife's enjoyment of her rightful status that within a few weeks her otherwise happy marriage of over five years was wrecked. ...Because of the continued presence of the mother-in-law, the Koch family, once united in domestic tranquility, became disturbingly fractious and discontented, culminating in a separation which might have been avoided had defendant taken reasonable and affirmative measures to eliminate the source of the friction and to save the marriage. Plaintiff gave evidence that after she left her husband she communicated with him and on one occasion said, "there was so much love between us, it couldn't have all died." She continued, "He didn't say anything to that." Plaintiff also told the court that she would go back to live with her husband if his mother were to live elsewhere.

The husband chose a position of neutrality when it was within his probable power to effectuate a solution of the familial difficulties. We hold, in the circumstances of this case, that the departure of the wife from the household was not obstinate but was justified and the separation is to be regarded as consensual on defendant's part...

Reversed and remanded for a determination of reasonable support and maintenance for plaintiff and the minor child of the marriage and the entry of judgment based thereon in favor of plaintiff.

D. Performance Outside of One Year

The fourth class of contract that falls within the statute of frauds is one that cannot be performed within one year.[13] The requirement that a contract must be in writing if it cannot be performed within one year may overlap with other classes of the statute of frauds.[14] For example, when Sam offers to give Mary certain personal property in exchange for a promise in consideration of marriage, the agreement falls within the statute of frauds because it is one in contemplation of marriage. But if Sam offers to give Mary certain personal property within two years in exchange for a promise to marry, the contract is not to be performed within one year because the promise to transfer the property in consideration of marriage overlaps with a contract that will not be performed within one year. In both cases the contract requires a writing to be enforceable.

The following case attempts to define *performance within one year*.

Case 6.4

Thomas R. Guilbert V. Charles B. Gardner, Jr.
480 F.3d 140 (2007); 2007 U.S. App. Lexis 5273
U. S. Ct. of Appl. for the 2nd Circuit

OPINION BY: HALL

In December 1991, Charles Gardner Jr. ("Charles Jr.") and his sons Douglas Gardner ("Douglas") and Charles Gardner III ("Charles III")[1] approached plaintiff, a former co-worker and family friend, about joining their new print brokerage business.

---

[13] Restatement (Second) Contracts § 110 (1)(e) (1979); *see also id.* at § 130 (1979).

[14] *Id.* at § 110 cmt. b (1979).

Plaintiff later met with defendants to discuss the details of plaintiff's prospective employment. Plaintiff informed defendants that he had accumulated approximately $ 39,000 in pension funds at his present job. Charles Jr. allegedly told plaintiff that if he joined the company, in addition to his salary, defendants would establish a pension fund for him with an initial deposit of $39,000 and subsequent annual deposits of $ 10,000.

Plaintiff accepted the terms of the agreement ("the employment agreement") and began work in January of 1992. He worked for the company until it collapsed in 2000. In early 1992, plaintiff alleges that Charles Jr. wrote down the terms of the pension on a legal writing pad. This document has not been produced in discovery. In the summer of 1992, and on a number of occasions thereafter, plaintiff requested documentation of his pension, but none was provided. Plaintiff alleges that defendants orally assured him on numerous occasions that they had "taken care of" his pension benefits.

On August 24, 2000, August 31, 2000, and September 7, 2000, defendants tendered three checks, each in the amount of $ 1,178.98, to plaintiff as part of his salary. In addition, on August 28, 2000, defendants tendered a check for $ 9,131.00 as reimbursement for plaintiff's car lease. Each of these checks bounced. In September 2000, it became clear to plaintiff that defendants were not going to pay his past salary and had not established pension benefits for him. Plaintiff brought this action in August of 2002. Plaintiff's amended complaint set forth nine causes of action. Plaintiff's first cause of action alleged that defendants were liable to him for his pension benefits under ERISA, 29 U.S.C.A. § 1132 (a). The second cause of action alleged that defendants failed to comply with plaintiff's request for information pursuant to § 1132(c)(1) and failed to meet the notice requirements of § 1132(c)(3). As a 7result, plaintiff claimed that defendants were liable to him in such an amount as the court determined, up to $ 100 per day beginning on the date of each violation. Plaintiff's third, fourth, and fifth causes of action alleged breach of contract, promissory estoppel and fraud respectively.

New York law provides that an agreement will not be recognized or enforceable if it is not in writing and "subscribed by the party to be charged therewith" and if the agreement " [b]y its terms is **not to be performed within one year** from the making thereof."

* * * * *

This provision of the **Statute of Frauds** encompasses "only those contracts which, by their terms, 'have absolutely no possibility in fact and law of full performance within one year.'"

* * * * *

The Court of Appeals has concluded that, "under a plain reading" of the statutory language, "the provision relates to the performance of the contract and not just of one party thereto."

* * * * *

Thus, "full performance by all parties **must be possible within a year to satisfy the Statute of Frauds.**" If an agreement may be fairly and reasonably interpreted to permit performance within a year, the Statute of Frauds will not bar a breach of contract action no matter how improbable it may be that performance will actually occur within that time frame.

Conclusion

For the foregoing reasons, we affirm the district court's grant of summary judgment on plaintiff's ERISA claims as well as his fraud claim. We remand for further proceedings consistent with this opinion.

II. The Uniform Commercial Code

The statute of frauds is not only applicable in common law, but also under the Uniform Commercial Code as well. Under the Uniform Commercial Code (UCC 2–201) a contract for the sale of goods for the price of $500 or more requires a writing.[15] A "sale" consists of the passing of title from the seller to the buyer for a price (UCC 2–106). "Goods," on the other hand, means all things (including specially manufactured goods) which are movable at the time of the identification to the contract (UCC 2–105(1)). Therefore, if there is a "sale" of "goods" for $500 or more, the statute of frauds apply and a writing is required for the contract to be enforceable.

III. Exceptions to the Statute of Frauds
A. Exceptions Under the UCC

Under UCC 2–201, writing is not required when, between two merchants, within a reasonable time, a confirmation of the contract is received and the party receiving it has reason to know its contents, the requirement of a writing is satisfied. For example, suppose Joe calls Sam on the telephone and contracts with Sam to send him ten carloads of cantaloupe in consideration for $10,000. Sam assents to the oral contract. When Sam does not deliver the cantaloupes, Joe brings a cause of action for breach of contract. Sam can assert the statute of frauds as a defense because there was (1) a sale of (2) goods for (3) $500 or more and therefore the transaction falls within the statute of frauds and a writing is required. Sam wins.

However, if Joe, immediately after he had finished talking to Sam on the telephone, sent a memorandum to Sam confirming the oral agreement, then the memorandum will serve to satisfy the statute of frauds without a written and signed contract by both parties.[16] So Joe would win.

But if Sam, upon receiving the memorandum from Joe, writes back to Joe disclaiming the contents of the memorandum within ten days, a written contract between Sam and Joe is then required to meet the requirements of the statute of frauds. If Sam does disclaim the contents of the memorandum from Joe within ten days, Sam will win because a written contract is required and there is no written contract between Sam and Joe.[17]

Moreover, where the promisor orally agrees to purchase specially manufactured goods, which are not suitable for sale to others in the ordinary course of the seller's business, and if the promisee has made a substantial beginning on

---

[15] Restatement (Second) Contracts § 110 (2)(a) (1979).
[16] The Uniform Commercial Code § 2–201 (2) (1977).
[17] *Id.*

producing the goods, the transactions fall outside the statute of frauds and a writing is not necessary to enforce the contract.[18]

B. Exception under the Common Law

Under the common law, part performance will satisfy the statute of frauds. A writing is not required where the promisee seeking enforcement reasonably relies on the promise of the promisor and the conditions in the contract and thereafter changes his position based on his reliance, and when injustice can be avoided only by specific enforcement of the oral contract.[19] This is known as the *part performance doctrine.*[20]

For example, Sam and Joe agree to sell and buy, respectively, a parcel of land in an oral agreement. Joe delivers a partial payment for the property to ensure that future payments will be made, and if Joe subsequently takes possession of the property and makes permanent improvements on the land by building a fence around the property, digging a well, and adding a room to the house on the property, partial performance has been manifested. Sam will be estopped from requiring a writing to satisfy the statute of frauds under the doctrine of partial performance.

While the sale of real property requires a writing under the statute of frauds, partial performance will take the transaction out of the statute of frauds. The requirements for partial performance require (1) partial payment on the property, (2) taking physical and permanent possession of the property, and (3) making permanent improvements.[21]

On the other hand, in determining whether injustice can be avoided only by enforcement of the oral promise, the following circumstance is significant:

1. Are other adequate remedies, such as cancellation and restitution, available?
2. What is the degree of forbearance relative to the remedy sought?
3. Can forbearance be established by clear and convincing evidence?
4. What is the reasonableness of the action or forbearance?
5. Was the forbearance foreseeable by the promisor?[22]

---

[18] *Id.* at § 2–201 (3)(a) (1977).
[19] Restatement (Second) Contracts § 129 (1979).
[20] *Id.* at § 129 cmt. a (1979).
[21] Restatement (Second) Contracts at § 139 (1979).
[22] *Id.* at § 139 (1979).

Chapter 6

Vocabulary

1. Statute of Frauds
2. Interest in Land
3. Answering for the Debt of Another
4. Upon Consideration of Marriage
5. Performance Outside of One Year
6. The Uniform Commercial Code Statute of Frauds
7. Exceptions to the S/F Under the UCC
8. Exception to the S/F Under the Common Law

Review Questions

1. What is the issue in the *Reedy v. Ebsen* case?
2. What is the principle of law in the *Reedy* case?
3. What is the issue in the *Garland Company, Inc. v. Roofeo Company* case?
4. What is the principle of law in the *Garland* case?
5. What is the issue in the *Ruth Koch v. George Koch* case?
6. What is the principle of law in the *Koch* case?
7. What is the issue in the *Thomas R. Guilbert v. Charles B. Gardner, Jr.* case?
8. What is the principle of law in the *Guilbert* case?

Chapter 7

Mistake

I. Mistaken Belief
A. Mistake Defined

There are circumstances in which a mistake with respect to an agreement will allow either avoidance or a reformation of the contract. The notion of "mistake" extends to a belief that is not consistent with the existing fact as opposed to an act that is manifested as a result of an erroneous belief.[1] Rather, the mistake relates to the existing facts that the parties acquiesced to as the basis for making the agreement.

B. Mutual Mistake

When both parties are mistaken as to the basic assumptions on which the contract was made at the time that the contract is consummated, and if the mistake has a material effect on the agreed performance, the contract then becomes voidable at the option of the adversely affected party.[2]

The following case analyzes the issue of whether or not a mutual mistake of fact exists.

Margaret U. Williams v. Stephen Glash
789 S.W.2d 261 (1990); 1990 Tex. Lexis 65
S. Ct. of Texas

Case 7.1

OPINION BY: DOGGETT

OPINION: The question presented is whether execution of the release for personal injuries in this cause bars a subsequent suit for an injury unknown at the time of signing. The trial court granted summary judgment against Petitioners Margaret and David Williams based on execution of a release. The court of appeals affirmed. We reverse the judgment of the court of appeals and remand this cause to the trial court for further proceedings.

* * * * *

---

[1] Restatement (Second) Contracts § 151 (1979).
[2] *Id.* at § 152 (1979).

Margaret Williams ("Williams") was a passenger in her family car when it was struck from behind by a car driven by the respondent Stephen Glash. While damage to the Petitioners' car was apparent at the time of the accident, there were no observable injuries. Williams immediately contacted State Farm Mutual Automobile Insurance Company, Glash's insurer, who advised Williams to bring the car to its local office for an appraisal of the property damage claims. State Farm estimated the cost of repairs at $889.46 and provided Williams a check payable for that precise amount. At the State Farm office, Williams was asked to complete a claim form containing a question as to whether anyone had been injured by the accident. She checked "No" in response. There was no negotiating or bargaining for release of a personal injury claim; only property damage to the car was discussed. Nonetheless, the back of the check contained language purporting to release personal injury claims, providing that: The undersigned payee accepts the amount of this payment in full settlement of all claims for damages to property and personal injury, whether known or unknown, which payee claims against any insured under the policy shown on the face hereof, or their respective successors in interest, arising on or about the date shown. This release reserves all rights of the parties released to pursue their legal remedies, if any, against any such payee. This release language was never explained to nor discussed with Williams or her husband. The face of the check contained a State Farm code, "200-1", denoting the settlement of a property claim, rather than a separate code used by the insurer for personal injury claims. Petitioners subsequently endorsed the check over to the garage that repaired their car. Williams was later diagnosed as having temporomandibular joint syndrome ("TMJ"), causing head and neck pain, as a result of the accident. Both the trial court and the court of appeals found that suit for this injury was barred by execution of the release.

* * * * *

Petitioners seek to avoid the effect of the release, imploring this court to follow the "modern trend" of setting aside releases when the injury later sued for was unknown at the time of signing.

* * * * *

It is true that a majority of our sister states would, under a variety of theories, permit invalidation of the release under the circumstances presented in this case. The most common basis for invalidation is the doctrine of **mutual mistake**, which mandates that a contract be avoided "[w]here a mistake of both parties at the time the contract was made as to a basic assumption on which the contract was made has a material effect on the agreed exchange of performances." Restatement (Second) of Contracts § 152 Following the modern trend, the Restatement expressly recognizes avoidance of personal injury releases when, in view of the parties' knowledge and negotiations, the release language "flies in the face of what would otherwise be regarded as a basic assumption of the parties."

* * * * *

Under Texas law, a release is a contract and is subject to avoidance, on grounds such as fraud or mistake, just like any other contract.

* * * * *

We then turn to an application of the **mutual mistake** factors in this case. As this is a summary judgment case, the issue on appeal is whether State Farm met its burden of establishing that there exists no genuine issue of material fact, thereby entitling it to judgment as a matter of law. *City of Houston v. Clear Creek Basin Authority*, 589 S.W.2d 671, 678 (Tex. 1979).

* * * * *

Summary judgment evidence manifesting Williams' objective intent shows that she had no knowledge of the TMJ injury at the time of signing the release. She neither discussed nor bargained for settlement of a personal injury claim, and the amount of consideration received was the exact amount of the property damage to her car. State Farm similarly had no knowledge of the TMJ injury and, in fact, used a code on the check indicating the settlement of property damage claims only. The only evidence that these parties intended to release a claim for unknown personal injuries is the language of the release itself. This summary judgment evidence is sufficient to establish the existence of a genuine issue of fact as to whether the parties intended the release to cover the injury for which suit was later brought.

The doctrine of **mutual mistake** must not routinely be available to avoid the results of an unhappy bargain. Parties should be able to rely on the finality of freely bargained agreements. However, in narrow circumstances a party may raise a fact issue for the trier of fact to set aside a release under the doctrine of **mutual mistake**. Because there is some evidence of such circumstances here, we reverse the judgment of the court of appeals and remand this cause to the trial court for further proceedings consistent with this opinion.

C. Mutual Mistake of Fact and Mistake of Value
1. Mistake of Fact

The courts make a distinction between mutual mistake of fact and mutual mistake of value. As mentioned earlier, the court will allow reformation of a contract when both parties are mistaken as to *mistake of fact*.

The classical "Peerless" case illustrates the thinking of the court with respect to mutual mistake of fact.

Raffles v. Wichelhaus
159 Eng. Rep. 375 (1864), 2 Hurl. & C. 906
(Court of Exchequer 1864)

Case 7.2

[Editorial Note: What follows is not an opinion written by a judge. Rather, it is a report of the pleadings in the case, a report of the colloquy between the lawyers and judges during oral argument, and a report of the judgment—all prepared by an official court observer. It is from this tradition of an observer reporting about a case that we derive our current "Reporters" that contain opinions written by the court rather than the reports of observers.]

Declaration [Analagous to the modern day complaint]. ...For that it was agreed between the plaintiff and the defendants, to wit, at Liverpool, that the plaintiff should sell to the defendants, and the defendants buy of the plaintiff, certain goods, to wit,125 bales of Surat cotton, guaranteed middling fair merchant's Dhollorah, to arrive ex "Peerless" [ship] from Bombay; and that the cotton should be taken from the quay, and that the defendants would pay the plaintiff for the same at a certain rate, to wit, at the rate of 17d. per pound, within a certain time then agreed upon after the arrival of the said goods in England. …Averments; that the said goods did arrive by the said ship from Bombay in England, to wit, Liverpool, and the plaintiff was then and there ready and willing and offered to deliver the said goods to the defendants, &c. Breach: that the defendants refused to accept the said goods or pay the plaintiff for them.

Plea [Analagous to the modern day answer]. …That the said ship mentioned in the said agreement was meant and intended by the defendants to be the ship called the "Peerless," which sailed from Bombay, to wit, in October; and that the plaintiff was not ready and willing and did not offer to deliver to the defendants any bales of cotton which arrived by the last-mentioned ship, but instead thereof was only ready and willing and offered to deliver to the defendants 125 bales of Surat cotton which arrived by another and different ship, which was also called the "Peerless," and which sailed from Bombay, to wit, in December. Milward, [barrister representing the plaintiff] in support of the demurrer. …The contract was for the sale of a number of bales of cotton of a particular description, which the plaintiff was ready to deliver. It is immaterial by what ship the cotton was to arrive, so that it was a ship called the "Peerless." The words "to arrive ex 'Peerless,'" only mean that if the vessel is lost on the voyage, the contract is to be at an end. … It would be a question for the jury whether both parties meant the same ship called the "Peerless." That would be so if the contract was for the sale of a ship called the "Peerless;" but it is for the sale of cotton on board a ship of that name. …The defendant only bought that cotton which was to arrive by a particular ship. It may as well be said, that if there is a contract for the purchase of certain goods in warehouse A., [the defendant would not be]…satisfied by the delivery of goods of the same description in warehouse B. In that case there would be goods in both warehouses; here it does not appear that the plaintiff had any goods on board the other "Peerless." …It is imposing on the defendant a contract different from that which he entered into. …It is like a contract for the purchase of wine coming from a particular estate in France or Spain, where there are two estates of that name. The defendant has no right to contradict by parol evidence a written contract good upon the face of it. He does not impute misrepresentation or fraud, but only says that he fancied the ship was a different one. Intention is of no avail, unless stated at the time of the contract. …One vessel sailed in October and the other in December. The time of sailing is no part of the contract.

Mellish (Cohen with him)[barristers representing the defendant], in support of the plea. …There is nothing on the face of the contract to show that any particular ship called the "Peerless" was meant; but the moment it appears that two ships called the "Peerless" were about to sail from Bombay there is a latent ambiguity, and parol evidence may be given for the purpose of showing that the defendant meant one "Peerless" and the plaintiff another. That being so, there was no consensus ad idem [no agreement on the same thing], and therefore no binding contract. [There was a mutual mistake of fact]. He [plaintiff] was then stopped by the Court.

Per Curium. There must be judgment for the defendants. Judgment for the defendants, [the buyer].

2. Mistake of Fact or Value

In the classic *Sherwood v. Walker*, 33 N.W. 919 (1887), case involving "Rose 2d of Aberlone," a cow, the parties agreed to buy and sell a cow that both believed to be barren. After the parties agreed to the sale, the seller refused to deliver it, claiming that the cow was with calf and therefore not barren after all. The buyer claims that it matters not whether the cow is barren or fertile, that a contract was made between the parties to buy and sell Rose 2d of Aberlone, and therefore the contract should be binding. The seller refused to deliver the cow. In a lawsuit brought by the purchaser, the court discussed the distinction between a **mistake of fact** and a mistake that goes to the substance of the transaction, where both parties thought they were buying and selling a barren cow when in fact they were buying and selling a fertile cow.

Sherwood v. Walker
66 Mich. 568 (1887), 33 N.W. 919 (1887)
Supreme Court of Michigan

Case 7.3

MORSE, Justice.

Replevin for a cow. Suit commenced in justice's court; judgment for plaintiff; appealed to circuit court of Wayne county, and verdict and judgment for plaintiff in that court. The defendants bring error, and set out 25 assignments of the same.

* * * * *

...The Walkers [defendants] are importers and breeders of polled Angus cattle. The plaintiff is a banker living at Plymouth, in Wayne county. He [plaintiff, purchaser] called upon the defendants at Walkerville for the purchase of some of their stock, but found none there that suited him. Meeting one of the defendants afterwards, he was informed that they had a few head upon their Greenfield farm. He was asked to go out and look at them, with the statement at the time that they were probably barren, and would not breed. May 5, 1886, plaintiff went out to Greenfield, and saw the cattle. A few days thereafter, he called upon one of the defendants with the view of purchasing a cow, known as "Rose 2d of Aberlone." ...The second morning after this talk he was called up by telephone, and the terms of the sale were finally agreed upon. He was to pay five and one-half cents per pound, live weight, fifty pounds shrinkage. ...He requested defendants to confirm the sale in writing, which they did by sending him the following letter:

"WALKERVILLE, May 15, 1886.

T.C. Sherwood, President, etc.—DEAR SIR: We confirm sale to you of the cow Rose 2d of Aberlone, lot 56 of our catalogue, at five and half cents per pound, less fifty pounds shrink. We enclose herewith order on Mr. Graham for the cow. You might leave check with him, or mail to us here, as you prefer. Yours truly, HIRAM WALKER & SONS

On the twenty-first of the same month the plaintiff went to defendants' farm at Greenfield, and presented the order and letter to Graham, who informed him that the defendants had instructed him not to deliver the cow. Soon after, the plaintiff tendered to Hiram Walker, one of the defendants, $80, and demanded the cow. Walker refused to take the money or deliver the cow. The plaintiff then instituted this suit. After he had secured possession of the cow under the writ of replevin, the plaintiff caused her to be weighed by the constable who served the writ, at a place other than King's cattle-yard. She weighed 1,420 pounds… The defendants then introduced evidence tending to show that at the time of the alleged sale it was believed by both the plaintiff and themselves that the cow was barren and would not breed; that she cost $850, and if not barren would be worth from $750 to $1000; that after the date of the letter, and the order to Graham, the defendants were informed by said Graham that in his judgment the cow was with calf, and therefore they instructed him not to deliver her to plaintiff, and on the twentieth of May, 1886, telegraphed plaintiff what Graham thought about the cow being with calf, and that consequently they could not sell her. The cow had a calf in the month of October following.

It appears from the record that both parties supposed this cow was barren and would not breed, and she was sold by the pound for an insignificant sum as compared with her real value if a breeder. She was evidently sold and purchased on the relation of her value for beef, unless the plaintiff had learned of her true condition, and concealed such knowledge from the defendants. Before the plaintiff secured the possession of the animal, the defendants learned that she was with calf, and therefore of great value, and undertook to rescind the sale by refusing to deliver her. The question arises whether they had a right to do so. The circuit judge ruled that this fact did not avoid the sale and it made no difference whether she was barren or not. I am of the opinion that the court erred in this holding. I know that this is a close question, and the dividing line between the adjudicated cases is not easily discerned. But it must be considered as well settled that a party who has given an apparent consent to a contract of sale may refuse to execute it, or he may avoid it after it has been completed, if the assent was founded, or the contract made, upon the **mistake of a material fact**, …such as the subject-matter of the sale, the price, or some collateral fact materially inducing the agreement; and this can be done when the **mistake is mutual**…

* * * * *

If there is a difference or misapprehension as to the substance of the thing bargained for; if the thing actually delivered or received is different in substance from the thing bargained for, and intended to be sold, …then there is no contract; but if it be only a difference in some quality or accident, even though the mistake may have been the actuating motive to the purchaser or seller, or both of them, yet the contract remains binding. …

* * * * *

It seems to me, however, in the case made by this record, that the *mistake or misapprehension of the parties went to the whole substance of the agreement.* If the cow was a breeder, she was worth at least $750; if barren, she was worth not over $80. The parties would not have made the contract of sale except upon the understanding and belief that she was incapable of breeding, and of no use as a cow. It is true she is now the identical animal that they thought her to be when the contract was made; there is no mistake as to the identity of the creature. Yet the *mistake was not of the mere quality of the animal, but went to the very nature of the thing.* A barren cow is substantially a different creature than a breeding one. There is as much difference between them for all purposes of use as there is between an ox and a cow that is capable of breeding and giving milk. If the mutual mistake had simply related to the fact whether she was with calf or not for one season, then it might have been a good sale, but the mistake affected the character of the animal for all time, and for its present and ultimate use. She was not in fact the animal, or the kind of animal, the defendants intended to sell or the plaintiff to buy. She was not a barren cow, and, if this fact had been known, there would have been no contract. The mistake affected the substance of the whole consideration, and it must be considered that there was no contract to sell or sale of the cow as she actually was. *The thing sold and bought had in fact no existence.* She was sold as a beef creature would be sold; she is in fact a breeding cow, and a valuable one. The court should have instructed the jury that if they found that the cow was sold, or contracted to be sold, upon the understanding of both parties that she was barren, and useless for the purpose of breeding, and that in fact she was not barren, but capable of breeding, then the defendants had a right to rescind, and to refuse to deliver, and the verdict should be in their favor.

* * * * *

The judgment of the court below must be reversed [in favor of defendants], and a new trial granted, with costs of this court to defendants.

In the classical case of the sale of a Stradivarius violin, the parties agreed to buy and sell a violin for a nominal amount of money. Later it is discovered that the violin was not an ordinary violin, that it was in fact a Stradivarius violin worth millions of dollars. The seller sues to recover the Stradivarius violin, arguing that that there was a mutual mistake of fact. The general rule here is that the courts will set aside a contract wherein both parties are mistaken about the facts of the transaction, but a court will *not* set aside a contract where the parties are mistaken about the value of the goods in the transaction. The court ruled that the parties were not mistaken about the fact, i.e. that they were buying and selling a violin. Both knew they were buying and selling a violin even though the parties were **mutually mistaken about the value** of the violin. Hence the contract could not be rescinded.

3. Mistake of Price

The following case illustrates a mistake with respect to the price of the goods where each party had a different opinion about the price they agreed to.

Case 7.4

Estey Organ Company v. Lehman
111 N.W. 1097 (1907), 1907 Wisc. LEXIS 96
Supreme Court of Wisconsin

Defendant buyer appealed an order of the Circuit Court for Brown County (Wisconsin), which entered a judgment in favor of plaintiff seller in the seller's action to recover the purchase price of an organ and motor that was delivered to the buyer pursuant to an agreement of the parties.

JUDGES: James C. Kerwin, J.

OPINION:

KERWIN, J. ...The defendants claimed an agreement to purchase the organ and motor at $1750, and this question was found against them by the jury. ...They involve the main controversy in the case, namely, whether upon the evidence and the verdict the plaintiff was entitled to judgment. The purchase of the organ and motor was made by correspondence, and it is established that no price was agreed upon nor time of delivery fixed upon in such correspondence. It is also established by the evidence that defendants expected to get the organ for $1750, while the plaintiff expected to get $2300 for it, and understood it was selling it for that price, which was the regular selling price. It is therefore apparent that the **minds of the parties never met** upon the price before delivery of the organ. It is strenuously insisted, however, by counsel for appellants that where no price is agreed upon the law will imply one. The argument of counsel would have great force if there was no misunderstanding as to price. But where no price is agreed upon and there is a misunderstanding as to price, one party understanding it to be one sum and the other another, the doctrine invoked by counsel for appellants cannot apply. There being a clear misunderstanding as to price, the contract of sale was not complete until the price was agreed upon, and the law could not imply a price contrary to the understanding of the parties. ...We think it clear that the doctrine that the law will imply the parties intended a reasonable price where no price is agreed upon cannot apply to the case before us. The organ ordered was one of the style and size that plaintiff sold for $2300. The organ was shipped on January 22, 1904. On January 25th plaintiff mailed a letter, inclosing an invoice of the price, $2300 for the organ, and the balance, $101.05, for the motor, making $2,401.05, the amount sued for. The defendants received this letter January 30, 1904, and replied to it the same day, stating that the plaintiff had made a mistake as to the amount and demanding that the bill be corrected. Plaintiff replied February 4, 1904, confirming the amount of the invoice. In the ordinary course of mail this letter would reach defendants not later than February 7, 1904. One of defendants left Green Bay February 12, 1904, for Houghton, Michigan, and took the organ from the railroad company at that place and set it up. The defendants having received and retained the property with knowledge of the price the plaintiff expected to receive, and without any agreement express or implied for a different price, they cannot escape payment of the price stated in the invoice. ...The minds of the parties not having met upon the price prior to the time the property was received by defendants at Houghton, Michigan, it was their duty, when they received it with knowledge of the price, to refuse to accept it, unless they were willing to pay the price stated in the invoice. Having taken the property and converted it to their own use, they became liable to pay such price, which the evidence establishes was the regular selling price and a reasonable price.

We find no reversible error in the record, and think the judgment is right and should be affirmed. By the Court. …The judgment of the court below is affirmed [in favor of the plaintiff].

4.   Unilateral Mistake and Bearing the Risk

Where one of the parties to the agreement is mistaken as to the facts composing the agreement, the mistaken party will not be allowed to void the contract, and the risk resulting from the mistake will be allocated to the mistaken party.[3] For example, suppose that the owner of a parcel of land sells the land to Sam for the purposes of farming. Afterwards it is discovered that the land contains oil. The seller attempts to void the contract on the basis that he was mistaken with respect to what was underneath the land. The contract will not be set aside because the mistaken party, i.e. the seller, bears the risk of the mistake.

The following case addresses the issue with respect to a unilateral mistake.

Case 7.5

City of Lawrenceville v. Ricoh Electronics, Inc.
174 Fed. Appx. 491 (2006); 2006 U.S. App. LEXIS 7900
U. S. Ct. of Appl. for the 11th Circuit

Lawrenceville provides natural gas service to Ricoh, a manufacturer of thermal paper. Between 1990 and 1998, Lawrenceville installed four gas meters at Ricoh's facility. Although Lawrenceville apparently believed that all four meters measured gas consumption in hundreds of cubic feet, one of the meters (the "thermal" meter installed in 1996) actually measured gas consumption in thousands of cubic feet. As a result, from March of 1996 through October of 2002 Lawrenceville billed Ricoh for only about one-tenth of the gas Ricoh actually consumed through the thermal meter during that period. During an inspection of the thermal meter late in 2002, Lawrenceville realized its error and notified Ricoh that approximately $ 1.5 million in back payments and taxes was due and owing. When Ricoh did not pay, Lawrenceville filed suit in Georgia state court, and Ricoh removed to federal district court on diversity grounds. The parties filed cross-motions for summary judgment.

*****

The district court denied summary judgment to Lawrenceville and granted summary judgment to Ricoh. Lawrenceville's "breach of ordinance" claim alleged that the applicable utility rate was set by ordinance, and that Ricoh's refusal to pay was

---

[3] Restatement (Second) Contracts § 154 (1979).

"a violation of Ricoh's obligations under its agreement with [Lawrenceville] and its obligations under the ordinance." The district court, however, found that Lawrenceville had not submitted evidence of a valid ordinance on the matter. Instead, the court agreed with Ricoh that Lawrenceville's breach of ordinance claim should be recast as one for indebtedness on an account. This account was stated and binding on the parties, the court explained, because the bills in question had already been sent and paid. To reform the account based on a **unilateral mistake**, the court held, Lawrenceville had to show that reasonable diligence would not have prevented the erroneous under billing-and Lawrenceville presented no such evidence. Nor, the court found, did Lawrenceville present evidence that fraud or inequitable conduct by Ricoh had caused Lawrenceville's error. The district court further rejected Lawrenceville's reliance upon several cases involving electric utilities that had under billed their customers and later sued to recover additional payments. Finally, the district court denied Lawrenceville's request for attorneys' fees, because Lawrenceville's claims failed on the merits and there were no pertinent allegations of bad faith or wrongdoing.

* * * * *

Here, the district court found that Lawrenceville presented "no evidence suggesting that it employed reasonable care or argument that due diligence would not have prevented its erroneous under billing." *City of Lawrenceville*, 370 F. Supp. 2d at 1331. Lawrenceville disagrees, arguing that sworn statements produced on summary judgment indicate "the under-billing was caused by a single error in setting up the account, and [Lawrenceville] was not able to detect it despite significant procedures designed to detect billing errors." Even if Lawrenceville did raise a fact issue on this point, however, the district court properly noted that a **unilateral mistake merits reformation only where "fraud or inequitable conduct by the other party induces the mistake."** *See Prince v. Friedman*, 202 Ga. 136, 42 S.E.2d 434, 437 (Ga. 1947) ("Equity will not decree the reformation of an instrument because of mistake of one of the parties alone unmixed with any fraud or knowledge on the part of the other equivalent to mutual mistake."). As the district court explained, Lawrenceville presented no evidence suggesting that fraudulent or inequitable conduct by Ricoh caused Lawrenceville's mistake. *Thus, Lawrenceville was not entitled to reformation of the account* stated created when Ricoh paid Lawrenceville's bills in full and Lawrenceville accepted payment without objection.

* * * * *

In light of foregoing, we find no reversible error in the district court's decision to grant summary judgment to Ricoh and deny summary judgment to Lawrenceville) based on the account stated doctrine. Nor did the district court err in granting summary judgment to Ricoh on Lawrenceville's claim for attorneys' fees, which was predicated upon Lawrenceville's success on the merits.

Affirmed, motion for sanctions denied

Chapter 7
Vocabulary

1. Mutual Mistake
2. Mistake of Fact
3. Mistake of Value
4. Mistake of Price
5. Unilateral Mistake

Review Questions

1. What is the issue in the Margaret U. Williams v. Stephen Glash case?
2. What is the legal principle in the *Williams* case?
3. What is the issue in the *Raffles v. Wichelhous* case?
4. What is the legal principle in the *Wichelhous* Case?
5. What is the issue in the *Sherwood v. Walker* case?
6. What is the legal principle in the *Sherwood* case?
7. What is the issue in the *Estey Organ Co. v. Lehman* case?
8. What is the legal principle in the *Lehman* Case?
9. What is the issue in the *City of Lawrenceville v. Ricoh Electronics, Inc.* case?
10. What is the legal principle in the *Lawrenceville* case?

Chapter 8

Misrepresentation, Duress and Undue Influence

I. Misrepresentation Defined

Contracts are determined through the process of bargaining between the parties involved. This basic premise presupposes that the bargaining process has not been impaired by misrepresentation, duress or undue influence.[1] *Misrepresentation* is a false statement that is contrary to the facts.[2] Misrepresentation arises when the following elements are present:

1. The manifestation of an untrue statement.
2. The untrue statement or misrepresentation must be either fraudulent or material.
3. The misrepresentation must have induced the recipient to make a contract.
4. The recipient's reliance must have been justifiable.
5. Whether or not the recipient's reliance is justifiable depends on whether the representation is an (1) assertion of opinion, (2) an assertion of a matter of law, or (3) intentional assertion.

A. The Assertion was an Opinion

A statement of opinion is also a statement of fact. But a statement of fact reveals that a person is certain about the veracity or certainty of the statement. On the other hand, the person opining is basically saying, "I think this is true, but I am not sure."[3] Nevertheless, it is still an assertion. Whether or not the assertion of an opinion rises to the level of equating to one of the elements of misrepresentations depends on whether the recipient knows that it is an opinion and whether the recipient relies on the statement.[4] However, statements with respect to quantity, quality, value and price are virtually never statements of opinion.[5]

---

[1] Restatement (Second) Contracts § 159 (1979).
[2] *Id.*
[3] *Id.* at § 168 cmt. a (1979).
[4] *Id.* at § 168 (1979).
[5] *Id.* at § 168 cmt. c (1979).

B. The Assertion was a Matter of Law

An assertion involving a misstatement of a matter of law, whether it is an opinion or not, is understood in law as an assertion.[6] A recipient who relies on a misrepresentation of law to attempt to avoid a contract will fail because everyone is presumed to know the law, and the recipient knew or should have known the law that allegedly was misrepresented. With respect to matters of law, the recipient is left to draw his own conclusions. For example, if the seller of land misrepresents to the buyer that the property is zoned for commercial purpose, but then after the sale the buyer discovers that the property is actually zoned for residential purpose only, the court will reject a misrepresentation argument because the misstatement was that of a matter of law.[7] On the other hand, recipients may rely on those persons who work in a specialized profession and who deal with the law, such as lawyers, real estate agents, judges or insurance agents.[8]

C. The Assertion was Intentional[9]

Where an assertion by the promisor is made to the effect that he intends to carry out a particular action that will be favorable to the recipient if the recipient consummates the contract when in fact the promisor has no intent to carry out the action, the assertion of the intention is a misrepresentation if the recipient relays on it. For example, suppose a seller of land represents to the buyer that he intends to build a shopping center across the street, when infact, he has no intention of doing so. The assertion of intent by the buyer is a misrepresentation.[10]

D. Manifestation of Misrepresentation

The misrepresentation may manifest itself by acts, conducts or words. Misrepresentation may also arise because of ignorance as a result of carelessness or omitted language.[11] When the misrepresentation causes the other party to assent to the proposed contract by relying on the misstatement of facts, his assent is not effective as a manifestation of mutual assent.[12]

---

[6] *Id.* at § 170 (1979).

[7] Restatement (Second) Contracts § 170 cmt. b (1979).

[8] *Id.* at § 170 cmt. b (1979).

[9] *Id.* at § 159, Introductory note (1979).

[10] *Id.* at § 171 cmt. a (1979).

[11] *Id.* at § 159 (1979).

[12] *Id.* at § 163 (1979).

The manifestation of misrepresentation may have three types of consequences.

1. It may prevent the formation of a contract.
2. It may make a contract voidable.[13]
3. It may give rise to the reformation of a contract.

E. Misrepresentation by Concealment

"Where a vendor has knowledge of a defect in property which is not within the fair and reasonable reach of the vendee and which he could not discover by the exercise of reasonable diligence, the silence and failure of the vendor to disclose the defect in the property constitutes actionable misrepresentation by concealment."[14]

The following case illustrates the issue of misrepresentation with respect to withheld information.

Case 8.1

Griffith v. Byers Construction Co. of Kansas, Inc.
510 P.2d 198 (1973), 1973 Kan. LEXIS 488
Supreme Court of Kansas

JUDGE: Fromme, J.

The petitions allege that Byers developed and advertised the addition as a choice residential area. Prior to the time of development the addition was part of an abandoned oil field which contained salt water disposal areas which Byers knew or should have known would not sustain vegetation because of the saline content of the soil. It was alleged that Byers graded and developed the whole addition for home sites in such a manner that it became impossible for a purchaser to discover the presence of these salt areas. It further appears from allegations in the petitions and testimony in depositions that each of the plaintiffs selected a home site which was located within a salt water disposal area. After houses were constructed attempts to landscape the home sites failed. Grass, shrubs and trees were planted and died because of the saline content of the soil.

* * * * *

The facts of this case appear to be unique for, although many cases can be found on a vendor-builder's liability for the sale of a defective home...no cases are cited and we find none which discuss a developer's liability for defects arising from sterility of soil. The saline content of the soil of these home sites does not affect the structural qualities of the homes. The allegations of the petitions and deposition testimony indicate that landscaping is either impossible or highly expensive.

* * * * *

---

[13] *Id.* at §164 (1979).
[14] Phillip C. Griffith and Harriet A. Griffith v. Byers Construction Co. of Kansas, Inc. 510 P.2d. 198 (1973), 1973 Kan. LEXIS 488.

It is noted the judgments of the court were based on a determination of three questions of law: ...(2) Lack of privity in the fraud claims, ...We have answered the first question. As to the second question we do not believe the record conclusively establishes the inability of the appellants to support their charges of fraud nor did the trial court dispose of the motion on that ground. ...

* * * * *

The allegations of fraud appear to be viable issues for trial if nondisclosure of a known material defect in the lots constitutes actionable fraud as to the appellants. This court has held that the purchaser may recover on the theory of fraud from a vendor-builder for nondisclosure of defects. In *Jenkins v. McCormick*, 184 Kan. 842, 339 P. 2d 8, it is stated:

* * * * *

"Where a vendor has knowledge of a defect in property which is not within the fair and reasonable reach of the vendee and which he could not discover by the exercise of reasonable diligence, the silence and failure of the vendor to disclose the defect in the property constitutes actionable fraudulent concealment."...

* * * * *

This *Jenkins* rule approximates that stated in Restatement (Second) Torts, § 551 (Ten. Draft No. 12, 1966):

"(1) One who fails to disclose to another a thing which he knows may justifiably induce the other to act or refrain from acting in a business transaction is subject to the same liability to the other as though he had represented the nonexistence of the matter which he has failed to disclose, if, but only if, he is under a duty to the other to exercise reasonable care to disclose the matter in question." (2) One party to a business transaction is under a duty to disclose to the other before the transaction is consummated. "(e) Facts basic to the transaction, if he knows that the other is about to enter into the transaction under a mistake as to such facts, and that the other, because of the relationship between them, the customs in the trade, or other objective circumstances, would reasonably expect a disclosure of such facts."

* * * * *

"One who makes a fraudulent misrepresentation is subject to liability for pecuniary loss" (a) To the persons or class of persons whom he intends or has reason to expect to act or to refrain from action in reliance upon the misrepresentation; and "(b) For pecuniary loss suffered by them through their reliance in the type of transaction in which he intends or has reason to expect their conduct to be influenced."

* * * * *

Under the alleged facts of our present case, accepting the same in the light most favorable to the appellants, we must assume the appellee, Byers, had knowledge of the saline content of the soil of the lots it placed on the market. After the grading and development of the area this material defect in the lots was not within the fair and reasonable reach of the vendees, as they could not discover this latent defect by the exercise of reasonable care. The silence of the appellee, Byers, and its failure to disclose this defect in the soil condition to the purchasers could constitute actionable fraudulent concealment under the rule in *Jenkins v. McCormick, supra*. One who makes a fraudulent misrepresentation or concealment is subject to liability for pecuniary loss to the persons or class of persons whom he intends or has reason to expect to act or to refrain from action in reliance upon the misrepresentation or concealment.

Of course, the fraudulent concealment to be actionable has to be material to the transaction. A matter is material if it is one to which a reasonable man would attach importance in determining his choice of action in the transaction in question. ...There is little doubt in this case a prospective purchaser of a residential building site would consider the soil condition a material factor in choosing a lot on which to build his home. It materially affected the value and acceptability of the home site.

* * * * *

As to the claims of Reichart and the Griffiths in District Court Cases No. C-21627 and C-21629 the order of the district court entering summary judgment in favor of the appellee is...reversed as to the alternative claims based on fraud, and these cases are remanded with instructions to proceed in accordance with the views expressed herein.

F. Fraudulent Misrepresentation

On the other hand, the elements of the common law tort of fraudulent misrepresentation that a plaintiff must prove in order to recover damages are: (1) a false representation (2) in reference to a material fact (3) made with knowledge of its falsity (4) and with the intent to deceive (5) with action taken in reliance upon the representation.[15]

The following case analysis addresses fraudulent misrepresentation.

Case 8.2

Ralph Nader v. Allegheny Airlines, Inc.
445 F. Supp. 168 (1978), 1978 U.S. Dist. LEXIS 20244
U. S. Dist. Ct. for the Dist. of Columbia

JUDGES: United States District Judge Charles R. Richey.

This action arose from the denied boarding of the plaintiff Ralph Nader from Allegheny Airlines Flight 864 on April 28, 1972. A trial was held before the Court, sitting without a jury, on September 4 and 10, 1973, and a decision awarding nominal and punitive damages to plaintiff Connecticut Citizens Action Group (CCAG) and compensatory and punitive damages to plaintiff Nader was filed on October 18, 1973. The case is now on remand to this Court for final disposition in accordance with the decisions of the reviewing courts. ...

I. *Plaintiff Nader's Claim of a Statutory Violation*
1. Section 404(b) of the Federal Aviation Act, 49 U.S.C. § 1374(b) (1970), provides: No air carrier or foreign air carrier shall make, give, or cause any undue or unreasonable preference or advantage to any particular person, port, locality, or description of traffic in air transportation in any respect whatsoever or subject any particular person, port, locality, or description of traffic in air transportation to any unjust discrimination or any undue or unreasonable prejudice or disadvantage in any respect whatsoever.

---

[15] Ralph Nader v. Allegheny Airlines Inc., 445 F. Supp. 168 (1978), 1978 U.S. Dist. LEXIS 20244.

2. To recover damages pursuant to a Section 404(b) action, an allegedly oversold passenger must first show that the defendant air carrier refused to honor his boarding priority. It is undisputed herein that plaintiff Nader held a confirmed reservation on defendant Allegheny's Flight 864 from Washington, D.C. to Hartford, Connecticut, on April 28, 1972, that he complied with Allegheny's pre-boarding conditions, that he was entitled to a seat, and that the reservation was not honored by defendant Allegheny because the flight had been overbooked and all seats were occupied. Thus, as the Court of Appeals recognized, plaintiff Nader's priority was undeniably dishonored, and plaintiff therefore established a prima facie statutory violation. ...

II. *Plaintiff Nader's Fraudulent Misrepresentation Claim*

What this Court must decide is whether Allegheny's failure to disclose its overbooking policies to plaintiff Nader was a fraudulent misrepresentation.

The elements of the common-law tort of fraudulent misrepresentation that a plaintiff must prove in order to recover are: (1) A false representation (2) in reference to a material fact (3) made with knowledge of its falsity (4) and with the intent to deceive (5) with action taken in reliance upon the representation.

...The Court finds that plaintiff Nader has proved all of these elements by a preponderance of the evidence.

12. *Falsity*. It is undisputed that defendant Allegheny communicated to plaintiff that he had a "confirmed reservation" on Flight 864 on April 28, 1972. It is also undisputed that defendant at no time (not in its tariffs, advertising, or other communications to the public) communicated to the plaintiff the existence of its overbooking practice. Defendant contends that a reasonable person would recognize that a "confirmed reservation" is not an absolute guarantee, but rather is a "reasonable assurance," of being flown, because any given flight may be cancelled as a result of meteorological conditions, mechanical problems, or the like. Defendant further contends that plaintiff had such a "reasonable assurance" of being flown on Flight 864 on April 28, 1972, not-withstanding defendant's overbooking policy, because only a very small percentage of reservation-holders were ever bumped.

The Court agrees with defendant's first contention, but disagrees entirely with its second contention. The "reasonable assurance" of flight that the term "confirmed reservation" connotes is a guarantee of flight subject only to contingencies beyond the control of the airline. The expectation of a reasonable person receiving a "confirmed reservation" is that the airline will do everything within reason to assure that the reservation-holder is flown on the flight for which he has a "confirmed reservation." Merely because any reservation is necessarily subject to unforeseen and uncontrollable contingencies is not license for the airline deliberately to impose its own additional contingencies on the "confirmed reservation," and no reasonable person would interpret the term "confirmed reservation" to incorporate such a license. ...The Court thus finds that defendant's non-disclosure of its overbooking practice was misleading and created a false understanding as to the chance of being flown on Flight 864.

13. *Materiality*. A material fact is one to which a reasonable person might attach importance in choosing his course of action...in other words, it is a fact that could reasonably be expected to influence the conduct of a person with respect to the transaction in question. ... the chance of being flown on Flight 864.

The Court finds that the fact of the existence of defendant Allegheny's overbooking practice was such a material fact. There can be no doubt that the very essence of a "confirmed reservation" is the assurance of flight capacity. Thus, even though defendant contends that the statistical probability of any given passenger being bumped is not substantial, the knowledge that bumping is a possibility might well, for example, influence a reasonable person to arrive earlier for the flight than he otherwise would have. More-over, defendant's contention that the fact of the existence of its overbooking practice is not material and would not likely influence passengers' behavior is irreconcilable with its admission in oral argument before the Supreme Court that Allegheny might well lose substantial business if it unilaterally (i.e., without like action by other airlines) notified passengers of its overbooking practice.

14. *Knowledge of Falsity.* Defendant Allegheny clearly knew that its representation to plaintiff Nader that he had a "confirmed reservation" was false and misleading because it knew that its practice of overbooking subjected Mr. Nader's reservation to the risk of being dishonored.

15. *Intent to Deceive.* There can be no doubt that the nondisclosure of the existence of defendant's overbooking practice was the result of a conscious and deliberate policy implemented by Allegheny in order to deprive passengers of information about its overbooking practice so as not to distinguish Allegheny's reservation practices from those of its competitors.

16. *Reliance.* Plaintiff Nader relied on his confirmed reservation as an assurance that he would be accommodated on Allegheny's flight, and the Court finds that such reliance was reasonable. Prior to April 28, 1972, plaintiff Nader was unaware of Allegheny's intentional overbooking policy. Although he knew from prior experience that other airlines had occasionally bumped passengers with confirmed reservations, he was unaware of Allegheny's overbooking practice, especially since the other airlines had always explained their over-sales as purely accidental rather than the result of a deliberate overbooking practice. If Allegheny had revealed the existence of its overbooking practice to Mr. Nader, the Court finds that because of the importance that he attached to the fulfillment of his speaking engagement in Hartford, he would have taken appropriate steps to protect against the risk of bumping, such as arriving earlier at the gate, arranging for an earlier flight, or arranging an alternative way to travel to Hartford. Allegheny's purpose in making confirmed reservations is to induce just such reliance by persons making travel arrangements, and there is no basis to assume that Mr. Nader should have realized that his reservation was subject to the risk of overbooking. For these reasons, the Court finds that plaintiff Nader justifiably relied on defendant's representation that he had a "confirmed reservation" as a reasonable person would construe that term. ...

17. *Duty.* It is well-established in this jurisdiction that: "[A] statement in a business transaction, which, while stating the truth as far as it goes, the maker knows or believes to be materially misleading because of his failure to state qualifying matter is a fraudulent misrepresentation; also that a statement containing a half-truth may be as misleading as a statement wholly false and thus that a statement which contains only those matters which are favorable and omits all reference to those which are unfavorable is as much a false representation as if all the facts stated were untrue..."... Thus, concealment or suppression of a material fact is as fraudulent as a positive direct

misrepresentation." ...It is also well-established that there is a duty upon one who undertakes to speak "not only to state truly what he tells" but also not to "suppress or conceal any facts within his own knowledge which materially qualify those stated. If he speaks at all he must make full and fair disclosure."

In the instant case, defendant Allegheny intentionally failed to disclose to plaintiff Nader information within defendant's possession—the existence of its overbooking practice— ...which materially qualified the meaning of its statement to plaintiff Nader that he had a "confirmed reservation," and this omission was misleading...and defendant knew it to be so. ...Thus, defendant Allegheny had a duty to disclose the existence of its over-booking practice and its failure to do so subjects it to liability for the common-law tort of misrepresentation.

*****

IV. Plaintiffs' Entitlement to Punitive Damages on Their Fraudulent Misrepresentation Claims

23. Both plaintiff Nader and plaintiff CCAG pray this Court to assess punitive damages against the defendant for its fraudulent misrepresentation. Since only plaintiff Nader is entitled to recover from Allegheny for its fraudulent misrepresentation, the Court can only consider the appropriateness of a punitive damages award to plaintiff Nader.

*****

29. Having concluded that punitive damages are appropriately awarded herein, the Court must determine the appropriate amount of punitive damages to be awarded. In its initial decision, this Court assessed punitive damages in the amount of $50,000 against defendant Allegheny—$25,000 in favor of plaintiff Nader, and $25,000 in favor of plaintiff CCAG. Upon reconsideration of the entire record herein, including defendant's submissions and arguments with respect to its asserted "good faith" defense, the Court concludes that an award of $15,000 punitive damages is appropriate in the circumstances of this case. ...The Court finds that an award of $15,000 in punitive damages will adequately serve to punish defendant Allegheny for its willful and wanton policy of nondisclosure and misrepresentation and will adequately serve to deter defendant from engaging in such practices in the future. The Court is aware that in this jurisdiction it is appropriate in assessing punitive damages to consider the amount of attorneys' fees incurred by the prevailing plaintiff in the course of this litigation, ... and the Court recognizes that the award of $15,000 will not fully compensate plaintiff Nader for the value of the many, many hours expended by his able counsel in pursuing this litigation to a successful conclusion. Nevertheless, in the circumstances of the present case, the Court concludes that the award of punitive damages should be limited to an amount adequate for the purposes of punishment and deterrence, and the Court concludes that the award of $15,000 in punitive damages is fair and reasonable and appropriate to satisfy the objectives of the law in applying punitive damages.

*****

ORDERED, that judgment be entered for plaintiff Ralph Nader on both his statutory discrimination and his common-law misrepresentation claims in the total sum of $10 for compensatory damages and on his common-law misrepresentation claim in the sum of $15,000 for punitive damages. ...

II. Duress and Undue Influence

A. Duress

Duress and undue influence address the notion that a bargain can be created under improper pressure by one of the parties.

There are two types of *duress*. In the first case, one of the bargaining parties compels the other party to acquiesce to the bargain by physical force when the bullied party has no intention of engaging or entering into a contract. This type of physical pressure and duress does not cause the conduct of the pressured party to rise to a contract. Therefore, where one is compelled by physical duress to a bargain that appears to be a manifestation of mutual assent when in fact the party under duress does not intend to engage in the bargain, the agreement does not rise to a manifestation of assent.[16] The result is that there is no contract or there is a void contract.[17]

In the second case, one of the bargaining parties threatens the other to acquiesce to the bargain. If a party's manifestation of assent arises as a result of a threat that leaves the threatened party without any alternative, the contract is voidable and can be avoided by the threatened party.[18] The threat may manifest itself by words or conduct but must leave no alternative to the threatened party. However, the threat itself does not have to be as severe as life, mayhem or imprisonment. In other words, the threat must arouse such fear as to preclude a party from exercising free will and judgment of a person's ordinary firmness.[19]

The following case focuses on the degree of the threat to rise to duress

---

Fred A. Quinn v. United States Fidelity & Guaranty Co. 163 Minn. 320 (1925), 204 N.W. 156 (1925) Supreme Court of Minn.	**Case 8.3**

OPINION BY: Holt

George A. Quinn, the son of plaintiffs, was cashier in a Minneapolis bank. Defendant had given its bond indemnifying the bank against loss from defalcation of the cashier. On April 18, 1923, George revealed to his parents that he was short [at the bank]. About the same time defendant and the bank discovered his misappropriation of the funds of the bank. Defendant at once set about to secure itself against the loss it knew would follow when the full extent of George's defalcation was ascertained and the bank would seek recourse on the bond. The result was that on May 11, 1923, plaintiffs

---

[16] Restatement (Second) Contracts § 174 (1979).

[17] *Id.* at § 175 (1) cmt. a (1979).

[18] *Id.* at § 175 (2) (1979).

[19] *Id.* at § 175 cmt. b (1979).

borrowed $1,075 from a nephew, which they turned over to defendant's agents, and also deeded to them their homestead, their all, in trust for defendant.

* * * * *

The sole question on the appeal is whether the evidence supports the verdict of the jury and the findings of the court that the money was obtained and the conveyance made under **duress**. The court charged the jury that plaintiffs could not recover unless they had satisfied the jury affirmatively that the money and deed were thus obtained, saying "**duress** is such pressure or constraint as compels a person to go against his will and virtually takes away his free agency and destroys the power of refusing to comply with the unlawful demand of another."

* * * * *

It is quite apparent from the testimony of plaintiffs and their situation that the jury were justified in finding that defendant's agents made it appear to the old people that, if the payment was made and the home conveyed, their son would remain unmolested, otherwise the law would take its course. It stands to reason that plaintiffs, who in a lifetime of toil had only been able to acquire a home, would not have parted therewith and gone in debt over a $1,000 in addition to help out this surety before it had made good the loss to the bank, unless the impending prosecution of their only child forced them. It was not for their default. They were not in defendant's debt. It is true, about three weeks elapsed between the discovery of his plight and the transaction, so they had time to consider and take advice. But they sought no legal advice. All their efforts seemed to have been devoted to attempting to borrow from relatives so as to satisfy defendant's demands.

The case of Foley v. Greene [citation omitted] is similar to the instant case in that there was no evidence of direct threats, and nevertheless it was held a question of fact whether there was **duress**. Where there is **duress**, the victim thereof cannot be said to be in *pari delicto* with the party to the agreement who procured it by the unlawful pressure. It is difficult to see how one who by **duress** is so robbed of his free will that the law regards his contract as voidable is in position to make an agreement to compound a crime. Our statute makes the taker and not the giver of the consideration for an agreement to stifle prosecution guilty of crime.

Of course, where there is a free and voluntary payment or conveyance to prevent prosecution of a person or a near relative the parties are left as found. It is only where the one making the payment or conveyance is shown to have been pressed thereto by express or implied threats of disgrace, disaster to person or property, or criminal prosecution, so that he could not have exercised any choice or free will in the matter. Having in mind the quantum of proof required in a case of this sort, we still think the evidence here made it a question of fact for the jury and the trial court whether the plaintiffs were impelled by the fear of threatened imprisonment of their only child to give their all, and more, to defendant's agents, under the belief that he would go free so that they did not make the payment or execute the deed voluntarily. …where two persons conspire together to do an act forbidden by law to one of them, the doing of it by joint agreement is a violation of law as to both." The case involved an illegal contract to the making of which both parties entered without a hint of **duress**.

The orders are affirmed [in favor of plaintiff.]

B. Undue Influence

When a person is under the domination of another and is influenced by unfair persuasion as a result of their relationship, thereby causing the subordinated person to act in contract in a manner that is inconsistent with his own welfare, such a persuasive act is called *undue influence*.[20] A contract entered into while under undue influence is voidable by the subordinated person.[21] Influencers who may manifest undue influence based on their relationships to the affected party include a child, parent, husband, wife, relative, clergyman, an elderly person, an illiterate person or patient.[22] The test to determine whether an undue influence exists is whether the contract was produced by seriously impairing the free and competent exercise of the subordinated party's exercise of judgment.[23]

Some of the factors in determining whether undue influence exists include:

1. The unfairness of the resulting bargain.
2. The unavailability of independent advice.
3. The susceptibility of the person persuaded.
4. The relationship of the parties involved in the transaction.[24]

The following case illustrates the relationship and circumstances under which undue influence may manifest itself.

Hyatt v. Wroten **Case 8.4** 43 S.W.2d 726 (1931); 184 Ark. 847 (1931) Supreme Court of Arkansas JUDGE: McHaney, J. The subject of this controversy is the will of John L. Wroten executed by him and properly attested on the first day of September, 1928. He died in November, 1929, at the age of 75. In this will he bequeathed $5 each to the appellees, three of whom are his children and one a grandchild. Of the remainder of his estate he devised and bequeathed one-fourth thereof to the board of trustees of the Arkansas Masonic Home and School and by the fourth paragraph thereof he gave the entire remainder of his estate "to my faithful housekeeper, Mrs. Lula Garner." He appointed W. W. Prewitt as the executor of his will, and directed that the executor sell all his real and personal property in the manner provided by law, and, after the payment of his debts, he should make the distribution of the estate in the manner above set out. The chief beneficiary,

---

[20] Restatement (Second) Contracts § 177 (1) (1979).

[21] *Id.* at § 177 (2) (1979).

[22] *Id.* at § 177 cmt. a (1979).

[23] *Id.* at § 177 cmt. b (1979).

[24] *Id.* at § 177 cmt. b (1979).

Lula Garner, died intestate in December, 1929, leaving surviving her the contestees, J. R. Hyatt and M. M. Hyatt, her brothers and only heirs at law.

* * * * *

Thereupon the [lower] court found from the verdict that it was the intention of the jury to sustain the will as to the bequest in favor of the Masonic Home and School, and against the will as to the bequest in favor of Lula Garner and instructed judgment accordingly. From this judgment both sides have appealed.

* * * * *

The facts are, briefly stated, that the testator was 75 years old at the time of his death and Lula Garner was 40 or 50. She had been living with him as his housekeeper about five years at the time of his death, and it appears that she exercised a great influence over him— "was always willing to do anything she wanted him to do," as one witness put it. She went with him almost everywhere in his car, and, when she did not go with him, she would walk out to the car and see him off. The evidence further discloses that there were three bedrooms in the house where they lived alone, one on one side of the hall and two on the other; that she occupied a bed in the room adjoining the testator's bedroom with a door opening from one to the other. She was seen to "wash his neck and ears and put his shoes on him," and he was seen with her in the house with nothing on but his shirt and underwear with her adjusting his neck tie. The testator was a married man, his wife being confined in the State Hospital for Nervous Diseases for many years prior to her death which happened prior to that of the testator. While no witness testified directly that the testator and Lula Garner were guilty of illicit relations, the facts and circumstances testified to were such as to justify the jury in inferring such relationship. We think the fact that they thus lived together for four or five years in the same house alone and with adjoining rooms with a door between, as said by this court in *Alford v. Johnson*, 103 Ark. 236, 146 S.W. 516, "was amply sufficient to justify the jury in finding that their relations were meretricious and adulterous." And, as was said in the same case: "There can be no doubt that a long continued relation of adulterous intercourse is a source of great mutual influence of each of the parties over the mind and person and property of the other. ...." When, therefore, undue influence is charged, the fact that the person accused of exercising it lived in illicit relations with the testator is properly admitted in evidence, to be considered by the jury, and from such testimony the jury may draw an inference of fact of such undue influence.

* * * * *

The proof further shows that the testator was ever ready to do whatever she wanted done and to do, things about the farm in the way she directed it to be done. Also that he was suffering from hardening of the arteries and high blood pressure which the physicians said tended to lower his mentality and break down his will power. Being subject to her influence in matters of minor importance when coupled with that wicked influence which arises from an illicit relation, we are forced to the conclusion, or at least the jury was justified in so finding, that he disinherited his own children and gave his property to his paramour, or a major portion of it, as a result of a baneful influence operating with great force on a diseased body and a waning will power. We think that if such relation existed between the testator and Lula Garner, as the jury has evidently found, when taken in connection with the bequest to her, this of itself is sufficient evidence of all undue influence exerted by her over the testator as to justify the verdict against the will. ...

* * * * *

Undue influence is generally difficult of direct proof. It is generally exercised in secret, not openly, and, like a snake crawling upon a rock, it leaves no track behind it, but its sinister and insidious effect must be determined from facts and circumstances surrounding the testator, his physical and mental condition as shown by the evidence, and the opportunity of the beneficiary of the influenced bequest to mold the mind of the testator to suit his or her purposes. We cannot therefore say that there was not substantial evidence to support the jury's verdict.

* * * * *

We therefore conclude that the court correctly construed the verdict of the jury and entered judgment accordingly, sustaining the bequest to the Masonic Home and School and invalidating the bequest to Lula Garner. Affirmed.

Chapter 8

Vocabulary

1. Misrepresentation
2. Representation by Opinion
3. Representation by Concealment
4. Fraudulent Misrepresentation
5. Duress
6. Undue Influence

Review Questions

1. What is the issue in the *Griffith v. Byers* case?
2. What is the legal principle in the *Griffith* case?
3. What is the issue in the *Ralph Nader v. Allegheny Airlines* case?
4. What is the legal principle in the *Nader* case?
5. What is the issue in the *Fred A. Quinn v. U. S. Fidelity Y Guaranty Co.* case?
6. What is the legal principle in the *Quinn* case?
7. What is the issue in the *Hyatt v. Wroten* case?
8. What is the legal principle in the *Hyatt* case?

Chapter 9

Performance of Contracts

I. Performance

Contracting parties generally have the expectation that the performances they promise to one another will be performed. Therefore, what is generally found in contracts is a laundry list of the performances expected by each party. However, as a general rule, contracting parties normally do not list the consequences of nonperformance.[1]

A. Expectations of Good Faith Performances

Contracting parties of an agreement not only have expectations that their counterparts' promises will be kept, but also that the performance agreed to will be carried out according to the agreement. Sometimes the parties are not clear about the performance, or one of the parties is unable to perform fully, so it is the job of the courts to insure that the parties act in good faith, thereby manifesting a sense of fairness in their performance.[2]

The following case illustrates the breach of several promises and several performances. It is followed by an analysis of good faith and dealing with failure to perform.[3]

Star Credit Corporation v. Cecilio Molina
298 N.Y.S.2d 570 (1969), 59 Misc. 2d 290 (1969)

Case 9.1

JUDGE: Irving Younger, J.

On July 25, 1966, Mr. and Mrs. Cecilio Molina signed a retail installment contract whereby they bought a freezer from Peoples Foods, Inc. for $1,222.15. On the next day, Peoples Foods, Inc., assigned the contract to Star Credit Corporation (for convenience, called "Star").

On July 30, 1966, Mr. Molina signed another retail installment contract, this time obliging himself to pay $445.82 to Peoples Food Packaging Corporation for a quantity of frozen and packaged foods. On the same day, Peoples Food Packaging Corporation assigned the contract to Star.

The freezer and one third of the frozen and packaged foods were delivered to the Molinas, who made payments of $169.75 on account of the first contract and of

---

[1] Restatement (Second) Contracts § 231 (1981).
[2] *Id.* at § 231 cmt. a (1981).
[3] *Id.* at § 231 cmt. d (1981).

$111.47 on account of the second. They never received the remaining two thirds of the foods because Peoples Food Packaging Corporation went out of business. When they stopped making payments, Star brought this action against Molina to recover the balance due on both contracts, together with late charges and attorneys' fees. Molina counterclaimed for the payments of $169.75 made on account of the first contract.

* * * * *

Grasping what the statutes offer, the sellers included in each of the contracts with Molina a printed clause as follows:

"This agreement may be assigned without notice to Buyer. The Buyer agrees not to assert against an assignee a claim or defense arising out of the sale under this contract provided that the assignee acquires this contract in good faith and for value and has no notice of the facts giving rise to the claim or defense in writing within ten days after such assignee mails to the Buyer at his address shown above notice of the assignment of this contract."

Star urges that it is the assignee of both contracts, that it acquired them in good faith and for value, that it gave the Molinas notice of the assignments, and that the Molinas did not within 10 days send Star a written statement of the facts giving rise to their claims and defenses, from all of which Star concludes that the Molinas' claims and defenses are not cognizable against Star.

* * * * *

We turn to the question whether Star acquired the contracts in good faith. …'**Good faith**' means honesty in fact in the conduct or transaction concerned"—and, in their Official Comment on the section, add that the phrase "means at least what is here stated." In short, "**good faith**," as used in the code, stands for "honesty" and perhaps more. …

Star argues that it is an entity separate from both Peoples Foods, Inc., and Peoples Food Packaging Corporation; that it never sold anything to Molina; and that it did not participate with the sellers in the behavior which gives rise to Molina's claims and defenses. Hence, Star urges, its conduct has been "honest in fact."

Were this case of businessman dealing with businessman, Star's argument would have considerable appeal. …This, however, is not a case which can be decided on the principle of caveat emptor. It is more than a commercial event. Although Molina was literate, they are hardly sophisticated enough to understand the "cut-off" provision of the contracts they signed. There was no parity of bargaining power between Molina and their sellers. If Molina is indeed "cut off" from asserting their claims and defenses, they will be required without further remedy to pay for foods they will never receive. For these reasons, we hold that "good faith," as used in section 9-206, means more than "honesty in fact" when, in circumstances such as those presented here, an assignee seeks to bar a consumer from asserting against the assignee claims and defenses to the underlying obligation.

* * * * *

We are therefore persuaded that the sellers entered into these contracts not primarily to sell a freezer and food to Molina, but primarily to obtain commercial paper for assignment to Star; and that Star accepted the assignments with full knowledge of the seller's conduct and intention. Accordingly, we hold that Star is not an assignee of these contracts "in **good faith**" and thus is not entitled to the protection of the "cut-off" provisions of section 9–206.

* * * * *

Molina argue finally that the sellers have breached these contracts. In order to decide the issue, we must determine precisely what the agreement was. As stated at the beginning, there were two documents, one dated July 25 and the other July 30. Mrs. Molina testified (and we accept her testimony) that a single salesman called upon her and in one interview sold her a "food plan"—food and a freezer to keep it in. She signed the freezer contract on that day, and her husband signed the food contract five days later when the first delivery of food was made. The freezer contract bears account number 8383, and the food contract number 5–8383. Each contract refers on its face to the possibility that a document would be attached providing for a plan or program," in which event the contract and the attachment are to be deemed a single agreement. While each contract names a separate corporation as seller, the address of these corporations is the same. The contracts are on substantially identical printed forms, and both were assigned to Star by the same person signing as vice-president of the seller named in each contract. The evidence persuades us that these are in fact not two contracts but a single agreement, contained in two memoranda, for the purchase of a food-and-freezer plan. The sellers' performance under this agreement was substantially defective. Only one third of the food was delivered. It was central to the bargain that food be supplied so that Molina could make efficient use of the freezer. Molina has not had a material part of what the sellers promised them.

When an obligor's performance is substantially defective, the obligee may rescind the agreement. (*Callanan v. Keeseville, Ausable Chasm & Lake Champlain R. R. Co.*, 199 N. Y. 268.) Here, Molina rescinded the agreement after receiving and consuming one third of the food for all of which they had promised to pay $445.82. They have already paid to Star a total of $281.22, which exceeds one third of $445.82 by $132.61. They have also had the use of the freezer since its delivery to them in July, 1966. I find that the fair value of this use is $132.61.

* * * * *

Accordingly, on the entire case, judgment will be entered dismissing the complaint and the counterclaim without costs to either side. Star shall of course have the right to repossess the freezer.

B. Effect of Performance and Nonperformance

The duty and obligations of the promisor are discharged when they are fully performed. It is essential that the performance be performed completely according to the promise and expectation of the parties.[4] Otherwise a breach for total or partial nonperformance may occur, resulting in a claim for either partial, total, or nominal damages.[5]

Where the performances are to be exchanged simultaneously, there is an expectation by both parties that the performance will be performed according to the promises made. However, either party may refuse to perform or delay his own performance unless he is substantially assured of the forthcoming performance

---

[4] Restatement (Second) Contracts § 235 (1981).

[5] *Id.* at § 236. (1981).

from the other party. If one party is not substantially assured, he may delay performance until he has received such assurance or until the performance is actually forthcoming.[6] But in order to delay performance, the nonperformance by the other party must be material.

To resolve whether or not the nonperformance is material, the following must be determined:

1. The extent to which the injured party will be deprived of the expected benefit.
2. The extent to which the injured party can be adequately compensated.
3. The extent to which the nonperformer will suffer forfeiture.
4. The likelihood that the nonperformer will cure his failure.
5. The extent to which the nonperformer acted in good faith and fair dealing.[7]

C. Breach by Nonperformance: Claim for Damages

Where promises are made between the promisor and the promisee for an exchange of performances, the breach by nonperformance will give rise to a claim for total breach, but only if it so substantially impairs the value of the contract to the injured party at the time of the breach.[8] But in the case below, the building subcontractor was entitled to the entire contract price only when it had rendered the entire contracted performance. But where he rendered only "substantial performance" the contractor is only entitled to a contract price less than the cost of completion.[9]

Case 9.2

> Schaff Brothers, Inc. v. American Fidelity Fire Insurance Co.
> 376 So. 2d 172 (1979), 1979 La. App. LEXIS 3059
> Court Of Appeal of Louisiana, Fourth Circuit
>
> OPINION BY: J. Redmann
>
> In this suit against a surety for the $7000 balance of a $55,000 subcontract price, on plaintiff's moving for summary judgment a defense affidavit by the general contractor's supervisor asserted four items of nonperformance of the contract: (1) nondelivery of the manufacturer's specifications and instructions for the heating

---

[6] *Id.* at § 238 cmt. a (1981).

[7] *Id.* at § 241 (1981).

[8] *Id.* at § 243 (1981).

[9] Schaff Brothers, Inc. v. American Fidelity Fire Insurance Company, 376 So. 2d 172 (1979), 1979 La. App. LEXIS 3059.

and air conditioning equipment, (2) nondelivery of equipment warranties, (3) constant leaking of a water fountain, and (4) nonperformance of checking duct thermostat operation. The trial court nevertheless granted summary judgment for the entire balance plus statutory attorney's fees. We reverse on the basis that the affidavit showed there was a dispute of material fact.

The law is clear that a building subcontractor is entitled to the entire contract price only when it has rendered the entire contracted performance, and that if it has rendered only "substantial performance" it is only entitled to contract price less cost of completion.

If the four items of nonperformance be established then plaintiff is not entitled to the full balance on the price. It may well be that the case must be considered one of **substantial performance,** in which it ultimately falls to defendant to prove the amount of the cost of remedying the minor nonperformance. But to defeat a motion for summary judgment for the price of a fully performed contract, defendant need show only that it disputes that the contract was fully performed, and need not further show the cost of remedying nonperformance a cost which plaintiff might itself dispute. That would amount to trying the dispute by affidavit, and that the law does not authorize.

The general contractor was entitled to every bit of performance the contract requires of plaintiff, just as plaintiff is entitled to every cent of the price as an equivalent. There is a dispute as to whether some bits of the contracted performance were performed. One therefore cannot say as a matter of law that plaintiff is entitled to the full price; the defense affidavit indicates that entitlement is only to price less cost of completion.

Reversed.

D. Repudiation of Performance

Repudiation occurs when the promisor affirmatively states to the promisee that he will no longer perform on the promise and therefore repudiates his agreement articulating the performance. The repudiation will impair the value of the contract to the injured party and will result in a total or partial breach, thereby giving rise to a claim for damages.[10]

E. Excusing Nonperformance

Where the injured party acquiesces to excuse the promisor from performing the contract, the nonperformance by the promisor is excused. Similarly, when the injured party accepts partial performance with knowledge that the remaining performance will not be performed because of special conditions, the remaining performance will be likewise excused. The case below illustrates another reason for excusing nonperformance.

---

[10] Restatement (Second) Contracts § 250 (1981).

Case 9.3

Florida Power Corporation v. City Of Tallahassee
18 So. 2d 671(1944), 154 Fla. 638 (1944)
Supreme Court Of Florida

OPINION BY: Chapman, J.

The City of Tallahassee and the Florida Power Corporation, on August 25, 1936, entered into a contract for the purchase and sale of electric energy. This contract was to remain in force and effect and binding upon the parties for a period of twenty years, with optional extension privileges in behalf of the city. Article 1 of the contract made it the duty of the power company to maintain two separate and independent transmission lines and two independent sources of electrical energy.

* * * * *

The service which the company agrees to furnish to the city shall be continuous and uninterrupted, and both of the company's said sources of electric energy shall be kept available for such purpose, unless the company is prevented from delivering electric energy hereby agreed to be furnished by the Act of God, or cause or causes beyond its control, or by any emergency in which the company may be compelled to act to prevent injuries to life, person or property of another, but where flood or drought is claimed to be an act of God, it shall not be excused where the same could have been reasonably anticipated and provided against, but even where interruptions are excused by act of God or for causes beyond the control of the company, the company shall be diligent in restoring its service after any such interruption, and if such service can be continued from any of the sources of electric energy available to the company, the same shall be promptly resorted to and electric energy supplied therefrom, and the company agrees to keep such sources of electric energy immediately available to meet any such emergency, and interrupted service shall be excused only until the company by the exercise of such diligence as the emergency demands can make available any of its sources of electric energy and deliver the same to the city.

* * * * *

It is further agreed that should the said interruptions exceed a total of twelve (12) hours per month for any two consecutive months, and said interruptions, defects or failures result from the company's negligence, the city may terminate this agreement by ninety (90) days' written notice to the company, and at the expiration of the said ninety (90) days period, all rights of the company under this contract shall cease, and the company shall within thirty (30) days thereafter begin the removal of all its physical property situated in the City, as provided for in Article III hereof."

* * * * *

The record reflects that on October 7, 1941, early in the morning, a hurricane blowing up from the Gulf of Mexico, struck Tallahassee and environs. The wind reached a high velocity, rain or sheets of water, accompanied the wind, and these natural elements continued, without serious interruption, for several hours and extended over a large and broad area about the City of Tallahassee and beyond. The equipment and facilities of the power company used in the generation of electric energy were so affected by the hurricane that it failed and omitted to deliver to the City o Tallahassee the required electric energy on October 7, 1941, for a period of 10.2 hours as required by the terms of its contract with the City of Tallahassee. The formula fixing the penalties for the "outage" embodied in the contract, when translated into money, approximates the sum of $2,659.83, and said sum was by the city deducted from the amount due the power company. The power company protested the action of the city and asserts that the unlawful deductions cannot be sustained by the terms of the contract.

*****

The *prior clause* of Article 12 of the contract makes it the duty of the power company to furnish to the city continuous and uninterrupted service of electric energy from both sources which shall be available for such purpose, unless the power company is prevented from delivering electric energy… by the Act of God or cause or causes beyond its control or by an emergency in which the company may be compelled to act to prevent injuries to life, person or property of another, but where drought or flood is claimed to be an Act of God it shall not be excused where the same could have been reasonably anticipated and provided against.

The cause for not supplying the electric energy on October 7, 1941, as provided for, was due and directly traceable to the hurricane that affected the facilities and equipment of the power company and rendered it impossible to supply or deliver to the city energy for 10.2 hours. It is not disputed that the hurricane struck Tallahassee and vicinity or that the equipment and facilities of the power company were disorganized for the period. The only justifiable reason for not delivering the electric energy is when so prevented by an Act of God. The city contends that the Act of God provisions are inapplicable to the third paragraph of Article 12 of the contract. The law makes a part of the subsequent paragraphs of Article 12 of the contract a justification for **non performance** or failure to deliver to the city electric energy, the Acts of God or cause or causes beyond the control of the power company.

*****

We therefore conclude that the hurricane visiting the City of Tallahassee and vicinity on October 7, 1941, for a period of several hours which disorganized and affected the equipment and facilities of the power company and thereby prevented a delivery to the City of electric energy for 10.2 hours, in light of the cited authorities, was an Act of God and a legal **justification for the non delivery** for the period of the energy as provided for by the terms of the contract.

*****

The final decree appealed from is reversed, with directions for further proceedings in the lower court, not inconsistent with the views herein expressed. It is so ordered.

F. Request for Adequate Assurance

As a general rule, a promisee has no right to demand assurance from the promisor that the performance will be performed according to their agreement. But, where the promisee has grounds to believe that the promisor will not perform on the promise, and that nonperformance would give the promisee a claim for damages for total breach, the promisee may demand adequate assurance of the performance due and may, if reasonable, suspend any performance until he receives such assurance or performance.[11]

The following case provides an analysis concerning adequate assurance.

---

[11] Restatement (Second) Contracts § 251 (1981).

Case 9.4

Ranger Construction Company v. Dixie Floor Company, Inc.
433 F. Supp. 442 (1977), 1977 U.S. Dist. LEXIS 16272
U. S. Dist. Ct. for the Dist. of So. Carolina

JUDGE: Hemphill J.

This action arises from a contract between the parties under which the defendant was to furnish all materials and labor for the installation of resilient flooring in the Clinical Science Building at the Medical University of South Carolina at Charleston. The complaint alleges that defendant refused to perform the work specified in the contract for the agreed price of $52,601 and that as a result, the plaintiff was required to enter into a second contract to have the flooring installed at a substantially higher cost. The plaintiff is seeking judgment against defendant for the additional amount which it alleges it was required to pay to have the contract performed, $22,268.

* * * * *

The defendant, in its answer, admitted that there was a contract between the parties, that the copy of the contract attached to the complaint was a true and correct copy, and that it had refused to perform its work under the subcontract. However, the defendant argues that its actions were justified in that the plaintiff had wrongfully withheld payment for work which the defendant had performed under a separate and distinct contract on a job in North Carolina.

The defendant alleges that shortly before it entered into the contract in issue, it had entered into another similar contract with the plaintiff which was completed in Hickory, North Carolina, on May 7, 1974. Thereafter the plaintiff, without apparent justification, refused to make payment as due under the contract, and, in order to collect the same, the defendant was forced to bring an action against the plaintiff in the United States District Court for the District of North Carolina and reduce its claim to judgment. Defendant finally received payment under this prior contract on June 7, 1976.

In April 1975, the plaintiff requested that the defendant begin work under the present contract. The defendant contends that as a result of the plaintiff's refusal to pay under the North Carolina contract, the defendant had substantial doubt as to both the plaintiff's ability and willingness to pay it for any performance it might render on the South Carolina contract. Accordingly, the defendant requested that the plaintiff provide it with **assurance of performance** and alleges that the plaintiff failed to do so in a satisfactory manner.

It is the defendant's position that the plaintiff's breach of the North Carolina contract constituted "reasonable grounds for insecurity" under § 2–609 of the Uniform Commercial Code (§ 2–609 of the S.C. Code Ann.) Section 2–609 of the S.C. Code reads:

Right to adequate assurance of performance.

(1) A contract for sale imposes an obligation on each party that the other's expectation of receiving due performance will not be impaired. When reasonable grounds for insecurity arise with respect to the performance of either party the other

may in writing demand **adequate assurance of due performance** and until he receives such assurance may if commercially reasonable suspend any performance for which he has not already received the agreed return.

* * * * *

(3) Acceptance of any improper delivery or payment does not prejudice the aggrieved party's right to demand adequate assurance of future performance.

(4) After receipt of a justified demand failure to provide within a reasonable time not exceeding thirty days such assurance of due performance as is adequate under the circumstances of the particular case is a repudiation of the contract.

The defendant urges that summary judgment is inappropriate in this case because under § 2–609 the question of whether or not the plaintiff's breach of the former con-tract was "reasonable grounds for insecurity" under this section constitutes a question of fact which should be reserved for the jury.

* * * * *

The defendant argues, however, that the plaintiff's wrongful failure and refusal to pay the defendant under the North Carolina contract was a clear indication of the plaintiff's prospective unwillingness and prospective inability to pay defendant for any performance that it might render in South Carolina, and that it was therefore excused from performance or at the very least was entitled to receive assurance of performance from the plaintiff. The defendant bases its position on the well-recognized principle of prospective failure of consideration which is embodied in § 280 of the Restatement of Contracts. That section reads: Manifestation by One Party of Inability to Perform or of Intention Not to Perform.

(1) Where there are promises for an agreed exchange, if one promisor manifests to the other that he cannot or will not substantially perform his promise, or that, though able to do so, he doubts whether he will substantially perform it, and the statement is not conditional on the existence of facts that would justify a failure to perform, and there are no such facts, the other party is justified in changing his position, and if he makes a material change of position he is discharged from the duty of performing his promise.

* * * * *

Under the theory of anticipatory repudiation, there is a question of fact for the jury involved in determining whether the plaintiff's refusal to pay the defendant under their North Carolina contract constituted a manifestation to the defendant that the plaintiff could not or would not substantially perform his promise under the contract. For this reason, summary judgment in this matter is inappropriate.

Therefore, for the foregoing reasons, plaintiff's motion for summary judgment is denied.

AND IT IS SO ORDERED.

Chapter 9

Vocabulary

1. Performance
2. Material Nonperformance
3. Repudiation of Performance
4. Excusing Nonperformance
5. Adequate Assurance

Review Questions

1. What is the issue in the *Star Credit Corp. v. Cecilio Molina* case?
2. What is the legal principle in the *Molina* case?
3. What is the issue in the *Schaff Brothers v. American Fidelity* case?
4. What is the legal principle in the *Schaff* case?
5. What is the issue in the *Florida Power Corp. v. City of Tallahassee* case?
6. What is the legal principle in the *Florida Power* case?
7. What is the issue in the *Ranger Construction v. Dixie Floor* case?
8. What is the legal principle in the *Dixie* case?

Chapter 10

Discharge of Contract

I. Unperformed Performance
A. Impracticability of Performance

As a general rule, the obligee (the recipient of the performance) will be discharged from an executed contract when it becomes impractical for the obligor (performer) to discharge his obligations. There are three basic situations under which this circumstance occurs:

1. When the obligor shows that some circumstance has made his own performance impracticable.[1]
2. When some circumstance has occurred on the part of the obligee, thereby frustrating the obligor's obligation to perform the contract.[2]
3. When the obligor claims that he will not receive performance from the obligee because of some circumstance that discharges the obligee's obligation on the performance on the grounds of impracticability or frustration.[3]

The underlying assumption and basis for discharging the obligor's obligation due to **impracticability of performance** and **frustration of purpose** is that there is an expectation on the part of both parties that such extraordinary circumstances will not occur.[4] The basic element of impracticability is that the cause for nonperformance must be some extreme or unreasonable difficulty that could not reasonably be expected to be within the contemplation of the parties at the time that they made their contract.[5]

The following case addresses the issue of **impossibility of performance**.

Case 10.1

Dominion Video Satellite Inc. v. Echostar Satellite L.L.C.
430 F.3d 1269 (2005); 2005 U.S. App. Lexis 26656
U. S. C t. Appl., 10th Cir.

OPINION BY: TACHA

This case began in 2003 when Plaintiff-Appellee Dominion Video Satellite, Inc. ("Dominion") claimed that Defendants-Appellants EchoStar Satellite Corporation and

---

[1] Restatement (Second) Contracts § 261 (1979).
[2] *Id.* at § 265 (1979).
[3] *Id.* at § 267 (1979).
[4] *Id.* at Chapter 11, Introductory Note.
[5] In re: David's & Unique Eater, 82 B.R. 652 (1987), 1987 Bankr. LEXIS 2162.

Echosphere Corporation (collectively, "EchoStar") were in breach of a lease agreement between the parties and sought to have the matter arbitrated as required by the agreement. After holding hearings on the dispute, the arbitration panel found in favor of Dominion and granted it $ 2,438,178 in damages. Dominion moved the District Court to confirm the award, pursuant to the Federal Arbitration Act, 9 U.S.C. §§ 9 and 13. EchoStar vigorously opposed both the arbitration panel's decision as well as Dominion's motion to confirm by filing numerous motions and supporting memoranda.

Both Dominion and EchoStar operate direct broadcast satellite systems ("DBS") that are licensed and regulated by the Federal Communications Commission.Dominion's network, known as "Sky Angel," offers predominantly Christian programming on approximately twenty channels. EchoStar's network, known as the "DISH Network," offers a wide variety of programming on over 500 channels. Prior to 1996, Dominion could not broadcast its Sky Angel network to DBS consumers because it did not own any satellites. At the same time, EchoStar could not meet its consumer's needs because, although it owned a satellite, it did not own sufficient FCC broadcastings license rights to serve its market.

* * * * *

In 1996, Dominion and EchoStar executed a mutually beneficial contract entitled "Direct Broadcast Service Transponder Lease, Channel Use and Programming Agreement" ("Agreement"). Under the terms of the Agreement, EchoStar leases eight transponders[1] from its broadcasting satellite to Dominion and in return Dominion subleases six of these frequencies back to EchoStar with accompanying FCC license rights. Thus, this Agreement gives Dominion a platform from which to broadcast the Sky Angel network and provides EchoStar increased capacity to serve its market.

* * * * *

In December 2002, EchoStar began broadcasting several predominantly Christian channels on the DISH Network. After attempting to persuade EchoStar that the Programming Exclusivity provision prohibited such action, Dominion sued to enjoin EchoStar from broadcasting these programs. After three days of hearings, during which the District Court was thoroughly briefed on the merits of the underlying dispute, the District Court granted Dominion a preliminary injunction. In so doing, the District Court noted that EchoStar's arguments on the merits of the underlying contractual dispute—included claims regarding federal preemption [and] legal **impossibility [of performance]**…

* * * * *

Under the defense of **impossibility of performance**, a party's breach of its contractual obligation will be excused when "changed circumstances have rendered the promise vitally different from what reasonably should have been within the contemplation of both parties when they entered into the contract." *Colo. Performance Corp. v. Mariposa Assocs.*, 754 P.2d 401, 407 (Colo. Ct. App. 1987) (quotation omitted). EchoStar claims that the FCC regulations, which were promulgated in 1998 and require EchoStar to reserve four percent of its programming capacity for educational or informational purposes, make it impossible for it not to broadcast Christian programming. EchoStar's bare allegations, which are not supported by the record, do not establish evidence in support of this contention, however, and we will therefore not vacate the arbitration award on this basis.

* * * * *

> EchoStar has failed to show that the arbitration panel acted fraudulently or with a manifest disregard for the law. We therefore affirm the District Court's order confirming the final award. Because we also find EchoStar's appeal of the District Court's order to be frivolous, Dominion may file a motion seeking reasonable attorneys' fees within fifteen days of the filing of this opinion; EchoStar will then have fifteen days to respond. Finally, we conclude that the District Court did not abuse its discretion in awarding Dominion $ 63,436.02 in attorneys' fees and costs under 28 U.S.C. 1927.
>
> Affirmed.

B. Commercial Impracticability

When one of the party's performances has become impracticable, through no fault on his part and by the occurrence of some unexpected event, his duty to execute the performance is discharged as a result of a *commercial impracticability*.[6] In other words, some unexpected intervening activity has caused the suspension of the performance through no fault of the party promising performance.[7] The concept of "impracticability" is usually reserved for "acts of God," or acts of third parties preventing the performance.

The principal inquiry in an impracticability analysis, then, is whether there was a contingency for nonoccurrence as a basic assumption underlying the contract. It is often said that this question turns on whether or not the contingency was "foreseeable" on the rationale that if it was, the promisor could have sought to negotiate explicit contractual protection ahead of time.[8] As a general rule the standard of impossibility is objective rather then subjective, i.e. the question is whether the thing can be done, not whether the promisor can do it.[9] The following case makes a distinction between impossibility of performance and impracticability of performance.

Wilma Miller v. Mills Construction, Inc 352 F.3d 1166 (2003); 2003 U.S. App. LEXIS 25608 U.S. Ct. Appl, 8 Cir.	Case 10.2

CIRCUIT JUDGE: Lay

Mills, a general contractor in Brookings, South Dakota, contracted with the City of Brookings to construct the Brookings AgriPlex, a series of buildings to be used

[6] Restatement (Second) Contracts § 261 (1979).
[7] *Id.* at § 261 (1979).
[8] Specialty Tires of America, Inc. v. The City Group/Equipment Financing, Inc. 82 F. Supp. 2d 434 (2000), 2000 U.S. Dist. LEXIS 994 [hereinafter *Specialty*].
[9] *Id.* Specialty.

for various purposes. One of the buildings to be constructed was a steel clear span arena 286 feet long by 209 feet wide. Due to the building's size and the fact that its construction would require the use of cranes, Mills decided to subcontract with a steel erection company for construction of the arena. Double Diamond, a steel erection company located in Lincoln, Nebraska, submitted a bid for the project, which Mills accepted. The parties entered into a subcontract dated March 18, 1998, under which Double Diamond agreed to provide the labor and equipment and Mills agreed to provide the prefabricated steel and other component parts for the building. Mills obtained the prefabricated steel for the building from American Buildings Company ("ABC"). Mills agreed to pay Double Diamond a total of $ 209,875 under the subcontract.

* * * * *

Under the subcontract, the delivery of materials was to begin the week of April 6, 1998. However, Mills, through ABC, did not make its first delivery until April 15, 1998, and some of the materials needed for the early stages of the building were not delivered until later shipments. As a result, construction was delayed. When Double Diamond was able to begin working on the building, it discovered numerous problems with the component parts supplied by Mills. Many of the steel components did not fit together properly, some of the mainframes were twisted, and other parts were missing or the wrong length.

Double Diamond reported the problems to Mills, who told Double Diamond to contact ABC directly. Double Diamond made numerous calls to ABC, but ABC did not resolve the problems. On May 12, 1998, Double Diamond ceased working on the project and informed Mills and ABC that nothing else could be done until the problems were corrected. On May 14, 1998, Wilma Miller wrote a letter to Mills, ABC, the City of Brookings, and the project architects, in which she recounted the problems, encountered during construction and expressed concern about the structural integrity of the structure.

* * * * *

On May 15, 1998, Dave Roberts, an ABC representative, visited the construction site to examine the structure. A videotape of his inspection documented the many problems with the structure and materials. Before leaving the site, Roberts concluded that the structure did not need additional bracing and would be fine unless hit by a tornado. Later that evening, the structure collapsed in the wind. A climatologist testified that the wind speed at the approximate time of the collapse was thirty-five miles per hour, but he also noted that an observer at the scene reported wind speeds of nearly fifty miles per hour at the time of the collapse.

* * * * *

After the collapse, Double Diamond submitted to Mills an invoice dated May 21, 1998, in the amount of $119,928 for work completed on the project up to the date of collapse.

* * * * *

On June 30, 1998, Double Diamond informed Mills that it would not return to work on the project unless Mills paid the balance due on the $ 119,928 invoice and executed a new contract with Double Diamond for completion of the project. When the parties did not reach a new agreement, Mills completed the project on its own.

* * * * *

On February 22, 1999, Double Diamond filed what amounted to a breach-of-contract claim against Mills, seeking damages in the amount of $ 139,875.

* * * * *

Mills denied liability and asserted counterclaims based on negligence and breach of contract for failure to construct in a good and workmanlike manner. One of Mills' affirmative defenses was that Double Diamond breached the contract and was not entitled to recover because it voluntarily discontinued work on the project after the collapse, and failed to return to work despite numerous requests by Mills.

* * * * *

Mills further argues on appeal that the district court erred by failing to find that Double Diamond was excused from performance of the contract. Mills asserts that absent a finding that Double Diamond was excused from performance, Double Diamond breached the contract by refusing to return to the project and is not entitled to recover. ...Another basis for excusing Double Diamond's performance is the district court's recognition that Mills made Double Diamond's performance under the contract impossible.

The doctrine of **impossibility of performance** provides an excuse for nonperformance of contractual obligations caused by supervening or existing conditions not contemplated by the parties. The Restatement (Second) of Contracts § 261 speaks in terms of **impracticability of performance** rather than impossibility. South Dakota recognizes the doctrine of **commercial impracticability** found in § 261 as an excuse from performance "due to extreme and unreasonable difficulty, expense, injury or loss involved." Groseth Int'l, Inc. v. Tenneco, Inc., 410 N.W.2d 159, 167 (S.D. 1987).

The South Dakota Supreme Court has stated that "as a general rule, unexpected difficulty, expense, or hardship involved in performance will not excuse performance where performance has not become objectively impossible." However, it also has recognized that performance may be excused "where very greatly increased difficulty is caused by facts not only unanticipated, but inconsistent with the facts that the parties obviously assumed would likely continue to exist." The question of whether performance has become **commercially impracticable** generally is considered to be a question of law.

* * * * *

The impossibility of completing performance was caused by the collapse, which we view as unanticipated given the assurance by ABC's representative that nothing further needed to be done to protect the structure from collapse. The collapse was also inconsistent with the facts the parties assumed would continue to exist, namely that the structure would remain standing. On these facts, we conclude that Mills' provision of defective materials and the resulting collapse made it **commercially impracticable** for Double Diamond to complete construction of the arena by June 30, 1998, as required by the contract, thereby excusing Double Diamond's performance. Accordingly, Double Diamond did not breach the contract.

* * * * *

For the reasons set forth in this opinion, we AFFIRM the...judgment in favor of Double Diamond.

C. Supervening Impracticability

Where performance of a promise is rendered impossible because of a *supervening* event, the duty of the promisor is discharged. This means that where the existence of a specific person is essential for the performance of a duty, his death or incapacity will make the performance impractical. There is a basic and fundamental assumption that the party with the duty to perform the contract will not die before the performance of the duty.[10]

Similarly, where the existence of a specific thing is essential to the performance of a duty, then the destruction of that thing will cause the performance to be impractical. There is a presumption that the specific thing will come into existence or the specific thing will be in existence at the time that the performance is due.[11]

The third type of impracticability of this kind is one that rises as a result of an intervening government regulation or law. Again, there is a basic assumption that the expected duty is not one that contravenes some regulation or law at the time of the performance.[12]

Finally, the fourth type of impracticability is temporary impracticability of performance. It occurs when the duty to perform is temporarily suspended because of temporary intervening impracticability. Unlike the other impracticability situations, here the performance of the duty is simply suspended temporarily until such time as the duty can later be performed once the temporary impracticability has passed.[13]

The doctrines of impossibility and impracticability have grown to recognize that relief is most justified if unexpected events inflict a loss on one party and provide a windfall gain for the other, or where the excuse would save one party from an unexpected loss while leaving the other party in a position no worse than it would have been without the contract.[14]

D. Frustration of Purpose

Frustration of purpose occurs when there is a change in circumstances that makes one party's performance virtually worthless, thereby frustrating the purpose in making the contract.[15] There are three basic requirements to manifest

---

[10] Restatement (Second) Contracts § 262 (1979).

[11] *Id.* at § 263 (1979).

[12] *Id.* at § 264 (1979).

[13] *Id.* at § 269 (1979).

[14] Specialty Tires of America, Inc. v. The Cit Group/Equipment Financing, Inc., 82 F. Supp. 2d 434 (2000).

[15] Restatement (Second) Contracts § 265 cmt. a (1979).

frustration of purpose. First, that which has been frustrated was the principle purpose for making the contract. Second, the frustration must be substantial and severe. Third, the nonoccurrence must have been a basic assumption for making the contract.

While the doctrines of frustration of purpose and impossibility of performance are akin, frustration is *not* a form of impossibility of performance: It more properly relates to the consideration for performance. Under such doctrines performance remains possible, but is excused whenever an event supervenes to cause a failure of the consideration or practically a total destruction of the expected value of the performance. The applicability of the doctrine off rustration depends on the total or nearly total destruction of the purpose for which, in the contemplation of both parties, the transaction was entered into.

The following case distinguishes between temporary impossibility of performance and permanent impossibility of performance.[16]

Gene Autry v. Republic Productions, Inc.
180 P.2d 888 1947, 30 Cal. 2d 144 (1947)
Supreme Court of California

Case 10.3

JUDGES: In Bank. Shenk, J. Gibson,

This is an appeal by the plaintiff from a judgment declaring the rights and obligations of the parties under contracts between them and in effect at the time of the plaintiff's enlistment in the United States Army in 1942.

Prior to his enlistment the plaintiff, Gene Autry, was a motion picture actor dramatizing western or cowboy roles. The defendant, Republic Productions, Inc., was a producer of western photoplays. On September 22, 1938, the parties entered into a written agreement by which the defendant engaged the plaintiff's services as an actor in ten photoplays during one year commencing July 1, 1938, the plaintiff to receive $6000 for each of the first two, and $10,000 for each of the remaining eight. ...

...On April 20, 1942, the plaintiff was ordered to report for physical examination under the Selective Service Act, and was placed in Class 1-A. On May 11, 1942, the parties executed a further written agreement by which the defendant was granted an additional option for one year commencing upon the expiration of the last option of the 1938 agreement and during which eight plays were to be photographed for a compensation of $15,000 each. Included in that agreement was a paragraph numbered 24, providing: "In the event that the Artist [plaintiff] shall be required to serve in the armed forces of the United States pursuant to the Selective Service Act, or shall volunteer for such service, the parties hereto will agree upon their mutual rights and obligations hereunder in view of such military service."

---

[16] Caroline A. Lloyd v. William J. Murphy, 153 P.2d 47 (1944), 25 Cal.2d 48 (1944), 1944 LEXIS 299.

The plaintiff enlisted in the Army on July 26, 1942. At that time there remained five plays to be photographed under the third option. The plaintiff rendered no service to the defendant after his enlistment.

* * * * *

On June 17, 1944, the plaintiff served on the defendant a notice of termination of the agreements and employment thereunder by reason of military service.

The [trial court] judgment declares that the contracts between the parties had not been terminated; that the plaintiff's military service suspended performance for a time equal to the period of military service; that after his discharge from the Army the plaintiff would be bound to carry out the unperformed portion of the contracted employment by appearing in five and eight photoplays under the third and fourth options respectively of the 1938 agreement, and eight photoplays under the additional option of the 1942 agreement...

The controversy presents the question of the effect of the plaintiff's military service on the rights of the parties under the contracts and their conduct there under. The plaintiff places reliance in part on the **doctrines of frustration and impossibility** to sustain his contention that the court's conclusions and judgment are unsupported. This court has recently considered the history and nature of the **doctrine of frustration as an excuse for nonperformance**. ...There it was pointed out...that although the doctrines of frustration and impossibility are akin, frustration is not a form of impossibility of performance. It more properly relates to the consideration for performance. Under it performance remains possible, but is excused whenever a fortuitous event supervenes to cause a failure of the consideration or a practically total destruction of the expected value of the performance. ...As stated in *Lloyd v. Murphy* the purpose of contracts is to place the risks of performance upon the promisor. Without extended discussion, the foregoing authorities demonstrate that, strictly speaking, there is here not a failure of the consideration or the destruction of the value of performance in the sense contemplated by the doctrine of frustration. (1) Furthermore, if the parties have contracted with reference to a state of war or have contemplated the risks arising from it they may not invoke the doctrine of frustration. ...

"**Impossibility**" is defined in section 454 of the Restatement of Contracts, as not only strict impossibility but as impracticability because of extreme and unreasonable difficulty, expense, injury, or loss involved. **Temporary impossibility** of the character which, if it should become permanent, would discharge a promisor's entire contractual duty, operates as a permanent discharge if performance after the impossibility ceases would impose a substantially greater burden upon the promisor; otherwise the duty is suspended while the impossibility exists. The trial court's judgment indicates that the controversy was resolved upon the theory of **temporary impossibility** and suspension due to military service.

At the time of the 1938 agreement the contingency of the entry of the United States into the Second World War was not expressly contemplated by the parties. Looking at that agreement alone, the war and the plaintiff's military service were supervening fortuitous events which rendered **performance impossible**. Had the parties not entered into further agreement, and in the absence of a validly exercised extension of the 1938 agreement, the controversy between them might properly be resolved solely by a determination of the question of impossibility. In *Havens v. Rochester Ropes, Inc....* it was indicated that entry into military service effected permanent discharge of an employment contract. The defendant cites no authority holding that military service results in a **temporary impossibility**. However, in view of our conclusions herein, it becomes unnecessary to treat more specifically the question whether the plaintiff's mere entry into military service resulted in a permanent discharge of the 1938 agreement.

* * * * *

(6) However, assuming, as the trial court concluded, that the plaintiff's military service constituted a **temporary impossibility** of performance, then it becomes necessary to determine the effect of paragraph 24 upon the rights and obligations of the parties following the plaintiff's discharge from military service. ...The parties are not deprived of reliance thereon in the event of the happening of the contingency with which it expressly deals. On the contrary the special provision then becomes effective as a modification of their agreements. The mere failure to come to agreement did not operate to restore or revive the original terms which were abrogated.

* * * * *

From the foregoing it follows that the judgment should declare that in the absence of a new agreement to continue the relationship of the parties, there is no duty upon the plaintiff to perform services for the defendant after his discharge from military service.

The judgment is reversed.

II. Discharge of the Contract
A. Discharge by Assent

The obligee (creditor) may assent to discharge the debt of the obligor (debtor) of his own volition, but the discharge will not be effective unless it is (1) made for consideration, (2) made under circumstance in which the "promise being discharged would be discharged without consideration or the discharge has induced forbearance on the part of the obligor.[17] But where the obligor has either performed in whole or in part, the obligee may manifest a discharge of the obligor's duties without consideration.[18]

The obligee can show his serious intent to discharge the obligation and duty of the obligor by destroying, cancelling or surrendering the document incorporating the obligation of the obligor[19] whether or not there is a breach of contract.[20]

B. Discharge by Substituted Performance

The obligee may accept something other then the expected performance from the obligor: He may accept a *substituted performance* that differs from the

---

[17] Restatement (Second) Contracts § 273 (1979).
[18] *Id.* at § 275 (1979).
[19] *Id.* at § 274 (1979).
[20] *Id.* at § 277 (1979).

original performance, in which case the obligor's duty will be discharged.[21] And where the obligor is in agreement, a third party may substitute a performance on behalf of the obligor, thereby discharging the obligor's duty of performance to the obligee.[22]

C. Discharge by Novation

A *novation* is a substituted contract that replaces the first contract and exculpates one of the parties from the obligations of the contract by substituting a third party. For example, suppose that a homeowner contracts with a contractor to build an additional room on the house. Later the contractor and the home-owner agree that it would be best if a third party contractor build the additional room instead of the first contractor. A second contract is then created in which only the homeowner and the third party contractor are bound. The homeowner agrees to set aside the original contract with the primary contractor, then creates a new contact, or a novation, with the third party contractor. When the third party breaches the contract because of his negligence in building the new room, the first contractor is not liable because he has been discharged from the contract due to the novation. Only the third party contractor is liable (as reflected in the chart below).

The existence of a novation must manifest (1) a previous valid contract, (2) an agreement by all the parties to a novation, (3) a valid new contract, and (4) the destruction of the primary contract.[23]

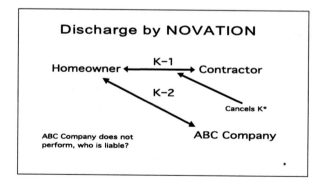

---

[21] Restatement (Second) Contracts § 278 (1979).
[22] *Id.* at § 278 (2) (1979).
[23] *Id.* at § 280 (1979).

D. Accord and Satisfaction

Where there is a dispute with respect to a sum intended to settle a claim between two parties, if one of the parties offers a lesser amount in full settlement of the claim and the other party accepts the sum offered and subsequently deposits the money in the bank, the party that accepted the money will be estopped from attempting to collect additional money because the claim was settled through an *accord and satisfaction*.

The elements of an accord and satisfaction are (1) that there is an amount in controversy (in other words, there is an unliquidated debt), (2) a lesser amount is paid by the debtor, and (3) the lesser amount is accepted by the creditor.

The following case illustrates the concept of accord and satisfaction.[24]

Mullinax v. Shaw
239 S.E.2d 547 (1977), 143 Ga. App. 657 (1977)
Court of Appeals of Georgia

Case 10.4

OPINION BY: J. WEBB

Dr. Allan F. Shaw provided over a two-year period extensive dental services to Mrs. Mullinax for which she paid him a total of $2550. She complained to Dr. Shaw about the fitting of the upper plate, particularly because her lip would not stretch over her front teeth and was getting "puffy." She went to the dentist several times and he would take off a little of the cusped. Her last visit was on March 11, 1974 because that morning about four o'clock she said she felt a muscle in her upper lip break. Her husband accompanied her, and after some discussion Dr. Shaw gave her a check for $700 on which was typed "endorsement of this check releases Dr. Allan F. Shaw from any further obligation, professionally and financially." Mrs. Mullinax read the words on the back of the check and the next day signed the check, deposited the funds to her account, and has spent the money. Almost two years later, March 3, 1976, Mr. and Mrs. Mullinax filed their complaints.

* * * * *

The trial court concluded that the use of its "equitable power in setting aside the accord is not justified" and granted summary judgment for defendant.

"'When a party makes an offer of a certain sum to settle a claim, the amount of which is in bona fide dispute, with the condition that the sum offered, if taken at all, must be received in full satisfaction of the claim, and the party receives the money, he takes it subject to the condition attached to it, and it will operate as an **accord and satisfaction**. ...The same ruling applies where the claimant, instead of receiving money as a settlement of his claim, receives a check or draft from the other party in full settlement of the claim. ...Where, without the practice of any fraud upon her, a plaintiff accepts, in full satisfaction of her claim, a lesser amount than what she claims is due her, there is an accord and satisfaction, and she is not entitled to a recovery. ...

---

[24] Restatement (Second) Contracts § 281 (1979).

"[T]he creditor could not accept the check and repudiate the conditions which the debtor had attached thereto, but that in accepting the one he automatically and as a matter of law accepted the other and agreed thereto. Had the creditor, while in the very act of appropriating the proceeds of the check, loudly declared his disagreement with the terms upon which the tender was made, and such declarations had been communicated to the debtor, under the controlling decisions of this court he would nevertheless and despite such declarations have been held as a matter of law to have agreed to all of the conditions attached to the tender." ...

"If there existed a question in appellee's [assignor's] mind relative to release or payment, or if they were unsatisfactory, the release and draft should have been returned to the appellant. ...Instead, appellee [assignor] cashed the draft and used the proceeds. He is bound by the release. ...

* * * * *

Judgment affirmed [in favor of defendant].

E. Rescission by Agreement

An agreement by *rescission discharges* all of the duties required in the performance of both parties.[25] A discharge of a contract manifests itself when both parties to the contract agree to discharge one another of the remaining obligations of the reciprocal performances by rescinding each other's duties.

F. Release

Releases are agreements in writing created to immediately discharge the maker of the release upon the happening of a certain condition. For example, insurance companies often offer payment for property losses to the insured if the insured signs a release not to pursue the claim any further.

The elements of an effective release are (1) an agreement between the parties, the insurance company and the insured, (2) the occurrence of an event, such as an accident, (3) some consideration in exchange for the release, and (4) signature of the party discharging the duty.[26]

A release contract is similar in nature to the contract not to sue except that here the obligee, the party to whom the debt is owed, promises to never sue the obligor or debtor or not to sue for a measured period of time. Effectively, any action against the obligor after the contract not to sue is consummated will be barred.[27]

---

[25] Restatement (Second) Contracts § 283 (1979).
[26] *Id.* at § 284 (1979).
[27] *Id.* at § 285 (1979).

Moreover, the duties in a contract will be discharged when the contract is altered such that the alterations are fraudulent or material. The alteration becomes material where the duties vary the legal relations with the maker or substantially vary the obligations in the contract.[28] But if the party knows of the alteration and acquiesces to the changes in the contract, the alteration will be allowed as a substitution for the original intent of the parties and the contract will not be discharged.[29]

---

[28] *Id.* at § 286 (1979).
[29] *Id.* at § 287 (1979).

Chapter 10
Vocabulary

1. Impracticability of Performance
2. Commercial Impracticability
3. Supervening Impracticability
4. Frustration of Purpose
5. Discharge of Contract
6. Discharge by Substituted Performance
7. Novation
8. Accord and Satisfaction
9. Rescission
10. Release

Review Questions

1. What is the issue in the *Dominion Video Satellite Inc. v. EchoStar Satellite* case?
2. What is the legal principle in the *Echostar Satellite* case?
3. What is the issue in the *Wilma Miller v. Mills Construction, Inc.* case?
4. What is the legal principle in the *Wilma Miller* case?
5. What is the issue in the *Gene Autry v. Republic Productions* case?
6. What is the legal principle in the *Gene Autry* case?
7. What is the issue in the *Mullinax v. Shaw* case?
8. What is the legal principle in the *Mullinax* case?

Chapter 11

Third Party Beneficiaries, Assignments and Delegation

I. Third Party Beneficiaries

As a general rule, at common law, only those that are at "privity" with each other have any rights or duties with respect to contracts. However, the courts recognize *third party beneficiaries* as an exception to this general rule.

There are two types of beneficiaries, intended and incidental beneficiaries.[1] *Intended beneficiaries* are those created when the promisor and the promisee agree in their contract for a third party beneficiary to benefit by their agreement. Intended beneficiaries, although not at privity in contract with each other, acquire the right to enforce the promise by the promisor. *Incidental beneficiaries* do not acquire this right.

The following case illustrates the two types of beneficiaries.

<table>
<tr><td>

William F. Martin v. R. M. Edwards
548 P.2d 779 (1976), 219 Kan. 466 (1976)
Supreme Court of Kansas

OPINION BY: HARMAN

    This is an action brought by one allegedly owning a "carried interest" to determine his rights in certain oil and gas leases principally located in Rice and Ellsworth counties and for an accounting of the proceeds of those leases from the lessee. Trial to the court resulted in a judgment for the latter from which plaintiff has appealed. The principal issue is whether plaintiff became a third party beneficiary entitled to enforce a contract between the lessees.

* * * * *

    The trial court first found that any recovery by appellant Martin had to be predicated upon a third party beneficiary contract. It further found there was never a promise made or conferred by appellee to create a separate interest in the leases in favor of appellant Martin; that any interest of appellant Martin was to be carved out of and granted to him by Sidney from Sidney's interest.

    Generally, where a person makes a promise to another for the benefit of a third person [beneficiary], that third person [beneficiary] may maintain an action to enforce the contract even though he had no knowledge of the contract when it was made and paid no part of the consideration. ...But it is not everyone who may benefit from the performance of a contract between two other persons, or who may suffer from its nonperformance, who is permitted to enforce the contract by court action. Beneficiaries

</td><td>

Case 11.1

</td></tr>
</table>

---

[1] Restatement (Second) Contracts § 302 (1979).

of contracts to which they are not parties have been divided into three classes: **Donee beneficiaries, creditor beneficiaries** and **incidental beneficiaries**. Only those falling within the first two classes may enforce contracts made for their benefit. …These third person beneficiaries are…as follows:

"…(1) Such person is a **donee beneficiary** if the purpose of the promisee in obtaining the promise of all or part of the performance thereof, is to make a gift to the beneficiary, or to confer upon him a right against the promisor to some performance neither due [nor supposed] or asserted to be due from the promisee to the beneficiary; (2) such person is a **creditor beneficiary** if no intention to make a gift appears from the terms of the promise, [and at least one of the parties to the contract is a creditor] and performance of the promise will satisfy an actual [or supposed] or asserted duty of the promisee to the beneficiary; (3) such person is an **incidental beneficiary** if the benefits to him are merely incidental to the performance of the promise and if he is neither a **donee beneficiary nor a creditor beneficiary**." …(Accord: Restatement of the Law of Contracts, § 133, pp. 151–152. Restatement, Contracts, 2d, Revised Tentative Draft, 1973, § 133, pp. 285–286, divides contract beneficiaries into two classes—intended and incidental).

* * * * *

Various tests have been used elsewhere in drawing the line between classes of beneficiaries. In *Burton v. Larkin*, this court held: "It is not every promise made by one to another from the performance of which a benefit may inure to a third, which gives a right of action to such third person, he being neither privy to the contract nor to the consideration. The contract must be **made for his benefit** as its object, and he must be the party intended to be benefited in order to be entitled to sue upon it." …Under this test a beneficiary can enforce the contract if he is one who the contracting parties intended should receive a direct benefit from the contract. …We think this test is sound and are content to reaffirm it. Contracting parties are presumed to act for themselves and therefore an intent to benefit a third person must be clearly expressed in the contract. …It is not necessary, however, that the third party be the exclusive beneficiary of all the promisor's performance. The contract may also benefit the contracting parties as well. …

The judgment is affirmed.

A. Creditor Beneficiaries

Say for an example that a creditor advances credit to the promisee, thereby establishing a creditor-debtor relationship in the amount of $1000. Thereafter, the promisee contracts with a promisor, wherein the amount owed by the promisor to the promisee is also $1000. The promisor and the promisee agree in their contract that the promisor, instead of paying the promisee on the contract, pays the third party creditor beneficiary. However, both the promisor and the promisee may later modify the contract to amend the rights of the beneficiary[2] unless

---

[2] Restatement (Second) Contracts § 311 (2) (1979).

the beneficiary has changed his position by relying on the contract between the promisor and promisee.[3] This contract creates a duty on the part of the promisor to pay $1000, which can be enforced by the third party creditor beneficiary.[4] (No knowledge or assent by the beneficiary is necessary for rights to be vested in him). Note that the promisor has overlapping duties to pay $1000 either to the promisee or the third party creditor beneficiary, but not to both.[5]

The following case illustrates the concept of creditor beneficiary.

Case 11.2

Town & Country Homecenter v. Ronald W. Woods
725 N.E.2d 1006 (2000), 2000 Ind. App. LEXIS 444
Court Of Appeals of Indiana

JUDGES: BAKER, Judge

The facts most…reveal that in June 1992, Lynn Fellows contracted with Ronald Woods to build a house. Fellows paid Woods $10,000 as down payment and applied for a mortgage with NCB to cover the remaining balance, which was due at closing. Woods purchased materials for the house from T&C. On September 23, 1992, Fellows received a letter from T&C entitled "a routine letter" (the pre-lien notice) which stated that T&C could perfect a lien against his property if payment was not received for the materials. Fellows brought the letter to the attention of Tom Gineris, the NCB representative handling his mortgage. Gineris responded that there was no problem, that similar situations arose "all the time" and that the letter would be addressed at closing.

The closing on Fellows' house occurred on October 13, 1992. Prior to the closing, T&C did not communicate with anyone at NCB regarding the bill owed by Woods. At the closing, Gineris questioned Woods about liens against the property. Woods acknowledged the existence of a mortgage held on the property by Tri-County Bank & Trust. Woods also confirmed that he had not completed payment to T&C but stated that he would pay T&C from the check he received at the closing. Gineris required that Woods sign a vendor's affidavit which stated that there were no liens on the property and that there were "no unpaid claims for labor done upon or materials furnished for the real estate in respect of which liens have been or may be filed." NCB then issued one check in the amount of $40,321.90 to Tri-County for Woods' construction loan and a second check to Woods in the amount of $59,229.17. Before doing so, Gineris asked Fellows if he was "comfortable" with disbursing the funds to Woods, based on Woods' statement that he would pay T&C from the proceeds. Fellows said, "That would be fine."

On January 11, 1993, T & C filed a mechanics lien against Fellows' residence with the Montgomery County Recorder, asserting it was owed $32,866.12. On January 7, 1994, T&C filed a complaint seeking to foreclose the lien, naming Woods, Fellows, NCB and the Montgomery County Treasurer as defendants. However, Fellows and the Montgomery County Treasurer were dismissed from the action. T&C's mechanics lien

---

[3] *Id.* at § 311 (3) (1979).
[4] *Id.* at § 304 (1979).
[5] *Id.* at § 305 (1979).

was ultimately released because the notice to Fellows did not comply with statutory limits. Evidence was submitted by stipulation and deposition testimony presented by T&C and NCB. The trial court then made its decision without hearing or jury, as agreed by the parties. It entered its order and judgment in favor of NCB and against T&C on December 17, 1998. T&C filed a motion to correct errors, which the trial court denied. T&C now appeals.

* * * * *

II. Third-Party Beneficiary Status

T&C first claims that it is the third-party beneficiary of the agreement between mortgagee NCB and mortgagor Fellows which permitted Fellows to take out a mortgage for his home. Specifically, T&C argues that NCB had a fiduciary duty to Fellows and T&C to exercise reasonable care that T&C be paid and that it breached that duty in disbursing funds to Woods knowing that T&C had not been paid.

We note that, in order to prevail upon a claim that one is a third-party beneficiary to a contract, a plaintiff must prove:

(1) A clear intent by the actual parties to the contract to benefit the third party;
(2) A duty imposed on one of the contracting parties in favor of the third party; and
(3) Performance of the contract terms is necessary to render the third party a direct benefit intended by the parties to the contract.

In this case, NCB's representative Gineris stated to Fellows that T&C's pre-lien notice would be "addressed" at the closing. We do not see in this statement a promise that T&C would be paid. Rather, at most, any promise amounted to a commitment to protect Fellows' interest by addressing the notice at the closing, where it was indeed addressed. After Woods informed Gineris that he would pay T&C with the check he was to receive from NCB, Gineris required Woods to sign a vendor's affidavit which stated that there were "no unpaid claims for... materials furnished for the Real Estate in respect of which lien have been or may be filed."

Fellows stated that NCB's payment to Woods, based on Woods' statement that he would pay T&C, was "fine." Thus, we do not see on NCB's part a commitment to ensure payment to T&C. Furthermore, even if a contract were established by Gineris' remark that the pre-lien notice would be addressed, the evidence presented does not demonstrate that NCB and Fellows had a "clear intent" to benefit T&C, as required under Indiana law.

T&C also contends that it was the intended beneficiary of the agreement between Gineris and Fellows. Specifically, it asserts that it is a **"creditor beneficiary"** under the Restatement of Contracts and therefore is entitled to bring suit based on the agreement of Gineris and Fellows.

Section 302 of the Restatement (Second) of Contracts (1981) provides that:

(1) Unless otherwise agreed between promisor and promisee, a beneficiary of a promise is an intended beneficiary if recognition of a right to performance in the beneficiary is appropriate to effectuate the intention of the parties and either:

(a) the performance of the promise will satisfy an obligation of the promisee to pay money to the beneficiary; or (b) the circumstances indicate that the promisee intends to give the beneficiary the benefit of the promised performance.

Restatement (Second) of Contracts, § 302 (1981). Furthermore, the Comments to § 302 define a **creditor beneficiary** as "the type of beneficiary covered by (1)(a)," that is the beneficiary of a promise to pay the promisee's debt.

In this case, T&C is not a **creditor beneficiary** because such a beneficiary is one who is a creditor of the promisee. Here, the promisee was Fellows, and T&C was not his creditor. Thus, the analysis which T&C asks us to perform does not apply.

*****

In conclusion, we find that, while NCB had a duty to protect Fellows, it had no duty to protect T&C, inasmuch as T&C was not a third-party beneficiary to its agreement with Fellows. As a result, the trial court properly entered judgment against T&C.

Judgment affirmed.

B. Donee Beneficiary

Similarly, an intended third party *donee beneficiary* is created when a donee-donor relationship is established where, for example, the donor first promises to give a $2000 gift to the donee. The donor then creates a contract with the promisor wherein the promisor agrees to pay the amount of $2000 to the donee. In the contract, the parties agree that instead of the promisor paying the donor directly, the $2000 will be paid to the donee beneficiary who is the intended beneficiary.[6] Accordingly, the rights of the creditor and the donee beneficiaries are the same. The following case addresses the issue of donee beneficiary.

Barbara Ann Baker v. Bank of Northeast Arkansas   **Case 11.3**
611 S.W.2d 783 (1981), 271 Ark. 948 (1981)
Court of Appeals of Arkansas

Lawson Cloninger, Judge.

This aspect of the case involves the cross-complaint filed in the original action by Barbara Ann Baker against the Bank of Northeast Arkansas. The cross-complaint stated that it was the intention of Rebecca Self for the certificates to pass to Barbara Ann Baker, and it was the fault of the bank that they did not. Barbara Ann Baker asked for a money judgment against the bank in the event she was not found to be the owner of the certificates. Her theory was that she was the beneficiary of a third party contract and that the bank was negligent. No additional testimony or proof was presented upon remand from this Court. The chancellor found that the bank had made mistakes but held that Barbara Ann Baker could not maintain her claim because she had no contractual relationship with the bank. This appeal is from that decision.

*****

---

[6] Restatement (Second) Contracts § 304 cmt. d (1979).

The chancellor, in making his ruling, commented that, "…Mrs. Self here deposited this money in the bank; and wanted it to go to this Mrs. Baker, survivor here. But still, Mrs. Baker didn't contribute anything to it. …There was no contract with Mrs. Baker, with the bank, that she could enforce at all…" Later on the chancellor stated that "Mrs. Baker had no right in this account here, unless it was done exactly right. The bank fouled up, there's no question about it."

The Arkansas Supreme Court has held that a contract made for the benefit of a third party is actionable by such third party. *Lovell v. Mariana Federal Savings and Loan Association* 264 Ark. 99, 568 S.W. 2d 38 (1978). The appellant is a **donee beneficiary**… He is a '**donee beneficiary**' if it appears from the terms of the promise in view of accompanying circumstances that the purpose of the promisee in obtaining the promise of all or part of the performance is to make a gift to or confer right of action upon the beneficiary.

The definition in *Coley v. English*, 17 Am. Jur. 2d, Contracts, § 311, states that: A person other than the promisee who will be benefited by the performance of the promise is a **donee beneficiary** where it appears that the purpose of the promisee in obtaining the promise was to make a gift to the beneficiary. In other words, a **donee beneficiary** is one to whom the promisee intends to make a gift of the performance by the promisor.

It is not necessary that consideration move to the obligor from the third party beneficiary. If there is consideration between the parties, then a standard contract is created. There must be consideration between the obligor and the obligee, but the absence of consideration or contract between the obligor and the third party beneficiary is the fundamental characteristic of a third party beneficiary contract. Rebecca Self supplied consideration to the bank in the form of a $5000 deposit, and the provision requested by Rebecca Self was for the direct benefit of appellant. The benefit intended to accrue to the appellant grew out of the contract itself, and appellant's interest was not a mere incident.

We find that appellant has proved a breach on the part of appellee and is entitled to judgment. …There was ample testimony to show that Rebecca Self intended that the three certificates were to pass to Barbara Ann Baker upon Mrs. Self's death, and that Mrs. Self effectively conveyed that intention to appellee. All three certificates were issued in the name of Rebecca Self or Barbara Ann Baker, either or the survivor of either. The loss to appellant arose because of the failure of appellee to follow its own procedures.

The judgment of the trial court is reversed and the cause remanded with directions to enter judgment for appellant (Baker) on her cross-complaint.

C. Incidental Beneficiary

When examining the facts, if it is found that the promisee intends that a third party should benefit from the contract, then that third party is an intended beneficiary who has enforceable rights under the contract against the promisor. On the other hand, if the contract reflects no intent to benefit a third party, then any third party beneficiary to the contract is merely an "incidental beneficiary" who has no enforceable rights under the contract.[7]

---

[7] In the Matter of the Estate of Evelyn I. Atkinson, Deceased, Court of Appeals of Ohio, 1991 Ohio App. LEXIS 4455 (1991).

The following case illustrates the circumstances under which a third party beneficiary becomes an incidental beneficiary.

In The Matter of The Estate of Evelyn I. Atkinson,
1991 Ohio App. LEXIS 4455
Court of Appeals of Ohio

JUDGES: Hadley, J. Evans and Shaw, JJ., concur.

Evelyn Atkinson ("Atkinson") died on June 21, 1989. Prior to that time, arrangements were made with two individuals for loans. On August 8, 1985, Atkinson made a written arrangement captioned "Loan Agreement" with Larry C. Copeland ("Copeland") which provided for a repayment schedule in the amount of $64,366.20. The written arrangement also stated that in the event of Atkinson's death prior to loan termination, "Remainder of loan to be paid to BARBARA MORRIS, 1016 Woodland Drive, Lima, Ohio." The probate schedule of assets valued this loan at $64,366.20.

On March 10, 1988, Atkinson made a written arrangement captioned "Promissory Note" with Daniel J. Kline ("Kline"), whereby Kline would repay Atkinson $40,000. This written arrangement provided that, "In the event of Atkinson's death, the Promissory Note shall be assigned to Barbara Morris." The probate schedule of assets values this note at $30,000.

Atkinson's will does not mention either the note or the loan arrangement. The loan arrangement and promissory note were included with the probate assets. On November 14, 1989, Appellant filed exceptions to the inventory, arguing that she was a third party beneficiary of the loan arrangement and the note and therefore, these items should not be included in the schedule of assets

* * * * *

The parties stipulated that if the probate court found these arrangements to be valid third party intended beneficiary contracts, then they would not be included in Atkinson's estate. Therefore, the determining issue is whether Barbara Morris was an incidental third party beneficiary or an intended third party beneficiary. The test is stated as follows:

"In applying Ohio state law...the district court applied the 'intent to benefit' test to distinguish between **incidental beneficiaries** and beneficiaries with enforceable rights. Under this analysis, if the promisee...intends that a third party should benefit from the contract, then that third party is an 'intended beneficiary' who has enforceable rights under the contract. If the promisee has no intent to benefit a third party, then any third-party beneficiary to the contract is merely an '**incidental beneficiary**', who has no enforceable rights under the contract."

* * * * *

Appellant's second assignment of error alleges that the trial court's finding of Barbara Morris as an **incidental beneficiary** was contrary to the manifest weight of the evidence. The record indicates that the probate court based its decision on the facts and circumstances alluded to by the parties and the language of the note and the loan. This finding indicates there was some competent, credible evidence on which the trial court based its decision on. ...Therefore, this assignment of error is overruled. Barbara Morris was an incidental third party beneficiary.

The judgment of the trial court is affirmed.

D. Defenses against the Beneficiary

Where the beneficiary attempts to assert his rights to enforce a contract against the promisor, the promisor has several defenses. The first defense is that for rights to vest in the beneficiary, the contract between the promisor and the promisee must be valid. If the contract is void, voidable or unenforceable, then the rights of the third party beneficiary are subject to the same infirmity.[8] Similarly, if the contract is deficient because of absence of mutual assent, lack of consideration, impracticability, against public policy, failure of performance, lack of capacity, fraud, or mistake, the rights of the beneficiary are permanently suspended and discharged or modified accordingly.[9]

II. Assignment and Delegation
A. Assignment and Delegation

With respect to the principles of assignment and delegation, rights are assigned while duties are delegated. Assignments and delegation can be either oral or in writing unless the transaction falls within the statute of frauds, in which case the agreement must be in writing.

Assignments require an intention by the assignor to manifest an assignment. An assignment is the transfer of a right by the owner (assignor) to another party called the assignee.[10] A delegation of duties is the transfer of duties from the delegator to the delagatee. Duties can only be delegated and cannot be assigned; rights can only be assigned and cannot be delegated. The obligor who has a duty to perform on a contract may not delegate his duties if they are personal in nature without the consent of the obligee.

B. Assignment of Rights

A contractual assignment is the intentional transfer of a right from assignor to assignee. Upon the manifestation of the assignment, the obligations of the obligor to the assignor are extinguished and the assignee acquires the rights of the obligor's performance.[11] For example, Mary contracts to sell an XLS computer to Joe for $400. Mary then assigns her contractual right to Sam to receive the $400 from Joe. Mary, the assignor, no longer has any rights to collect the money from Joe. Sam, the assignee, now has the right to collect the $400 from Joe.

---

[8] Restatement (Second) Contracts § 309 (1) (1979).
[9] *Id*. at §309 (2) (1979).
[10] Restatement (Second) Contracts § 317 (1979).
[11] *Id*. at § 317 (1979).

There are certain circumstances under which a contractual right cannot be assigned:

1. Where the assignment of the contractual rights from the assignor to the assignee would materially alter the duties of the obligor.
2. Where the burden or risk would materially increase for the obligor.
3. Where the assignment would materially impair the return performance to the obligor.
4. Where the assignment would materially reduce the value of the contract to the obligor.[12]
5. Where the assignment is forbidden by statute or public policy.[13]
6. Where the contract forbids an assignment.[14]

C. Assignments of Future Rights

As a general rule, a contract to make a future assignment of a right is not an assignment.[15] An assignment to right of payments that have not yet come into existence is only a promise, and the right to payment will only vest when the right itself arises.

The following case addresses the issue of distinguishing between future and present rights assignments.

Case 11.5

George J. Stathos v. William F. Murphy, Sr.,
26 A.D.2d 500 (1966), 276 N.Y.S.2d 727 (1966)
Supreme Court of New York

JUDGE: Breitel, J. P

The issue is whether an assignee of an interest in a lawsuit is entitled to recover the allocable proceeds of a settlement as against a judgment creditor of the assignor whose judgment was recovered and whose restraining notice was served subsequent to the assignment but before the settlement of the lawsuit. Although the issue is one that has arisen with some frequency in the past, the application of the rule has been surrounded with some confusion.

In the instant case, Special Term, after a reference and hearings before the Special Referee, held that the judgment creditor was entitled to prevail, presumably adopting the view of the Special Referee that the assignment related to subsequently acquired property and therefore could not take effect until the settlement moneys were in hand. ...

---

[12] *Id.* at § 317 (2) (1979).
[13] *Id.* at § 317 (2)(b) (1979).
[14] *Id.* at § 322 (1979).
[15] *Id.* at § 330 (1) (1979).

The confusion in this area of the law arises primarily from a failure to distinguish between the **assignment of future rights**, such as future wages, revenues on contracts yet to be made, and the like, regarded as after-acquired property, and the **assignment of present rights**, typically choses in action, which have yet to ripen into deliverable assets, particularly money. While there may be many practical contingencies or even conditions stipulated in the realization of choses in action, such contingencies or conditions alone do not negate the fact that a present right exists and is being effectively transferred. A further distinction should be kept in mind between the assignment of a cause of action, an interest in a lawsuit, or a chose in action, however termed, and an assignment of the proceeds or a share of the proceeds of a judgment or settlement to be obtained in the future. This, of course, is the difference between a present transfer and a transfer to take effect in the future. If the authorities are analyzed within a proper classification they are largely reconcilable in result if not always in their *rationes decidendi*.

The first question in this case, then, is the nature of what was purportedly assigned. George Stathos, one of the plaintiffs and the assignor, instituted this action in March, 1958 to recover corporate stock and money. In June, 1964 the action was settled for $65,000 to be paid to specified persons as their interests might appear. At issue in this present appeal is the share allocable to George Stathos of $13,665.50 claimed by his judgment creditors, Seaways Shipping Corp. and Rio Palmea Compania Naviera, S. A. At Special Term it was also claimed by the co-plaintiff Kirkiles to the extent of $8,601.25 by virtue of an agreement with Stathos, and by Victoria Stathos, the mother and assignee of George Stathos, to the extent of $5,065.25. 1 On the appeal, there remains only the assertion of the assignee's claim in the full sum of $13,665.50, the Kirkiles' claim having been disallowed.

The assignment to Victoria Stathos was dated May 25, 1959 and the Special Referee found: "The credible proof shows that at the time this assignment was made, Stathos was indebted to his mother for at least $30,000. Victoria Stathos' uncontroverted testimony establishes that her son owed her this sum of money. ... Nothing in the record warrants the conclusion that any of the loans made by her to her son were ever intended as gifts. ...On the contrary, it clearly appears that the assignment was made by Stathos for good and valuable consideration, in an amount perhaps exceeding this sum of $30,000."

* * * * *

The assignment in usual form purported to "grant, assign and convey...all my right, title and interest in the cause of action now pending...entitled...wherein I [Stathos] am plaintiff. ..."

From the foregoing recital it is evident that the subject of the assignment was a fully matured claim for breach of contract. No future interest or "after-acquired" property was involved. The claim, of course, was quite uncertain as to realization because it was disputed and being seriously litigated. Indeed, the eventual amount of the settlement was a fraction of the pleading claims of $869,800 and $376,500. Notably, the assignment was of the cause of action and not of an interest in a future judgment or fund.

The next question is whether the assignment in this case took effect instantly or matured as a transfer only after the proceeds of the settlement were at hand.

There is no doubt that the assignment of a truly future claim or interest does not work a present transfer of property. It does not because it cannot; no property yet exists. However, equity has long recognized such a purported transfer as an agreement or promise to transfer when the capacity to transfer arises—hence, one form of the equitable assignment enforceable in equity with the inchoate right receiving no or only limited recognition at law. Quite different is the assignment of a present claim not yet matured, or disputed, or dependent upon future conditions. There has never been any doubt that such an assignment was one of a presently-existing interest. Difficulty only arose because there might not be an immediate action at law available to enforce the claim, and the unmatured claim would be the best example. However, even in such case, while law and equity were still separated, equity would provide whatever recognition or protection was necessary, but always considering the transfer as one of a present interest. But, for the purposes of this case, an existing right was transferred for which there was a pending mode of enforcement and the assignor lost the power to transfer to another or to create rights in his creditors pre-empting those of the assignee. And, of course, the problems engendered by the separation of law and equity should no longer plague us.

* * * * *

...Mrs. Stathos was the assignee of a present interest in an existing chose in action, based on contract, and uninhibited by rule of decision or statute limiting its assignability for reasons resting in public policy. The Stathos assignment was even an unconditional chose in action, contingent only on the practical burdens and risks of proof and enforcement of the underlying claim.

Accordingly, the judgment should be modified, on the law and on the facts, to allow claimant-appellant her full claim to the proceeds to which her assignor was entitled and disallowing the claims of claimants-respondents, with costs and disbursements to claimant-appellant against claimants-respondents.

D. Partially Effective Assignments

Where the assignor makes an effective assignment to the assignee, the rights of the assignor are extinguished and the same rights then arise in the assignee. But if the assignment is found to be conditional, revocable, or voidable, the assignor may retrieve the assignment from the assignee, thus restoring the rights back to the assignor.[16]

E. Gratuitous Assignments

An assignment that is transferred without consideration is considered to be gratuitous and therefore becomes revocable and the rights of the assignee are terminated. The conditions upon which a gratuitous assignment can be terminated are the death of the assignor, incapacity of the assignor, subsequent assignment by the assignor, or notification by the assignor to the assignee of

---

[16] Restatement (Second) Contracts § 331 (1979).

revocation of the assignment.[17] For example, Joe gives Sam a promissory note for $1000. Sam transfers and assigns the promissory note to his daughter as a gift for her birthday. Before the daughter (assignee) gives notice to Joe (obligor), Sam (assignor) revokes the assignment to his daughter, thereby terminating her rights to the assignment.

On the other hand, a gratuitous assignment ceases to be revocable where (1) the assignment is in writing, signed or under seal and delivered by the assignor, (2) the assignee obtains payment or satisfaction of the obligation, (3) there is a judgment against the obligor, or (4) there is a new contract by novation between the obligor and the assignee or the assignee transfers consideration to the assignor.[18] A gratuitous assignment also becomes irrevocable under equitable principles to the extent that it avoids injustice when the assignor induced forbearance on the part of the assignee and the assignee relied on the assignor's inducement.[19]

F. Restriction on Assignments
1. Contract Prohibiting Assignment

A contract agreement that prohibits the assignment of the contract itself restricts only the transfer of the required performance to the assignee.[20] However, the parties to the contract can agree to restrict the assignment of rights but cannot restrict the assignment of a right to proceeds from insurance, negotiable instrument or to damages for breach of the entire contract.[21]

2. Obligors Assent to the Assignment/Delegation

It is not required that the obligor assent to the assignment. But his assent will preclude subsequent objections when the performance becomes burdensome, duties are modified, or the risk increases.[22] Therefore, when the obligor assents in a contract to future assignment of rights or where the obligee assents to a future delegation of performance of a duty, the assignment of rights by the obligor and the delegation of duties by the obligee are enforceable notwithstanding any subsequent objections.[23]

---

[17] *Id.* at § 332 (1979).
[18] *Id.* at § 332 (1979).
[19] Restatement (Second) Contracts § 332 (4) (1979).
[20] *Id.* at § 322 (1) (1979).
[21] *Id.* at § 322 (2)(a) (1979).
[22] *Id.* at § 317 cmt. a (1979).
[23] *Id.* at § 323 (1) (1979).

3. Restriction on Assignment of Guarantees

As a general rule, contract rights can be assigned unless they involve obligations of a personal nature or if there is some public policy against the assignment. However, special rules govern the assignability of guaranties, and these rules involve the characterization of the guaranty as special or general. A special guaranty is usually not assignable.[24] The following case illustrates this issue.

Case 11.6

Finance America Private Brands, Inc. v. Harvey E. Hall, Inc.
380 A.2d 1377 (1977), 1977 Del. Super. LEXIS 92
Superior Court of Delaware

OPINION BY: J. CHRISTIE

This matter is before the Court on a motion for summary judgment by the defendant, Anna Belle Hall. The pertinent facts are not in dispute. Harvey E. Hall, Inc. (HEH, Inc.) was an appliance store which purchased appliances from Sylvania Electric Products, Inc. (Sylvania). Using what appears to be a conventional commercial floor plan agreement, the costs of acquiring the goods were financed by John P. Maguire & Co., Inc. (Maguire).

As additional security, Sylvania and Maguire required that Harvey E. Hall and his wife, Anna Belle Hall, personally guarantee the debts of HEH, Inc. to the amount of $25,000. The Halls met this requirement on July 29, 1966 by signing a form entitled "Guaranty of Past and Future Indebtedness" with Sylvania Electric Products, Inc. and/or John P. Maguire & Co., Inc. as addressees. The signatures on this form are not challenged.

Approximately two years after the execution of the guaranty, Maguire assigned all its rights and interest in the financing plan, including the guaranty in question, to plaintiff, Finance America Private Brands, Inc. (FIN.AM.). On April 9, 1976, FIN. AM. took all rights, title and interest of GTE Sylvania (formerly Sylvania Electric Products, Inc.) to the guaranty by assignment.

It appears that in 1968, when FIN.AM. took over the financing from Maguire, loan procedures continued as they had before; FIN.AM. merely took Maguire's place in the triangular financing arrangement. FIN.AM. continued to extend credit to HEH, Inc. HEH, Inc. closed in September of 1975. Harvey E. Hall, one of the signers of the personal guaranty had died in early 1971.

The $6,823.61 which plaintiff seeks in this suit results from a default on payments due from HEH, Inc. to FIN.AM. on inventory sold from August 31, 1974 to November 26, 1974. There is no dispute that a sum is owed, it is only the personal liability of Anna Belle Hall that is in issue.

* * * * *

---

[24] FinanceAmerica Private Brands, Inc. v. Harvey E. Hall, 380 A.2d 1377 (1977), 1977 Del. Super. LEXIS 92.

Anna Belle Hall raises as her defense the claim that the personal guaranty ran only to Sylvania and/or Maguire and could not be effectively transferred to FIN.AM. Thus, she says she cannot be held personally liable for credit extended by FIN.AM. to HEH, Inc., where FIN.AM. was not an obligee of her personal guaranty.

There are two issues for the Court to decide. First, what kind of guaranty was this? Second, was it assignable? A contract of guaranty is the promise to answer for the payment of some debt or the performance of some obligation by another on the default of that third person who is liable in the first instance. …

There are two types of guaranties. An instrument of guaranty addressed to all persons generally, or "to whom it may concern" may be enforced by anyone to whom it was presented who acts upon it. This is a general guaranty. A guaranty which is special is addressed to a particular person, firm or corporation, and, when so addressed, only the promisee named in the instrument acquires any rights under it. …

Generally, contract rights can be assigned unless they involve obligations of a personal nature or there is some public policy against the assignment. Williston, Contracts, Third Ed. § 412. However, special rules govern the assignability of guaranties, and these rules involve the characterization of the guaranty as special or general. As indicated, a special guaranty is usually not assignable. …

* * * * *

This latter point is important. Williston has said that "the commonest type of right subject to assignment is one for the payment of money, and such assignment is effective not only as against a principal debtor, but as against a guarantor." Williston, Contracts, Third Ed. § 412. However, this does not support the plaintiff's position that since it was only a money payment which was guaranteed, the guaranty was freely transferable. What Williston was saying is that a debt (which may have originated in a guaranty) is transferable. A creditor can assign his right to receive money to another who then has the right to receive it. The guarantor then continues to guarantee the transferred debt.

I find that this guaranty was a **special guaranty**. It is specifically addressed to Sylvania Electric Products, Inc. and/or John P. Maguire & Co., Inc. and consistently refers to the guaranty of the obligation unto you (Sylvania and Maguire). Note also that there are no words of assignability in the guaranty. It may not be necessary to specifically provide for assignability in the guaranty in order to make it assignable, but the absence of such language reinforces the conclusion that it was meant to be only for the protection of the named obligees.

This case does not involve the assignment of a debt; rather, it involves an attempt to **assign a guaranty**. The guaranty was a special one to Sylvania and/or Maguire but the debt arose from financial dealings between FIN.AM. and HEH, Inc. which took place after one of the attempted assignments. Under the plaintiff's interpretation of the guaranty, Anna Belle Hall, the surviving signatory, would not merely continue to guarantee an obligation that had arisen between the original parties, but she would also guarantee any new debts to any subsequent assignees of the guaranty. This view would greatly expand the scope of the paper signed by the Halls for the protection of Sylvania and Maguire.

The majority rule, and the rule to be applied here, is that once a guaranty is correctly categorized as special, it is **not assignable** absent a specific assignability provision or other special circumstances not here present. I find the **special guaranty** is addressed to specific named obligees and was intended only for their benefit. Therefore, such guaranty is non-assignable.

* * * * *

Summary judgment is granted in favor of the defendant, Anna Belle Hall, against the plaintiff, Finance America Private Brands, Inc. The case will be dismissed.

IT IS SO ORDERED.

G. Assent by Assignee

As a general rule, where the assignor makes an assignment of rights to the assignee, it is essential that the assignee manifest intent to accept the assignment. The exception occurs when, for example, Sam contracts with Joe to sell a car. Joe, in return, transfers a promissory note to Sam. Subsequently, Sam assigns the promissory note to Charlie upon David's (Charlie's brother) request to give Sam consideration for the assignment. In this case Charlie is unaware of Sam and David's agreement, but the assignment is good even though Charlie does not manifest intent to become an assignee.[25]

H. Successive Assignees

Where the assignor makes an assignment of rights to an assignee and subsequently makes a second assignment of the same rights to a subsequent assignee, the rights of the first assignee are superior to the rights of the subsequent assignee.[26] This is called the "first in time first in right" rule. An exception to this general rule arises when the primary assignment is ineffective, revocable or voidable, either by the assignor or the subsequent assignee.[27]

I. Assignors Warranties

When an assignor makes an assignment of his right to an assignee, he warrants that (1) he will do nothing to defeat or impair the value of the assignment, and has no knowledge of any circumstance that would impair the value of the assignment to the assignee, (2) there are no limitations or defenses against the assignor that would flow to and against the assignee, (3) the rights assigned actually exist, (4) that the writing evidencing the right of assignment is real and actually exists at the time of the assignment, and

---

[25] Restatement (Second) Contracts § 327 (1979).

[26] *Id.* at § 342 (1979).

[27] *Id.* at § 342 (a) (1979).

(5) that the assignor is bound by his promises and affirmation underlying the assignment. But the assignment does not represent or warrant that the obligor is solvent or that he will perform the obligation evidence in the assignment. Nor does the warranty from the assignor to the assignee flow automatically to a sub-assignee unless it is agreed otherwise.[28]

J.   Defenses Against the Assignee

Upon the manifestation of an assignment, the assignee acquires the rights of the assignor and the obligor's obligations are transferred from the assignor to the assignee. The assignment to the assignee is valid but only to the extent that the obligor is under a duty to the assignor. Where the duty by the obligor to the assignor is voidable by the obligor or unenforceable by the assignor, the rights of the assignee will also be unenforceable.[29]

Suppose that Joe (obligor) is a minor who gives a promissory note to Sam. Subsequently, Sam assigns the promissory note to Mary (assignee). Joe then decides to assert his rights as a minor and revoke the contract with Sam. The assignment by Sam to Mary is then void and she accordingly has no rights against the obligor.

Where the obligor has defenses against the assignee before the obligor receives notification of the assignment of rights from the assignor to the assignee, the assignee will be subject to the obligor's defenses. For example, suppose that Joe (obligor) purchases a car from Sam and gives Sam a down payment and a promissory note. The car has a damaged engine and therefore Joe refuses to pay Sam for the car asserting the defense of lack of consideration. Suppose further, that Sam (assignor) then assigns the promissory note to Mary (assignee). Mary then gives notice to Joe that she has the promissory note and demands payment from Joe. Joe can assert the defense of lack of consideration against Mary because he had a defense against the payment of the note before he received notice from Mary (assignee). But if the defenses arise after the assignment of rights is made, then the obligor may not assert the defenses against the assignee.[30]

---

[28] Restatement (Second) Contracts § 333 (1979).
[29] *Id.* at § 336 (1) (1979).
[30] *Id.* at § 336 (2) (1979).

However, if the rights of the assignor are subject to discharge because of impracticability, public policy or nonoccurrence of a condition, the rights of the assignee are also subject to the same discharge even if the obligor has received notification of the assignment.[31] After the assignment is made, the assignor retains the power to discharge or modify the duty of the obligor except when after the assignee has given notice to the obligor of the assignment.[32]

III. Delegation of Duties (Performance)

Where an obligor has an obligation to render performance of a duty to an obligee, the obligor may delegate his duties of performance to a third party to perform the duty in his stead. But the delegation will be prohibited where:[33]

1. the delegation is contrary to public policy.
2. it is restricted in the contract creating the obligation.
3. the performance delegated is of a personal service.
4. the exercise of personal skills is involved.[34]

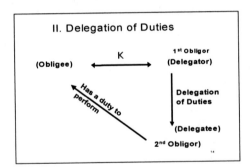

The following case addresses the issue of delegation of duties for personal services.

---

[31] *Id.* at § 336 (3) (1979).
[32] *Id.* at § 338 (1) (1979).
[33] *Id.* at § 318 (1) (1979).
[34] *Id.* at § 318 (c) (1979).

Case 11.7

The Macke Company v. Pizza of Gaithersburg, Inc.
270 A.2d 645 (1970), 259 Md. 479 (1970)
Court of Appeals of Maryland

JUDGES: Hammond, C. J.

The appellees and defendants below, Pizza of Gaithersburg, Inc.; Pizzeria, Inc.; The Pizza Pie Corp., Inc. and Pizza Oven, Inc., four corporations under the common ownership of Sidney Ansell, Thomas S. Sherwood and Eugene Early and the same individuals as partners or proprietors (the Pizza Shops) operated at six locations in Montgomery and Prince George's Counties. The appellees had arranged to have installed in each of their locations cold drink vending machines owned by Virginia Coffee Service, Inc., and on 30 December 1966, this arrangement was formalized at five of the locations, by contracts for terms of one year, automatically renewable for a like term in the absence of 30 days' written notice. A similar contract for the sixth location, operated by Pizza of Gaithersburg, Inc., was entered into on 25 July 1967.

On 30 December 1967, Virginia's assets were purchased by The Macke Company (Macke) and the six contracts were assigned to Macke by Virginia. In January, 1968, the Pizza Shops attempted to terminate the five contracts having the December anniversary date, and in February, the contract which had the July anniversary date.

Macke brought suit in the Circuit Court for Montgomery County against each of the Pizza Shops for damages for breach of contract. From judgments for the defendants, Macke has appealed.

The lower court based the result which it reached on two grounds: first, that the Pizza Shops, when they contracted with Virginia, relied on its skill, judgment and reputation, which made impossible a delegation of Virginia's duties to Macke; ...These conclusions are challenged by Macke.

In the absence of a contrary provision—and there was none here—rights and duties under an executory bilateral contract may be assigned and delegated, subject to the exception that duties under a contract to provide **personal services may never be delegated**, nor rights be assigned under a contract where delectus personae was an ingredient of the bargain. ...Crane Ice Cream Co. v. Terminal Freezing & Heating Co., ...held that the right of an individual to purchase ice under a contract which by its terms reflected a knowledge of the individual's needs and reliance on his credit and responsibility could not be assigned to the corporation which purchased his business. In Eastern Advertising Co. v. McGaw & Co., our predecessors held that an advertising agency could **not delegate** its duties under a contract which had been entered into by an advertiser who had relied on the agency's skill, judgment and taste.

The six machines were placed on the appellees' premises under a printed "Agreement-Contract" which identified the "customer," gave its place of business, described the vending machine, and then provided:

TERMS

1. The Company will install on the Customer's premises the above listed equipment and will maintain the equipment in good operating order and stocked with merchandise.
2. The location of this equipment will be such as to permit accessibility to persons desiring use of same. This equipment shall remain the property of the Company and shall not be moved from the location at which installed, except by the Company.
3. For equipment requiring electricity and water, the Customer is responsible for electrical receptacle and water outlet within ten (10) feet of the equipment location. The Customer is also responsible to supply the Electrical Power and Water needed.
4. The Customer will exercise every effort to protect this equipment from abuse or damage.
5. The Company will be responsible for all licenses and taxes on the equipment and sale of products.
6. This Agreement-Contract is for a term of one (1) year from the date indicated herein and will be automatically renewed for a like period, unless thirty (30) day written notice is given by either party to terminate service.
7. Commission on monthly sales will be paid by the Company to the Customer at the following rate: ...

We cannot regard the agreements as contracts for personal services. They were either a license or concession granted Virginia by the appellees, or a lease of a portion of the appellees' premises, with Virginia agreeing to pay a percentage of gross sales as a license or concession fee or as rent, ... and were assignable by Virginia unless they imposed on Virginia duties of a personal or unique character which could not be delegated, ...

The appellees earnestly argue that they had dealt with Macke before and had chosen Virginia because they preferred the way it conducted its business. Specifically, they say that service was more personalized, since the president of Virginia kept the machines in working order, that commissions were paid in cash, and that Virginia permitted them to keep keys to the machines so that minor adjustments could be made when needed. Even if we assume all this to be true, the agreements with Virginia were silent as to the details of the working arrangements and contained only a provision requiring Virginia to "install...the above listed equipment and...maintain the equipment in good operating order and stocked with merchandise." We think the Supreme Court of California put the problem of personal service in proper focus a century ago when it upheld the assignment of a contract to grade a San Francisco street:

"All painters do not paint portraits like Sir Joshua Reynolds, nor landscapes like Claude Lorraine, nor do all writers write dramas like Shakespeare or fiction like Dickens. Rare genius and extraordinary skill are not transferable, and contracts for their employment are therefore personal, and cannot be assigned. But rare genius and extraordinary skill are not indispensable to the workmanlike digging down of a sand hill or the filling up of a depression to a given level, or the construction of brick sewers with manholes and covers, and contracts for such work are not personal, and may be assigned."

Moreover, the difference between the service the Pizza Shops happened to be getting from Virginia and what they expected to get from Macke did not mount up to such a material change in the performance of obligations under the agreements as would justify the appellees' refusal to recognize the assignment. ...

* * * * *

Modern authorities...hold that, absent provision to the contrary, a **duty may be delegated**, as distinguished from a right which can be assigned, and that the promisee cannot rescind, if the quality of the performance remains materially the same. Restatement, Contracts § 160 (3) (1932) reads, in part: "Performance or offer of performance by a person delegated has the same legal effect as performance or offer of performance by the person named in the contract, unless, (a) performance by the person delegated varies or would vary materially from performance by the person named in the contract as the one to perform, and there has been no...assent to the delegation.

* * * * *

As we see it, the delegation of duty by Virginia to Macke was entirely permissible under the terms of the agreements. ...the Pizza Shops had no right to rescind the agreements. ...

Judgment reversed as to liability; judgment entered for appellant for costs, on appeal and below. ...

Chapter 11
Vocabulary

1. Creditor Beneficiary
2. Donee Beneficiary
3. Incidental Beneficiary
4. Third Party Defenses
5. Assignment of Rights
6. Gratuitous Assignments
7. Restrictions on Assignments
8. Successive Assignees
9. Assignors Warranties
10. Defenses against Assignee
11. Delegation of Duties

Review Questions

1. What is the issue in the *William Martin v. Edward Martin* case?
2. What is the legal principle in the *Martin* case?
3. What is the issue in the *Town & Country v. Ronald Woods* case?
4. What is the legal principle in the *Woods* case?
5. What is the issue in the *Barbara Baker v. Bank of Northeast Arkansas* case?
6. What is the legal principle in the *Baker* case?
7. What is at issue in the *In the Matter of Estate of Atkinson* case?
8. What is the legal principle in the *Atkinson* case?
9. What is the issue in the *Stathos v. Murphy* case?
10. What is the legal principle in the *Murphy* case?
11. What is the issue in the *Finance America Private Brands, Inc. v. Harvey E. Hall, Inc.* case?
12. What is the legal principle in the *Finance America* case?
13. What is the issue in the *Macke Co. v. Pizza of Gaithersburg* case?
14. What is the legal principle in the *Macke* case?

Chapter 12
Remedies

I. Remedies Based on Interest

There are three types of a promisee's interests that are protected under the rules of contract law. The first is "expectation interest," which represents the promisee's benefit of the bargain or the expectation of being placed in the same position that the promisee would have been in if the contract had not been breached. These damages include compensatory and incidental damages.

The second is "reliance interest," which represents the right of the promisee to recover remedies based on his reliance on the contract by being placed in the same position the promisee would have been in if the contract had not been consummated.

Finally, the third interest is "restitution interest." This is the notion that the promisee is to be restored or any benefit returned which he has previously conferred on the promisor.[1]

A. Recovery at Law or Equity

When a breach of contract occurs, the injured party has a right to recover either at law or in equity. If the injured party decides to recover money damages the action is *at law*. Where the injured party chooses to recover under principles *of equity*, he will seek remedies.

The recovery of damages at law against the breaching party includes an award for (1) damages in money, (2) adjudicating in favor of the rights of the parties, (3) awarding money to prevent unjust enrichment, and (4) enforcing an arbitration award. And (5) where the breach of contract causes little or no loss to the injured party, the court may award nominal damages.[2]

Recovery in equity includes (1) specific performance, (2) restoring specific things to prevent unjust enrichment, and (3) promissory estoppel.[3]

B. Expectation Interest Damages

Injured parties have a right to damages based on their expectation interest as measured by (1) the loss in the value to the injured party caused by the

---

[1] Restatement (Second) Contracts § 344 (1979).
[2] *Id.* at § 346 (1979).
[3] *Id.* at § 345 (1979).

promisor's failure of performance, (2) including other losses such as incidental or consequential loss caused by the breach, and (3) any other loss that the injured party has avoided by not having to perform.[4] These principles are delineated in the following case.

Case 12.1

>

BVT Lebanon Shopping Center, Ltd. v. Wal-Mart Stores, Inc.
48 S.W.3d 132 (2001), 2001 Tenn. LEXIS 142
Supreme Court of Tennessee

OPINION BY: Janice M. Holder

J.R. Freeman (Freeman) and Kuhn Brothers Co., Inc. (Kuhn Brothers) entered into a lease agreement in 1968 under which Kuhn Brothers agreed to lease space in The Center of Lebanon, a shopping center owned by Freeman. The lease provided for a guaranteed minimum rent and for additional rent calculated as a percentage of Kuhn Brothers's gross receipts (percentage rent). In 1981, the lease was amended, conditioned in part upon Wal-Mart's acquisition of Kuhn Brothers. The 1981 Amendment extended the lease to 1996; …and changed the permitted use from "retail promotional type store" to "discount department store."

The lease was amended again in 1985, following BVT's acquisition of The Center of Lebanon, to accommodate Wal-Mart's desire to expand its lease space from 50,000 square feet to 84,000 square feet. BVT agreed to pay for the approximate $1,500,000 in expansion costs, including the purchase of additional real estate and the buyout of a lease adjacent to the Wal-Mart premises; …

On October 5, 1994, BVT filed suit for **anticipatory breach** of the leasing agreement. BVT alleged that Wal-Mart intended to replace the Wal-Mart store with a Bud's Discount City (Bud's) and to open a new Wal-Mart Superstore in the area. BVT alleged that Wal-Mart breached an implied covenant of continuous occupancy. BVT also alleged that Wal-Mart breached the express "permitted use" clause of the lease, claiming that Bud's did not qualify as a "discount department store." BVT sought $4,689,526 in **compensatory damages**.

In May of 1995, Wal-Mart ceased operating its Wal-Mart store in The Center of Lebanon. In October of 1995, Bud's opened in the space previously occupied by the Wal-Mart store. Wal-Mart continued to pay the $272,000 annual base rent throughout this period. Bud's, however, never generated sufficient gross receipts to allow BVT to collect any percentage rent.

✶ ✶ ✶ ✶ ✶

On a trial of all of the remaining issues, the trial court found that Wal-Mart had breached both the express permitted use clause of the lease and an implied covenant of continuous occupancy. At trial, BVT proposed alternate **measures of damages**: 1) the present value of the lost future percentage rent alone, or 2) the diminution in the fair market value of the shopping center caused by Wal-Mart's withdrawal as the anchor tenant.

---

[4] *Id.* at § 347 (a–c) (1979).

The trial court found the proper measure of damages to be the present value of the lost future percentage rent for the duration of the lease term and awarded BVT $2,507,674 in damages for Wal-Mart's breach of contract. With respect to the Medco receipts claim, the trial court awarded BVT $108,759 in damages plus interest.

Wal-Mart appealed from the trial court's judgment. BVT filed a cross-appeal seeking **compensatory damages** based upon diminution in value. The Court of Appeals adopted the diminution in market value of the entire shopping center as the proper measure of damages and modified the trial court's judgment by increasing BVT's **compensatory damages** to $4,695,000. The Court of Appeals affirmed the trial court's judgment on all other issues. We granted review.

We granted appeal in this case to address: 1)…2) the proper **measure of damages** for Wal-Mart's breach of the implied covenant of continuous occupancy; and 3)…

* * * * *

The purpose of **assessing damages** in breach of contract cases is to place the plaintiff as nearly as possible in the same position she would have been in had the contract been performed, but the nonbreaching party is not to be put in any better position by recovery of damages for the breach of the contract than he would have been if the contract had been fully performed.

…Generally speaking, **damages** for breach of contract include only such as are incidental to or directly caused by the breach and may be reasonably supposed to have entered into the contemplation of the parties." …The general rule seeks to protect the non-breaching party's "expectation interest." …Subject to the limitations stated in §§ 350-53, the injured party has a right to damages based on his expectation interest as measured by:

   a. the loss in the value to him of the other party's performance caused by its failure or deficiency, plus

   b. any other loss, including **incidental or consequential loss**, caused by the breach, less

   c. any cost or other loss that he has avoided by not having to perform.

Diminution in value best serves the objective of protecting the non-breaching party's expectation interest when a covenant of continuous occupancy is breached

* * * * *

The majority correctly states the general goal of **contract damages**, which is to place the "injured parties 'in as good a position as they would have been in if the contract had not been breached.'" Indeed, the majority cites the test for **expectation damages** in section 347 of the Restatement (Second) Contracts as a correct formulation of this general goal. The Restatement measure of expectation damages provides, in a simple and straightforward manner, that the injured party has a right to damages based on his expectation interest. Measure of damages is not as precise as a fixed monthly amount, lost percentage rental income is clearly available when it can be proven to a reasonable degree of certainty, and the plaintiff has proven these damages to my satisfaction.

* * * * *

The Court of Appeals thus erred when it used appellee's expert. The case was thus remanded in order to resolve the conflicting evidence on the issue of diminution in value.

C. Reliance Interest Damages

When the injured party is not seeking damages based on expectation interest, he may recover damages based on his reliance interest, which includes expen-
ditures incurred as a result of preparing for the performance less the amount the
injured party would have incurred even if the contract had been performed.[5]

The following case illustrates the reliance interest issue.

Case 12.2

> Security Store & Mfg. Co. v. American Railways Express Co.
> 51 S.W.2d 572 (1932), 227 Mo. App. 175
> Court of Appeals of Missouri
>
> JUDGES: Bland, J.
>
> On October 1st, plaintiff wrote the defendant at Kansas City, referring to its letter
> of September 18th, concerning the fact that the furnace must be in Atlantic City not
> later than October 8th, and stating what Johnson had told it, saying: "Now, Mr. Banks,
> we want to make doubly sure that this shipment is in Atlantic City not later than
> October 8th and the purpose of this letter is to tell you that you can have your truck call
> for the shipment between 12 and 1 o'clock on Saturday, October 2nd for this." (Italics
> plaintiff's.) On October 2nd, plaintiff called the office of the express company in
> Kansas City and told it that the shipment was ready. Defendant came for the shipment
> on the last mentioned day, received it and delivered the express receipt to plaintiff. ...
>
> Plaintiff's president made arrangements to go to Atlantic City to attend the
> convention and install the exhibit, arriving there about October 11th. When he reached
> Atlantic City he found the shipment had been placed in the booth that had been
> assigned to plaintiff. The exhibit was set up, but it was found that one of the packages
> shipped was not there. This missing package contained the gas manifold, or that part of
> the oil and gas burner that controlled the flow of gas in the burner. This was the most
> important part of the exhibit and a like burner could not be obtained in Atlantic City.
>
> Wires were sent and it was found that the stray package was at the "over and
> short bureau" of defendant in St. Louis. Defendant reported that the package would
> be forwarded to Atlantic City and would be there by Wednesday, the 13th. Plaintiff's
> president waited until Thursday, the day the convention closed, but the package had not
> arrived at the time, so he closed up the exhibit and left. About a week after he arrived in
> Kansas City, the package was returned by the defendant.
>
> * * * * *
>
> [Plaintiff argues] "That relying upon defendant's promise and the promises of its
> agents and servants, that said parcels would be delivered at Atlantic City by October 8,
> 1926, if delivered to defendant by October 4, 1926, plaintiff herein hired space for an
> exhibit at the American Gas Association Convention at Atlantic City, and planned for
> an exhibit at said Convention and sent men in the employ of this plaintiff to Atlantic
> City to install, show and operate said exhibit, and that these men were in Atlantic City

---

[5] Restatement (Second) Contracts § 349 (1979).

ready to set up this plaintiff's exhibit at the American Gas Association Convention on October 8, 1926."

"That defendant, in violation of its agreement, failed and neglected to deliver one of the packages to its destination on October 8, 1926:

* * * * *

Plaintiff asked damages, which the court in its judgment allowed as follows: $147 express charges (on the exhibit); $45.12 freight on the exhibit from Atlantic City to Kansas City; $101.39 railroad and Pullman fares to and from Atlantic City, expended by plaintiff's president and a workman taken by him to Atlantic City; $48 hotel room for the two; $150 for the time of the president; $40 for wages of plaintiff's other employee and $270 for rental of the booth, making a total of $801.51.

* * * * *

In the case at bar defendant was advised of the necessity of prompt delivery of the shipment. Plaintiff explained to Johnson the "importance of getting the exhibit there on time." Defendant knew the purpose of the exhibit and ought to respond for its negligence in failing to get it there. As we view the record this negligence is practically conceded. The undisputed testimony shows that the shipment was sent to the over and short department of the defendant in St. Louis. As the packages were plainly numbered this, prima facie, shows mistake or negligence on the part of the defendant. No effort was made by it to show that it was not negligent in sending it there, or not negligence in not forwarding it within a reasonable time after it was found.

* * * * *

Defendant contends that plaintiff "is endeavoring to achieve a return of the status quo in a suit bases on a breach of contract. Instead of seeking to recover what he would have had, had the contract not been broken, plaintiff is trying to recover what he would have had, had there never been any contract of shipment;" that the expenses sued for would have been incurred in any event. It is no doubt, the general rule that where there is a breach of contract the party suffering the loss can recover only that which he would have had, had the contract not been broken, and this is all the cases decided upon which defendant relies. …But this is merely a general statement of the rule and is not inconsistent with the holdings that, in some instances, the injured party may recover expenses incurred in **relying upon the contract**, although such expenses would have been incurred had the contract not been breached. …

* * * * *

"*Compensation is a fundamental principle of damages* whether the action is in contract or tort. One who fails to perform his contract is justly bound to make good all **damages** that accrue naturally from the breach; and the other party is entitled to be put in as good a position pecuniarily as he would have been by performance of the contract."

* * * * *

The case at bar was to recover damages for loss of profits by reason of the failure of the defendant to transport the shipment within a reasonable time, so that it would arrive in Atlantic City for the exhibit. There were no profits contemplated. The furnace was to be shown and shipped back to Kansas City. There was no money loss, except the expenses, that was of such a nature as any court would allow as being sufficiently definite or lacking in pure speculation. Therefore, unless plaintiff is permitted to recover the expenses that it went to, which were a total loss to it by reason of its inability to exhibit the furnace and equipment, it will be deprived of any substantial compensation for its loss. The law does not contemplate any such injustice. It ought to allow plaintiff, as damages, the loss in the way of expenses that it sustained, and which it would not have been put to if it had not been for its reliance upon the defendant to perform its contract. There is no contention that the exhibit would have been entirely valueless and whatever it might have accomplished defendant knew of the circumstances and ought to respond for whatever damages plaintiff suffered. In cases of this kind the method of estimating the damages should be adopted which is the most definite and certain and which best achieves the fundamental purpose of compensation. ...Had the exhibit been shipped in order to realize a profit on sales and such profits could have been realized, or to be entered in competition for a prize, and plaintiff failed to show loss of profits with sufficient definiteness, or that he would have won the prize, defendant's cases might be in point. But as before stated, no such situation exists here.

* * * * *

While, it is true that plaintiff already had incurred some of these expenses, in that it had rented space at the exhibit before entering into the contract with defendant for the shipment of the exhibit and this part of plaintiff's damages, in a sense, arose out of a circumstance which transpired before the contract was even entered into, yet, plaintiff arranged for the exhibit knowing that it could call upon defendant to perform its common-law duty to accept and transport the shipment with reasonable dispatch. The whole damage, therefore, was suffered in contemplation of defendant performing its contract, which it failed to do, and would not have been sustained except for **the reliance** by plaintiff upon defendant to perform it. It can, therefore, be fairly said that the damages or loss suffered by plaintiff grew out of the breach of the contract, for had the shipment arrived on time, plaintiff would have had the benefit of the contract, which was contemplated by all parties, defendant being advised of the purpose of the shipment.

The judgment is affirmed.

D. Avoidable and Foreseeable Damages

The restatement of contracts encourages injured parties to attempt to avoid undue loss. Therefore, when the injured party can avoid damages without undue burden, he will not be allowed to recover those damages.[6] Similarly, where the breaching party has no reason to foresee the losses that might be incurred as a result of his breach, the injured party may not recover damages.[7] But losses may become foreseeable where the losses occur in the ordinary course of business[8] or the breaching party had reason to know that damages were going to be incurred as a result of the breach.[9]

---

[6] Restatement (Second) Contracts § 350 (1979).

[7] *Id.* at § 351 (1) (1979).

[8] *Id.* at § 351 (2) (1979).

[9] *Id.* at § 351 (2)(b) (1979).

In all circumstances, there is a requirement that damages can only be recovered where evidence can establish such damages with reasonable certainty.[10] In addition to damages, the injured party can recover interest from the time of the expected performance.[11]

E. Punitive Damages

Punitive damages are awarded by the court as a means of punishing the culpable party for causing the breach. Punishment falls within the realm of criminal law and therefore it is rarely given in cases dealing with breach of contracts. Hence, in rare instances the injured party can recover punitive damages but only if the breach is also a tort for which damages are recoverable.[12]

The test requires the following elements to be present in order to recover punitive damages:

1. The breaching party conduct must be reprehensible.
2. Some relationship between the ratios of punitive damages to actual damages.
3. Some comparison between civil and criminal penalties for similar conduct.

F. Liquidated Damages

The parties may, upon creating a contract, agree in advance on the amount of liquidated damages that may be recovered if either breaches the contract. Liquidated damages are the amount of clearly identified money the parties to the contract have agreed between each other to pay to the injured party in the event of a breach of contract.[13] The agreement to identify the liquidated damages in the contract saves the time of courts, juries, parties and witnesses and reduces the expense of litigation.[14] But where the liquidated amount is so unreasonable, large, or excessive that it has no relationship to the loss as a result of the breach of contract, the amount will be classified as a penalty and unenforceable by the court as a matter of public policy.[15]

---

[10] *Id.* at § 352 (1979).

[11] *Id.* at § 354 (1979).

[12] *Id.* at § 355 (1979).

[13] Restatement (Second) Contracts § 356 (1979).

[14] *Id.* at § 356 cmt. a (1979).

[15] *Id.* at § 356 (2) (1979).

II. Specific Performance

Specific performance is an alternative to recovering damages. It is used in equity as a means of enforcing a contract where the injured party does not seek damages for his injury but rather wants to have the promise in the contract enforced. It is intended to produce generally the same results as if the contract had been performed. A court of equity will grant specific performance at its own discretion.[16] But where damages are adequate or will be sufficient for the breach of contract, specific performance will not be granted.

To determine whether damages are adequate, the courts will look to the following:

1. the difficulty of proving damages with reasonable certainty
2. the difficulty of procuring a suitable money substituted award
3. the difficulty of collecting the award of damages[17]

Both **specific performance** and **damages** may be granted by the court if it finds it necessary to protect the injured party's expectation interest and to make him whole again.[18] The following case is such an illustration.

Case 12.3	Charles P. Butler v. A.E. Schilletter and Grace Schilletter 96 S.E.2d 661 (1957), 230 S.C. 552 (1957) Supreme Court of South Carolina JUDGE Bellinger: The defendant, A. E. Schilletter, has moved to require the plaintiff to elect between (a) his cause of action for specific performance on the equity side of the Court and (b) his cause of action for damages which is not appropriate to the cause of action for specific performance and is triable on the law side of the Court. The defendant, A. E. Schilletter, also put in an answer in which he admits that he and the plaintiff entered into the written contract set forth in the complaint and admits that he was fully paid for the property described in the complaint but alleges that there were certain restrictions that should be incorporated into the contract, and that he is willing to convey the lot in question if the restrictions can be incorporated into the conveyance. The written contract makes no reference to any restrictions and the defendant does not allege that there was a plan of subdivision recorded at the time of the contract in question setting forth any restrictions. It appears that the plaintiff desires to cut a road through the lot in question and the defendant does not want the road cut.

---

[16] *Id.* at § 357 (1979).
[17] *Id.* at § 350 (1979).
[18] *Id.* at § 359 (2) (1979).

As to the motion of defendant to require the plaintiff to elect whether to proceed on the equity side of the court in specific performance or on the law side of the court for damages the Court has repeatedly held that the plaintiff is entitled to any special damages that he may have suffered as a result of the delay in not conveying and at the same time be entitled to **specific performance** when his cause is a meritorious one. *Spencer v. National Union Bank of Rock Hill*, 189 S.C. 197, 200 S.E. 721, 723, was a case in which the Court held that damages in general could not be recovered in an action in specific performance but the Court further held, "But this does not mean, should **specific performance** be invoked and decreed, that the plaintiff may not recover any 'special damages' to which he may be entitled."

* * * * *

"A court of equity, when it acquires jurisdiction in a claim made for **specific performance**, can retain jurisdiction, and adjudicate all of the legal rights of the parties to the suit in conformity with justice, equity, and good conscience. The court is bound to see that complete justice is done to the parties before the court."

The plaintiff is entitled to recover any special damages that he may have suffered as a result of the defendant refusing to convey in accordance with the terms of the contract; therefore the defendants' motion requiring election is denied. *Culler v. Hydrick*, 162 S.C. 253, 160 S.E. 731, 733, contains a very fine discussion of remediable rights and election of remedies. In the Culler case the court held, "Damages arising out of fraud in the breach of the contract differ in kind and measure from those general damages resulting from the vendor's mere refusal to perform the contract of sale. The two causes of action, if pleaded, are not inconsistent, if they both arise out of the same transaction, or transactions connected with the same subject of action; and the doctrine of election of remedies in such case would not apply as between them."

* * * * *

…The Referee shall also at the reference take testimony as to any special damages suffered by the plaintiff and report his findings of fact and conclusions of law to this Court, respecting the dower interest of Mrs. Schilletter and as to any special damages suffered by the plaintiff.

* * * * *

Attention is called to the principle that **specific performance** is not a matter of absolute right but rests in the sound discretion of the court, which it is claimed cannot be properly exercised until a reference is had and all the attendant circumstances developed. But there are no equities set out in the answer warranting the denial of the relief sought. No showing whatsoever is made why appellant A. E. Schilletter, an experienced real estate man, should not carry out his contract. A summary order of **specific performance** is entirely proper.

* * * * *

The decree of the Court below is modified in the particulars above set forth and the case remanded for further proceedings, with leave to appellant Grace Schilletter to answer within twenty days after the filing of the remittiture.

A. Denial of Specific Performance

Specific performance will not be granted when the contract came into existence (1) because of a mistake, (2) the relief of specific performance would cause unreasonable hardship on the breaching party, (3) granting the specific performance would be grossly inadequate or unfair,[19] (4) granting it would run contrary to public policy,[20] (5) where the burden of enforcing or supervising the specific performance by the court would be substantially burdensome,[21] (6) where the performance requested is of personal service,[22] and (7) where the promisor has the power of terminating the contract.[23]

III. Restitution

Where the court has granted the injured party the right to set aside the contract, the parties to the contract are required to provide restitution. Restitution is the equitable principle wherein the law attempts to make the parties whole again by requiring each of the parties to return what was exchanged initially as part of the exchange of promises. Restitution will only be required when one or both of the parties have previously conferred a benefit to the other[24] by way of part performance or reliance.[25] But restitution will not be granted by the court if it would cause an injustice.[26]

The fact that a contract is unenforceable because it violates the rule of the statute of frauds does not prohibit the injured party from recovering in restitution unless otherwise stated in the contract.[27] Even when the contract is unenforceable because of impracticability, frustration or nonoccurrence of a condition, the injured party is still entitled to **restitution**.[28] In the following case the injured party is seeking **restitution** where he alleges the contract was both tainted and illegal.

---

[19] Restatement (Second) Contracts § 364 (1979).
[20] *Id.* at § 365 (1979).
[21] *Id.* at § 366 (1979).
[22] *Id.* at § 367 (1979).
[23] *Id.* at § 368 (1979).
[24] *Id.* at § 370 (1979).
[25] *Id.* at § 373 (1979).
[26] *Id.* at § 372 (1979).
[27] *Id.* at § 375 (1979).
[28] *Id.* at § 377 (1979).

Bessie DeMayo v. Leonard A. Lyons
228 S.W.2d 691 (1950), 360 Mo. 512 (1950)
Supreme Court of Missouri

OPINION BY: Aschemeyer

This appeal is from an order of the Circuit Court of Jackson County, Missouri, denying appellants' motion for an order of **restitution** in accordance with a mandate of this Court issued in *DeMayo v. Lyons*, 358 Mo. 646, 216 S.W. (2d) 436, where this Court reversed a judgment in favor of Frank DeMayo (plaintiff—now deceased) and against appellants (defendants). Appellants contend that a judgment for $33,669.69 should have been entered in their favor upon the motion for restitution.

* * * * *

The case originated as a suit for an accounting upon a partnership for the purchase and sale of whiskey. A judgment in plaintiff's favor for $22,004.09 was reversed by this Court on the ground that the contract between the parties was illegal and void since they were engaged in the business of selling intoxicating liquors without a license in violation of law. The facts relating to the transaction are more fully stated in the opinion of this Court upon the first appeal.

* * * * *

The foregoing facts were shown by appellants in support of their motion for **restitution**. Appellants' evidence also showed that plaintiff had sold all but a small quantity of the whiskey obtained by him upon the execution and Sheriff's sale and that he had received $25,987.00 upon such sales.

The judgment of this Court rendered upon the first appeal, reversing the judgment in plaintiff's favor, provided, in part, "that the said appellants be restored to all things which they have lost by reason of the said judgment." A certified copy of the judgment of reversal was, of course, incorporated in the mandate transmitted to the trial court. After the mandate had been lodged in the trial court, appellants filed their motion for an order of **restitution** seeking to be restored to all things they had lost under the reversed judgment.

In denying the motion for **restitution**, the trial judge stated that **restitution** was not a matter of right but, rather, one within the discretion of the Court so that it ought to be denied in view of the decision of this Court holding the contract between the parties to be illegal and void. The Court reasoned that the relief of **restitution** ought not to be granted appellants because "the law will leave transgressors, in the circumstances, where they place themselves." This is essentially the position taken by respondents upon this appeal since respondents argue that restitution was properly denied because: (1) appellants are not entitled to any relief under the partnership contract which was held to be illegal and void, and (2) in any event, after the reversal of the prior judgment, the trial court was vested with discretion which it exercised properly in denying restitution.

The general rule is that, upon reversal of a judgment against him, the appellant is entitled to **restitution** from the respondent of all benefits acquired under the erroneous judgment during the pendency of an appeal. This rule has been followed in Missouri in many decisions. …The right to **restitution** exists even though it is not expressly ordered by the appellate court upon the reversal of an erroneous judgment and a motion for **restitution** is a proper method of obtaining such relief in the trial court. ...

Respondents argue that the Missouri decisions have not recognized the right to **restitution** in a case where the appellant, who seeks such relief, is a party to an illegal contract which is void and contrary to public policy. It should be apparent that appellants are not seeking relief under the contract which was held to be void. The motion for **restitution** is not an action to recover upon such contract. It is an effort to be restored to those things which plaintiff had taken from them under an erroneous judgment of the trial court. The benefits secured by plaintiff under this judgment were obtained by execution. The process of the Court, issued under an erroneous judgment, was used to take property from the appellants and turn it over to plaintiff. The power and duty of the trial court to grant **restitution** under these circumstances is inherent and "is substantially the same which it exercises when its own process has been abused." ...The trial court should grant **restitution** "without reference to the peculiar nature of the controversy which it had erroneously determined." ...An appellant is entitled to **restitution** even though he is under a moral duty or obligation to make the payment which an erroneous judgment has attempted to coerce. ...

* * * * *

The judgment of the circuit court of Jackson County is reversed and the cause is remanded to that court with directions to enter judgment in accordance with this opinion in favor of appellants and against respondents upon appellants' motion for an order of restitution.

A. Denial of Restitution

Restitution will be denied unless the person seeking restitution returns or offers to return any interest in property that he has received unless the property, at the time of receipt, was worthless, destroyed or lost. Furthermore, the property must be in substantially the same condition as when it was received.[29]

IV. Election of Remedies

Where the injured party has a choice of more then one remedy, such as damages, specific performance or restitution, his choosing one remedy does not preclude him from asserting another remedy unless the chosen remedies are incongruent with one another or if the breaching party changes his position by relying on the injured party's selection of remedies.[30]

---

[29] Restatement (Second) Contracts § 384 (a) (1979).
[30] Restatement (Second) Contracts § 378 (1979).

Chapter 12

Vocabulary

1. Remedies
2. Recovery at Law
3. Recovery at Equity
4. Interest Damages
5. Reliance Interest Damages
6. Foreseeable Damages
7. Punitive Damages
8. Liquidated Damages
9. Specific Performance
10. Restitution
11. Election of Remedies

Review Questions

1. What is the issue in the *Lebanon Shopping Center v. Wal-Mart Stores* case?
2. What is the legal principle in the *Wal-mart* case?
3. What is the issue in the *Security Store v. American Railways Express* case?
4. What is the legal principle in the *Security Stores* case?
5. What is the issue in the *Butler v. Schilletter* case?
6. What is the legal principle in the *Butler* case?
7. What is the issue in the *Bessie DeMayo v. Leonard Lyons* case?
8. What is the legal principle in the *DeMayo* case?

Table of Cases

Index

without consideration, promise to
　pay an antecedent debt, 56–57
Counteroffers, 27–28
Craft v. Elder & Johnston Co. supra, 14
Creditor beneficiaries, 136–39
Criminal law, 163
Culler v. Hydrick, 165

D

Damages
　assessing, purpose of, 159
　avoidable and foreseeable, 162–63
　claim for, 114
　compensatory, 158, 159, 161
　contract, 159
　expectation interest, 157–59
　liquidated, 163
　measures of, 158, 159
　punitive, 163
　reliance interest, 157, 160–62
　restitution interest, 157
　specific, 164, 165
Death of offeror, 33
*Deborah L. Baldwin v. University of
　Pittsburgh Medical Center*, 4–5
Debt
　answering for, of another, 75–76
　promise to pay antecedent, 56–57
Defenses
　against the assignee, 150–51
　against beneficiaries, 142
Delegation
　of duties, 151–54
　obligors assent to, 146
Delivery of gift, 50–51
Denial
　of restitution, 168
　of specific performance, 166
Direct broadcast satellite systems
　(DBS), 122

Discharge of contract, 121–33
　accord and satisfaction, 131–32
　commercial impracticability,
　　123–25
　discharge by assent, 129
　discharge by novation, 130
　discharge by substituted
　　performance, 129–30
　frustration of purpose, 121, 126–29
　impossibility of performance, 121–
　　23, 125, 127–29
　impracticability of performance,
　　121–23
　release, 132–33
　rescission by agreement, 132
　supervening impracticability, 126
DISH Network, 122
Doctrines of frustration, 128
*Dominion Video Satellite Inc. v.
　Echostar Satellite L.L.C.*, 121–23
Donee beneficiaries, 136, 139–40
Duration of power to accept, 27
Duress
　physical, 105
　by threat, 105–6
　types of, 105
Duties, delegation of, 151–54

E

Early Retirement Incentive Program
　(ERIP), 8
EchoStar, 122, 123
Election of remedies, 168
Element of offer, 17
Employees at-will, 54
Employment Separation Agreement
　(ESA), 6
Enforceable contracts without
　consideration, 58–60
Equitable obligation, 56

CPSIA information can be obtained
at www.ICGtesting.com
Printed in the USA
FSOW02n0916070717
36041FS

9 781465 202383